To my invisibly real teachers,

I am honored to be your humble grasshopper.

My son, Dean,

From your first breath,
you have been loved unconditionally.

THE INVISIBLY REAL

*Multidimensional Conduct
& Communication Guide*

Michele Bigness

THE INVISIBLY REAL ©

The Invisibly Real, 2019 by Michele Bigness
Registered with the Library of Congress: September 2019

Cover and Book Design: Michele Bigness
Photo Credit: Andrea Pittori / Alamy Stock Vector

All rights reserved. Printed in the United States of America. No part of this book may be used or reproduced in any manner whatsoever without written permission except in the case of brief quotations embodied in critical articles or reviews.

The views expressed in this work are solely those of the author, unless indicated otherwise. The author of this book does not dispense medical advice or prescribe the use of any technique as a form of treatment for physical, emotional, or medical problems without advice of a physician, either directly or indirectly. The intent of the author is to offer information of a general nature to help you in your quest for emotional and spiritual well-being. In the event you use any of the information in this book for yourself, which is your constitutional right, the author assumes no responsibility for your actions.

Photos used follow copyright usage. The Invisibly Real uses photographs acquired from a variety of sources. Every effort has been made to ensure that no copyright has been infringed. Photos provided without reference or credit are labeled for the general public or created illustration of the author of this title.

Printed in the United States of America
First Edition: December, 2021

10 9 8 7 6 5 4 3 2 1

CONTENT

FAST FOOD BUDDHISM 8

THE CLIENT
BEHAVE TO BE-HAVE 13
WHAT CLIENTS ASK 24
LOVE EXCHANGES 40
LOVE TO LEAVE 50

THE PSYCHIC MIND
THE SILVER CORD 57
THE SIXTH SENSE 61
MEDIUMSHIP 73
CELEBRITY MEDIUMS 81
TIMELINES 87
DIVINATION 94

THE ABILITY
THE INVISIBLY FORCES 107
PSYCHIC INTELLIGENCE (PI/Q) 111
UNIVERSAL TIMESTREAM 107

THE HEAVENS
REINCARNATION 121
DEATH, KEYWORDS & WEIGH STATIONS 146
SPIRITS GUIDES 146
HEAVENLY HELLOS 158

THE ALTERNATE REALITIES
REALITY POTENTIALITY 174
THOUGHT REALITY 182
REALLY, HE SEES DEAD PEOPLE 193
PSYCHIC REALITY 212

THE WISE & THE A.S.S.
GLOBAL PHENOMENA 225
THE A.S.S. 235
HOTLINES & COLD READINGS 243

REFERENCE
AFTERWORD 259
SOURCE'S GUIDE TO ENLIGHTENMENT 267
MODALITIES, PRACTICES & TERMINOLOGY 274

CHAPTER TOPICS

THE ANSWER IS NOPE
LOSE YOUR MIND
LOVE TO ANSWER
DECEPTION AND SERIAL CHEATING
SOUL MIRRORS
QUESTIONS PSYCHIC ABILITY
QUESTIONS MEDIUM ABILITY
PHYSICAL PERCEPTIONS
SIGNS OF NATURAL INTUITION
SELECTING THE RIGHT READING
SCHEDULING & TIPS
SIGNS OF PSYCHIC ABILITY
PSI AND REINCARNATION
THE SUBSCONSCIOUS MIND
CLIENT PARTICIPATION
FUTURE VALIDATION
DIRECT COMMUNICATIONS
NEWS CLUES
PROPHECY, PREDICTIONS
FATE AND DESTINY
TAROT MYTHS
ASTROLOGY
THE MENTAL MATRIX
THE GATE KEEPERS
LIGHTS, DHARMA, ACTION!
THE EXPERIENCE OF DEATH
SOUL LEVELS
ARCTURIAN WEIGH STATION
JUPITER?
IDENTIFYING THE SOULMATE
TWIN FLAME
AKASHIC RECORDS
BOOK OF LIFE
SOUL CONTRACTS
WALK-INS
INTERVIEW WITH NINA

THE ELDERS, ANCIENTS, ANGELS
COSMIC GUIDES
VIVID DREAMING
VISITATION DREAMS
THE SOUL GOING HOME
THE TWINS AND GOD
THE CONVULSIONNAIRES
EDGAR CAYCE PREDICTIONS
ATTRACTIVE AURAS
PROTECTION RITUALS
ENERGY CLEANSING
EMPATHS
TELEPATHY
NEGATIVE THOUGHT TRANSFER
OUT-OF-BODY EXPERIENCE
COLLECTIVE SHIFTS
CHANNELING - ST. GERMAIN
TRUE CHANNELING
INSIGHTS FROM GHOSTS
GHOSTS, HOLD THE SUGAR
PARANORMAL SHOWS
THE ANGELIC HOST
EXERCISE 1 - CLAIRVOYANCE
EXERCISE 2 - CLAIRAUDIENCE
WHAT A PSYCHIC EXPERIENCES
EXTRAORDINARY ABILITIES
SUPER PSYCHIC CHILDREN OF CHINA
IF PSYCHIC ABILITY IS REAL, WHAT
THE CIA & STARGATE
DEBUNKERS
PSYCHIC VIGILANTES
THE ALLEGEDLY PEOPLE
PSYCHIC HOTLINES
SIGNS OF COLD READING
GENERALLY SPEAKING VALIDATION
WHEN TO LAUGH AND LEAVE

REFERENCES & ABBREVIATIONS

<u>Nina</u>	Name of the co-author and spirit guide
<u>DLO</u>:	abbreviation for Deceased Loved Ones
<u>channeled</u>:	psychically received communications
<u>client</u>:	or seeker, is the person requesting a reading
<u>PSI</u>:	general term for any ESP related abilities
<u>psychic</u>:	is referenced for any psi function or communication, i.e., mediumship, unless indicated otherwise

Understanding is the one-dimensional comprehension of the intellect. It leads to knowledge. Realization is three-dimensional — a simultaneous comprehension of head, heart, and instinct. It comes only from direct experience. You now see everything through a veil of associations about things, projected over a direct, simple awareness. You've 'seen it all before'; it's like watching a movie for the twentieth time. You see only memories of things, so you become bored. Boredom, you see, is fundamental nonawareness of life; boredom is awareness, trapped in the mind. You'll have to lose your mind before you can come to your senses.

— **Dan Millman, Way of the Peaceful Warrior**

INTRODUCTION

'Psychics have written books about their personal experiences, explained aspects of, but there isn't one book describing extra-sensory. You might also be surprised to hear the majority of Psychics do not consider asking their own guides to explain how psychic abilities communicate.' Nina

The words from my guide, Nina and inspiration for this book was a three year process with many new discoveries. First, was extensive research for books on ESP that went as far back as the mid-1800's. What I found fell into three categories of knowledge; 1) in-depth information for a specific expertise 2) surface-level understanding of internal functioning, with the last, 3) theories and inferences pieced together. Considering the irony connected to the skillset. the implications staggering. Not because it compromised the ability rather the presumption of its purpose. Every question was another domino to the next uncertainty, linking the exhausting number of conflicting opinions…until the last piece fell onto Nina's purpose. The uninformed seeker is vulnerable to the opportunist's playground, and the reason they exist. In case you missed it, that nugget was an aha! moment.

Our mutual goal is updating ESP's status, from the most speculated three letters in the world. Hopefully, you can connect all the moving parts and restore esoteric concepts that aren't mass produced.

So…welcome to The Invisibly Real – a guide explaining psychic ability inspired to educate the true seeker of invisibly wisdom.

Great things are not accomplished by those who yield to trends and fads and popular opinion. Jack Kerouac

REALITY IS DEFINED as a state or world representing *what actually exists*, as opposed to idealistic notions. The definition doesn't acknowledge reality is an ever-changing cycle of awareness subjective to the era it's conceived. Progress in discovery is a major influence witnessed over the centuries. Imagine the reaction of someone from when witches were burned at the stake being told paranormal shows are primetime. The new millennium did something no one saw coming – alternative reality was re-defined and re-shaped by popular demand.

The last decade, a global awareness shift was experienced by millions, ushering in the second generation of New Agers and eager to understand enlightened wisdom. Chapter zero discusses what the majority of people aren't aware of; it didn't go according to plan. Opportunism diverted the path into wholesale trends, instant access, instant results from instant expert's plagiarized cut-and-paste regurgitations. The reality of true wisdom has been taken hostage by page likes and the number of social media followers.

BUT, WHAT IF THE THOUSANDS OF PHILOSOPHIZING CUT AND PASTED PROFUNDITY WAS INSPIRED FROM A BONG HIT AND A BOTTLE OF WINE?

Or, **POST wisdom**; Plagiarized Opportunism Spiritual Trends. What does this have to do with psychic ability? Patience grasshopper. The answer requires a short trip back in time when tie-die and Janis Joplin eight-tracks was groovy and find why the current spiritual climate zigged, instead of a zagged.

THE DAWNING OF A NEW AGE

THE SIXTY'S, a decade of freedom fighters set in motion the counterculture, deeply rooted in Spiritualism, New Thought, the Human Potential Movement and Theosophical philosophies; each playing a pivotal role paving the way for a New Age of spirituality. By the early seventies, England was first to embrace the movement, drawn to past occult traditions rooted in Eastern philosophy. The brief backstory necessary to introduce the event many consider responsible for the popularity of The New Age. Jane Roberts groundbreaking dictations from a discarnate entity, published in *The Seth Materials*, generated broad-spectrum awareness flooding new thought concepts of *creating our own reality* into the mainstream; revolutionizing American thinking.

FLOWER POWER HIPPIES were the first to convert their psychedelic ways for existential reality. Mind-Body-Spirit found its groove in holistic health. The transcendentalists ushered in Reiki (ray-kee) aligning things called chakras from fingers creating swirly air symbols. The peculiar, but remarkably effective rituals spread by word of water cooler whispers sought alternatives to pharmaceutical's Mach 2 cautions of scrolling symptoms requiring a lot of toilet paper. Hypnosis took center stage discovering spontaneously quacking like a duck was optional. Subconscious upgrades were pursued by the avantgarde for clinical redirects – and, can you please make me forget *I ever met that a**hole who cheated on me* (um, no). Meanwhile, Oprah was promoting Eckart Tolle's, *Power of Now*, Book Clubs exchanged T*he Bridges Over Madison County* for *What the Bleep* and *The Secret*. Books on tape commuters redirected mental chatter into that hottie magnetically attracted to happy thoughts. *Ask and It Will Be Given* and *The Law of Attraction* vision boards, daily affirmations were co-created during colonic cleansings, before Yoga class, after Reiki, in between Acupuncture and purchasing herbal tea remedies for the anxiety trying to be present. The new kids on the metaphysical block were met with enthusiasm overload. Eventually, the secrets, laws and bleeps fast-paced **self-realization** balanced into a kindred mind meld fellowship of holistical-mysticals at Barnes & Noble's New Age aisle with a 2% Chai Tea in one hand and, of like mind, in the other. The once dubbed whack-a-doodles openly enjoyed the revels of the elysian-cabalistic coming of age period without the eye rolls from the, *why don't you think like me*, people. But, were we ready for the second wave of The New Age? The new millennia's, *I'm spiritual - not religious* was the first spiritual movement popularized by click bait social media trends.

MINDFUL-AWAKENED-ATTAINING CONSCIOUSNESS

The awakening consciousness transcending a deeper connection to self and Source impacted mainstream minds with the same magnitude as the *Seth Materials*. Globalizing the psyche demands required fast supply solutions for publishers. Or, why so many book titles include *…attract … awaken … secrets revealed, unleashing something within* and, *the power of.* When the consciousness craze slowed, mindfulness, was the new 'it' title. I summoned the Google gods, as it applies to current trends; mindfulness *is the consciousness activity of becoming intentionally aware of what one is aware of.* Really, that's a quote.

Yes, books are time consuming, costly and require minimalizing risks. But… adaptations to satisfy a Harry Potter trend and audiences seeking the enlightened path and psychic development – insert a wizard punchline. Fast forward, to the current publishing criteria requiring authors to include their social media presence. Decisions creating an infiltration of masquerading gurudom, splashing platitudes of esoteric musings, pep-rally exuberance and a lot of!!!!! Answered, (at the time) once again, by the Google gods entering *psychic development,* with the first listing from an author touting 25 years of experience. Wait for it. The author, teaching you how to be psychic, isn't psychic. Experiences touted, is based on, '*theoretical research,*' defined as; *attempts to gather knowledge about a phenomenon whose conclusions may not have any immediate real-world application.*

Psychic decepticons skyrocketed into the overflowing pay-per-minute hotlines, taking credit cards for fortune cookie predictions, love zombie potions, and spells of false hope. Psychics and spirituality were devolving into mass produced easy steps and fast results catering to instant, now, and immediately. The jury is still out, on who's more dangerous – the *you have a curse,* scammer or *popular and perky* opportunist with thousands of followers?

FAST FOOD BUDDHISM – 10 STEPS, 5 LAWS, 4 RULES

Want a psychic reading? No problem. Becky just bought a tarot deck and pretty sure she's ready to answer all your most intimate, life changing questions. Billy, a part-time cashier at Piggly Wiggly can show you how to unlock your empathic superpowers. No worries! If that isn't what you're looking for, BJ's popular CD (only $99.00) guarantees anyone can contact Ascended Master, St. Germain; who is also very busy making his rounds on YouTuber channels. We know, because people recite his words saying, "*I am the Ascended Master St. Germain and love purple.*" It's extra cool when someone's voice changes into an English accent. He isn't from England, (shrugs) I'm sure it will make sense later, though. Oh yeah, duh! Don't forget to check out Candy's newest post, "*Ten signs you met the most sacred, there's only one and super rare Twin Mate!*" Click the like button because next week she reveals her secrets to apply mascara without clumping! OMG!! She's so diverse! For you paranormal people, uhh... FYI... it's all about contacting the Plee-eighties, says Julie and Joe-Joe's hottest online spirituality group where anyone can post messages from evolved beings. So beautiful.

The last category is a bit trickier. Using credentials to shroud personal beliefs.

THE HIPPY-CRITICAL

A Psychiatrist's blog jumps into the fringe with starry-eyed thoughts on Astrology. My initial enthusiasm, given the profession, diminished into confusion by the second paragraph and dumbfounded climax. The analysis of the ancient practice could only be described as a painfully awkward. It was clear his evaluation was research solely on daily horoscopes that didn't extend beyond astrology websites from the drumroll moment, '*call me an idiot but believing you can tell me everything about my life just from the month I was born is ridiculous.*' Fair enough, Dr. Idiot and may he appreciate the irony in this quote. "*A physician without knowledge of astrology has no right to call himself a physician.*" — **Hippocrates** (Hippocratic oath)

PULPIT'S-FICTION

Why, a Priest, indeed. Because he used a modernized dais (blog) to inform his online flock that <u>all</u> psychics claiming they're involved with police investigations are frauds. "*Ask them what case or what they solved and the bragging turns into incoherent muttering.*" Using the same rules, <u>all</u> priests are pedophiles.

THE CLIENT

Who and what influences the mind, doesn't affect the human experience; it is how the human experiences. Bigness

BEHAVE & BE-HAVE

THE CLIENT, THE PSYCHIC AND THE ABILITY to reveal life's many mysteries, answers to heal the past, discover present opportunities and anticipate future possibilities. Clients are defined as the individuals seeking answers from the divine. Psychics are the individuals with heightened sensory perception to relay guidance, messages and answers, from the divine. The ability is the divine communicating through the psychic, to assist the seeker. Divine communication, is then determined by the degree of accuracy. But why is accuracy often decided by what *should be* received. Is it derived by *unqualified certainty*, or *confident uncertainty*, observing the unobservable unknowns – to clear up your confusion?

How people communicate is conveyed, in the thinking, making a request or indicating a need. Over the centuries, multiple sources rate abilities from physical observations assuming, what it is, without experiencing interactions directly. Anticipating responses imply competence to recognize the expectations of the ability. With confidence to advise on skills relevant to alternative means of expression, is aware interactions are receptive and crucial when engaged in multisensory occupations.

Clients aren't required to grasp the complexities of multidimensional communication. Learning how to participate, express expectations relating to immediate needs or interests. The purpose throughout, is for clients to have awareness of anything that can potentially affect readings, accuracy, and their desired goal. Since, the client's frame of mind plays a crucial role, I am acquiescing to Nina's perception as a spirit guide, to provide the first step towards effective communication.

Clients share in the relationship united by divine wisdom's interacting roles (continued below):

- Spirit guides are advanced beings aware of the seeker's thoughts, emotions, and intentions. Messages and guidance, given or not given, is concluded on how the information affects the seekers.
- The client is communicating directly to the spirit guide, or loved one, on the other side.
- The psychic or medium are intermediaries, relaying what's received, on the behalf of (like a UN interpreter).

The behaviors and exchanges are presented in short question-answer formats, with recommendations, when applicable. Keep in mind, examples of difficult behavior characteristics should focus on the profile's interaction functionality, not an individual's deficits. Lastly, the following were selected from real readings frequent enough to establish a grouping and relate to a wide spectrum, when clients...

WHEN CLIENTS….

try to trick the psychic

Giving wrong information to see if the psychic is legitimate, doesn't happen often but enough to mention. With the understanding of interacting with the spirit guide directly, and using deception to validate authenticity **is not a good idea. The obvious reason, is concern of legitimacy, and why a dedicated chapter on recognizing fraud is included. For** any victimized by a sociopath's fraud, first, that sucks and a big hug. Advice more effective is simply asking the (if) psychic to explain how they validate information.

worry about embarrassing or private matters

A psychic's empathic radar can sense a client's emotional state and reason for the confusion. Knowing how reading information is psychically received will help. First, psychics don't read minds, our spirit guides do and always respect a client's privacy. Since spirit guides run the show, if a secret is revealed, it would be something serious, like a situation connecting harm. Otherwise, your secrets are safe.

THE CLIENT

tell me whatever you get

It can be fun when a stranger describes what makes you – you, and private thoughts no one could possibly know or guess. Asking the psychic for whatever they get, is something I suggest all clients should include at some point in their reading for information, not known or considered important. This isn't suggested for clients looking for answers about specific situations, discussed next.

readings for mental clarity

A clarity reading, asking *whatever you get*, isn't suggested because the situations almost always come with intense emotional focus, that I'll elaborate on. Clarity, as the sole purpose to contact a psychic, wants answers desperate to ease obsessive thoughts cycling on the Ferris Wheel of why. Even though open to hearing answers, desperation creates resistant energy from what it wants to be true. The best approach is to let the psychic know what you want from the reading but first refer to the chapter on what's too much information.

responds with maybe, could be, i think so, sure, ok...

When clients give non-committal replies, one of three reasons is usually why; embarrassment or not sure how to answer fall into the lower percentages. Mostly, it's from the helpful good-intensions, bad-advice – every question is suspect of psychic phishing. Questions are sometimes necessary to make sure received information is accurately interpreted. Reframing validation is a technique used to strengthen their connection with the client. *'I'm hearing you want to know about your career. Is one of your questions concerning a recent promotion?'* See the last chapter on identifying scams.

i already knew that

What would you think if a psychic recited your exact thoughts, word-for-word? Maybe, *it doesn't get better than that*, right? Some clients become irritated and reply with; "*yeah, but I already knew that.*" Their irritation also applies to past and present details about the situation –

because they knew that, too. If future predictions don't align with a pre-established idea, *it doesn't make sense*, because it isn't, *what it should be*.

Suggestion: Tell a friend what to say, for free, or, the same, pay per minute.

yes, yes, what else...

This is a personality who uses chaos to control, and devoid of any self-accountability. From the start, the client consistently interrupts with, *yes, yes, it all makes sense. What else?* This continues until predictions are finally heard. It's futile to accommodate their demands and advice for newer psychics, if they decide to ignore how readings work, it's one of few exceptions to let the client take the lead knowing what is inevitable, after the reading. Later, they will begin mentally reviewing what was said. They won't have notes, or any information to establish trust and doubt sets in. Predictions are questioned, one by one, and their impatience kicks back in, that needs answers. Self-accountability not being their strong suit, re-create a modified substitution into the imagination. In this version, the client is well-behaved and patient while explaining to others how the stupid-head psychic didn't say one thing they could validate. The psychic is called a fake and schedules with a different psychic. Shampoo, rinse, repeat.

asks about the future

90% of clients dismiss future predictions that doesn't fit with current ideas, desires, or life situations. In other words, events, situations or conclusions that aren't already present to link it to. Communication validating the past and present is logically deduced as a different ability and precognition becomes the suspect variable. The client doesn't see the irony why they contacted a psychic and deciding future accuracy on only what 'makes sense.' To see how future timelines unfold; think of a television series with three seasons. A client with the above mindset, has watched only the first season and asks about the third season. The plot twists, change of cast members that were gradually introduced and occasional dramatic surprises are unknown and limits answers to only what makes sense in season one.

THE CLIENT

NOPE

you're reading my mind, right?

Nope, my guide is. People have actually said, "*You're not psychic. You're only reading my mind.*" A brain boggler every time I hear it. But wait, there's more and might take a second to wrap your head around.... skeptics have uttered the same words .... to reinforce psychic ability isn't real. One more. Someone I met personally, and discovered I was psychic believed keeping some imagined distance would prevent mind reading. Insert an hour of laughter for this entire paragraph.

True telepathic capability is able to tap into any individual's thoughts, as the over generalization. A psychic, can dialog telepathically with their guide or DLOs, but not the public. I don't know if I could communicate with a true telepath because I've never met one because of how rare the ability is, likened to telekinesis (moving objects with the mind). The number of telepaths is unknown and perhaps for the simple reason, how people would react. A secret held close to the vest, even from family and close friends who don't want their most private thoughts known.

psychic voyeurs

"*I'm sure you already know this. Did you see what happened to me last* (night, week, month)." Nope, sure didn't. "*I was sending you thoughts before our appointment. Did you get what I sent?*" Nope. Didn't feel a thing.

Abilities for the purpose to spy on others goes against a psychic's ethical code. Yes, there are rare exceptions but from guides, without provocation. We learn how to tune-in and tune-out, early to prevent the aethers version of going coo-coo for coco puffs.

but my friend said...

Nope, and thankful to the wonderful friends or family offering advice based on their experience. Why mentioned is because suggestions are typically given with the impression their experience represents a genuine reading. Without knowing there are different methodologies, can be counterintuitive.

BEHAVE & BE-HAVE

I only have one question

Nope, ha ha ha ha. You certainly do not. You have one question you're currently obsessing over. When I answer your one question, you will say, wait, wait, only one more question…does that mean….?????

free questions

Asking for free help is most often about paranormal activity, if their experiences mean they have psychic ability, the five page email describing a plague of dark critters or, my personal favorite – can I recommend a psychic who is less expensive. Nope, nope and nope. Long ago, I answered the free questions via email, as a goodwill gesture. Not one or two, every individual I replied to, turned into ongoing follow-ups, one more – please, I swear it's super quick with 10-pages of, omg! this is really important details they forgot to include. When you tell them no more never ending follow-ups, there isn't a thank you for the time given. Last, are free questions used as a con for free readings under the ruse if they prove genuine, blah, blah, schedule a reading.

is it true, psychics worship the devil?

Nope (and, sigh) and…yes, I've been asked. Usually, it's a partial Bible quote, then ask me, "is that the quote?" Might take a minute to catch why that's funny.

we have 3 minutes left; can you tell me…

Does anyone on the other side have a quick message for me? Will I get fired? Is my spouse cheating on me? Does my mother have cancer? Can you find out why I can't get pregnant? You think there's a ghost in my house because I think it's possessing my cat. I keep having a recurring dream of the world blowing up, what does it mean? Is my husband going to have a nervous breakdown because I think an alien tried having sex with me? Did my boyfriend/girlfriend cheat on me when I was in the hospital donating a kidney? My ex told me they might have Herpes; do I have Herpes? I met three women on a dating site, which one do you think I'll marry? My friend said her boyfriend has a micro-

THE CLIENT

penis; can you ask your guides how to make it bigger? Was I Cleopatra in a past life? Where is my brown shoe?

Nope. With a few minutes of remaining time the suggestion is for a quick review to see if any guidance received needs additional clarity.

do movies base psychic abilities accurately?

Nope. Media representations of clairvoyance, psychic ability, medium communication, tarot readings, telepathy, telekinesis or any form of ESP have yet to be accurately depicted in a movie, or television show.

Personal story watching a suspense movie with a friend. The entire movie plot took place in an airplane – did I mention my friend being an airline pilot? About twenty minutes in, he started to show signs of agitation with the occasional eye roll and "tssssttt" sounds. A few minutes later, it was apparent he was not getting through to the *'idiot pilot.'* He re-positioned himself a few feet from the wall mounted flatscreen to blurting out cockpit, thrust and fuselage to the fictitious pilot ignoring his rants of expertise. It was quite entertaining to watch, until Nicholas Cage portrayed a psychic with pre-cognitive ability but only one minute before the actual event. Use your imagination on how I responded.

LOSE YOUR MIND (PLEASE)

Disposition, attitude, and expectations absolutely impact how a client interprets guidance. This can be illustrated with identical readings experienced by two different personalities. The first, (client A) has a relaxed and easy-going disposition and (client B) tends to be anxious and sensitive. In this scenario, client A and B meet with the same psychic, and both present a calm and friendly manner, and identical situations. Client A's easy going persona is open and asks questions when the psychic's information isn't the preferred answer. Client B, has a calm demeanor on the outside but the psychic senses empathically, waves of anxiety. When answers are not desired responses are confused (I don't understand), may ask follow-up questions that eliminate or ignore key points and repeats details thinking the psychic doesn't understand.

People with open and loving dispositions are an absolute joy to talk to. Their personality can be feisty, gentle or a wise-ass that shares the experience with the psychic, even under duress. Not all personality traits interact with the intention of partaking in a mutual goal. Selected below are these attitudes.

the vip

The Very Important Person(a) doesn't request psychic help often. When they do, clues are recognized easily as; frequent interruptions, argue mundane points with apathetic replies, *yeah, I don't think so*. Asking to clarify inaccuracy is met feigned laughter (meaning they can't).

Comment: VIPs are unaware of how they affect others and wouldn't identify with the above description. Psychics may choose to warn x times before ending the appointment without a refund or tolerated.

spirituality experts

Enlightened individuals omit open and loving energy and always a pleasure to speak with. The spirituality expert isn't enlightened, doesn't walk the talk and gives irresponsible advice. Spirituality experts wait to be recognized by the psychic as an equal, and make it a point when it isn't.

Considering the topic, it could get lost in translation as competitive or putting a hack in their place. Not at all. Spirituality expert's ego are counterintuitive to what it stands for and interestingly, have the same energy signature as a skeptic.

the literal personality

People who process information literally aren't difficult psychic relay can be energy intensive and why found under this heading.

Psi language uses variable exchange sequences of literal, figurative, metaphors, symbols and relayed through the senses to perceive a stranger's experience. We, 'ish' with timeframes, might say Jack for Mack, see a symbol for birthdays or anniversaries. You get the idea.

Example: A received message includes timing of a past event, and rounded up as three months ago (ish). How this personality processes information, the reply might be, *nothing happened three months ago,* if timing was 2 months and 3 weeks ago.

Suggestion: Pay-per-minute won't be the best choice (grin). Schedule with someone reputable, and let the psychic know before the reading begins so you can manage the information together.

the closed door

People preparing to speak with a medium contacting a loved one get nervous and expected. Mediums usually give a few extra minutes explaining their methodology, and relevant details, to ease worries. The closed door prepares by putting in place mental safeguards, *when I hear..., I'll know it's them and you're a real medium.* To them, it's logical and makes sense because the DLO *should say it* and energetically locked, silently ignoring messages they don't realize are from their loved one.

If the Clairvoyant senses a resistance that energetically interferes, asks the client to be open to what comes in. If the medium detects they're still secretly holding onto the safeguards, the client usually laughs, and opens. Very few continue to hold onto control where the reading stops. It's important to add, resistance doesn't always interfere explained in further detail in the next chapter (explaining the energy of skeptics).

the open door

The first psychic or medium reading, the open door believes everything said, with or without validation. If it doesn't make sense, they're sure it will later. You'd think the description would be considered the perfect client. On the contrary; they terrify me. The same trust given to me, would also be given to those eventually seen in headlines wearing orange jumpsuits. We've all heard horrific stories about sociopaths playing psychic resulting in emotional and financial devastation.

Guidance: Reading only the topics of interest, including the later chapters identifying signs of fraud, isn't suggested. Each chapter contributes a vital piece of the bigger picture. exposes the signs to recognize different types of scams imposters use.

i can't be read

When a client thinks something about them defies psychic energy. I know of only three reasons when true; 1) a previous reading and the guide doesn't answer a question that could alter the outcome. The client re-interprets this into their general condition. 2) mental health concerns like paranoia, stalking, heightened obsession tendencies 3) inflexible attitudes the psychic doesn't want to read for.

they can't be read

There are individuals a psychic is prevented from reading with two identifiers. 1) the client's attitude is open, even eager 2) receiving psychically, is resistant until its understood, as off-limits. [Nina] Restricted access is specific to advanced souls undergoing a duration of challenges with the purpose of, ascending or fine-tuning. Therefore, few intuitives would have the occasion to read for this client and fewer, able to explain the reason answers are blocked at the soul level. Chapter 12, reviews the different soul levels, including indicators.

why is personal ascension important

Ascension is the act of rising to higher levels, defined by vibrational signatures. Vibrations, is a word associated spiritually describing the essence of a person or situation. Everything has its own vibrational signature; a planet, stars, people, words, colors, sounds, emotions, thoughts and so on. Lower equal what is less loving and higher as more loving. The level of transcendence is measured by the illusions transformed and held, creating a unique vibrational signature, or a key. Lower vibrations access lower planes, higher vibrations ascend into the universe.

CELEBRATING SPIRIT

real clients, real experiences, real connections

All my life I felt certain things. (The psychic) not only felt and found those same things but she spelled them out before me in such clarity that even my wife went to see her, and she too, was blown away. The best part was she required little to nothing from us and when the revelations began all we could do was listen.   J.O.

I've talked to many psychics and had as many different types of experiences. One of them was at a spiritual store that offered readings. I was curious why nothing she said was accurate and asked her a few questions. Well, it turns out she just started and the hiring process only required saying she was psychic, that's it. The bad ones out there give the good ones a bad reputation.

Listen to your intuition. Going to reputable places with reviews or only reading what they write isn't a guarantee. What's been working for me is listening to my own intuition. I look at their photo and see if it feels off or feels right. It's been accurate and tried it out by contacting 3 psychics with the same question. Every one gave the same answers and a couple of times, the exact words.   **B.P.**

I am by nature extremely skeptical but at the suggestion of a friend I contacted (a psychic) regarding a complex historical case. I told her nothing; the information she revealed was specific and astounding, turning me into a believer. She has the ability to describe places, events and people, both living and deceased. Two years and several readings later I still find her accuracy uncanny.   R.A.

That was the most beautifully different experience I have ever encountered. It was enlightening, reaffirming and most of all vindicating. I needed it all!! I am still digesting it, but I think each day to follow will be viewed differently because of it.   J.H.

WHAT CLIENTS ASK

To understand what exists outside of current perceptions, one is to learn about existence beyond its current perceptions. – Andromeda's Muse

THERE ARE THREE TYPES OF QUESTIONS; what clients frequently ask, don't consider to ask, or thought already known. Of the three, what is believed already known creates the biggest challenge, understood personally after discovering ideas that familiarity shaped into beliefs, then re-translated as, intuitively received. The first question presented, updated with Nina's answer, is an example of an energy resistance concept-turned-belief, from nothing more than a logical deduction.

why are nonbelievers hard to read for?

❰ *Psychics use universal energy but also rely on seekers to contribute to the triune connection. A seeker's energy is an agreement the universal guides acknowledge. Non-believers, skeptics or mindsets requesting guidance, simultaneously dictating to the universe how we are to provide, closes off the universal flow and this applies to any psi-connection. The function of psychics and guides are to assist the willing, not convince fears, or override demands.*

AUTHOR COMMENT: There is an accepted practice in spiritual circles regarding individuals not physically available where their higher-self acts as a surrogate for permission (I've never heard requests denied). According to Nina; the conscious energy of the individual is the determining factor. In other words, would the individual agree, if available to directly ask? If the answer is no, their higher self is also no. Healing, doesn't require an agreement; the body rejuvenating or not, determines the destiny's purpose.

are readings better in person?

A few psi abilities need a form of physical contact, like psychometry, or palm reading. Otherwise, distance is irrelevant for the simple reason the psychic communicates with their guides or loved ones, directly. Psychics who only offer in-person readings based on proximity might be inexperienced, and suggest asking before scheduling.

yes or no questions

Yes or no questions are handled differently. One advisor might answer questions exactly as given, another who understands the frame of mind, and mentally rephrases the question. Intentions might be for answers to be clearly outlined with the pertinent details. To clearly communicate the intended desire, avoid limiting specificity and expand your options about a current situation; *I'm interested in knowing if there is a future with...and, if yes, what is the guidance for this to happen?* Below are comparative suggestions:

Limiting - *Should I apply for a new job?* - **Opens choices** - *What can I do to advance my career? I would like to know if applying for a new job will benefit me and guidance on how to advance my career.*
Obsessive: *Will (that guy/girl) contact me?* Offers potential opportunities - *I would like to know what's coming up for me in romance?*

Another example is, Phrasing like this opens the question isn't restricted allowing answers to consider other available options.

how do clients sabotage their reading?

Scenario 1: after the psychic explains the reading process and just about to begin relaying information, the client verbally erupts spilling every detail, about the situation. Attempts are made by the psychic with a sophisticated methodology of – la, la, la, la over and over until they stop talking. Scenario 2: this is a combination of high anxiety, nervous tension anticipating what they will hear. The psychic says hello, and the reply is, "*my boyfriend...we've been together for 2 years, broke up with me a month ago for some (whore, tramp, bitch, demon spawn) and I've been calling and he won't answer. She won't let him, right? Say it...I already know...*"

WHAT CLIENTS ASK

Honestly, most clients in this heading are very sweet and always want to give them a big hug. So, if this is you, let us help you.

will a psychic tell me, or someone i love, will die?

No, 98%, with the remaining for specific exceptions. When aware of a terminal prognosis – it might be answered for those who live further away to make travel or other necessary arrangements. Another exception involves preventing a situation but may be presented in a way that doesn't scare the individual, preventing the result. The reason not all accidents, fatal or non-fatal, are forewarned has to do with interfering when slated as a pre-established destiny point.

helping the psychic

Helpful client #1: intensely focuses on their questions to mind meld with the psychic, before or during the reading, as a loving gesture to help the psychic. It isn't necessary but I always enjoy feeling their helpful energy.

Helpful client #2: interprets a psychic's listening silence as a request to help by giving more details (ssshhh - smiling). Clients who get chatty-nervous, please be aware people playing psychic often use silence as a ploy for over sharing. If they didn't let you know, ask why they are silent, otherwise, don't volunteer information.

Pretending helpful client #3: The VIP ongoing interruptions, and I can't be read personality under the guise of helping. Unaware why their energy affects the flow of information they interpret the psychic's challenge to read them as a compliment. As mentioned, I follow the, third time not charmed with the first gently, the second, firmly, the third time, concludes.

Another reason for shushing is my favorite clients hearing their excitement but… wanting to over share. I repeat la, la, la, la until they stop, laugh, apologize and we continue.

why is quiet sometimes needed?

Psychic communication is compared to; one foot in the conscious world and the other in the unconscious. During a reading a deeper trance may be required for: specific questions, to clear nervous energy felt empathically or because their spirit guide is relaying a lot of information, telepathically. It's the psychic – medium that never asks that might need to be considered.

will psychics tell me what to do?

There are times life feels overwhelming and just want someone to decide for us. It's important to understand a question that involves a psychic's code of ethics. Specifically, we are not to create dependency, or allow. We don't decide your life for you. We help you find the direction, explained, below.

A client is offered two job opportunities, both offering the same monetary benefits that appeal for different reasons:

1) offers a higher-level job title and 4 weeks' vacation time

2) the same position but includes traveling overseas with the option to work from home.

The guide explains details about the situation, not considered, *the client loves to travel but being a hands-on father with young children is important to him. In addition, there are recent health concerns for his elderly parents.* To help the client decide the guide presents a question, if traveling would create stress being unavailable for his kids or parents.

am i allowed to ask about someone else?

The heading focuses on what offers the extenuating details that decide what's allowed and not. Inquiries mostly ask about others to discover the past linked to why they did/didn't, present attitudes/feelings, and future intensions, actions/inactions. Questions about others <u>are answered</u> when the client's life choices, are directly affected. Questions <u>are not answered</u> for curiosity, including questions about their ex's new lover because they'll feel better knowing. Examples are:

A client wants to know about an ex-romantic partner...:

- that recently ended. It's intuited they moved on with no further contact. The answer helps the client remove false hopes and stop waiting. *Affects her choices and life.*
- currently in another serious relationship with someone else. Personal questions are posed 'to help them move on' when the actuality is psychic spying to satisfy curiosity. *None of their business.*

A client wants to know information about their employer:

- to <u>discover</u> what promotion opportunities are available, and, if so, the guidance to make that happen. *Affects decisions and life direction.*
- for inside track information to use as an advantage. The client's motivation is to <u>create</u> an advantage for self-gain.

The most perplexing client who believe the same strategies used on people will be hidden from the super psychic, telepathic, spirit guide their asking.

someone I love needs help... can I ask for them?

The more important question is, do they want you to ask? Loving intensions aside, clients don't always consider the individual would feel their privacy was invaded. When connected to romance to rationalize a partner's behavior trust the guides know how to determine the best and most effective information that benefits everyone involved.

how often can i get a reading?

Psychic Readings: can be scheduled, as needed, during challenging periods; not on the questions, previously asked. Contacting numerous psychics for the same question, is also asking spirit guides and will compromise future readings. Other than specific situations, generally twice a year is the average.

Medium readings to contact the same DLO can be scheduled, preferably once, no more than twice in the same year. Contacting mediums often prevents the healing process.

does the psychic know too much about me?

The psychic-client can be a strong bond developed over time when guided on intimate and personal concerns. Impartiality depends on each psychic's level of development (*discussed in the next section*). Every reading, should begin with an empty mind to receive a guide's wisdom.

can friends or family join my reading?

A personal story sheds light on this question. A good friend invited me to his mother's birthday party, with a heads up his sister-in-law wanted a reading. Being he was a close friend; I extended her a free reading. At the party there were 20 or so guests and decided the kitchen had the most privacy. What I received was very clear, not expecting her reply that nothing made sense. This continued for ten minutes until my friend sneaked into the kitchen for a beer, overhearing part of the conversation, and said, "*I only heard a couple minutes and can tell you; the situation sounds just like what is going on with my mom.*" Without waiting for a reply, he shouted for his mother to relay the same information. Fast forward, everything said was specific to her current situation.

What happened: Ultimately, guides decide and his mom's current crisis was prioritized over curiosity. The same when others join a medium reading, for support or to share the experience. The one requesting the reading will likely hear from their loved one, but might share their scheduled time, if a loved one wants to say hello. First time clients can get nervous before a reading, as the reason for others to join. Usually, the client's attention isn't fully engaged, constantly checking their reactions so they don't feel left out. Lastly, consider if topics might include private or sensitive information.

taking notes, and recordings

Years ago, it was a common practice for psychics to provide a cassette recording of the reading. After a few squeaky wheels took legal action due to technical problems occurring, the psychic community stopped, shifting the responsibility to the client. Fortunately, technology has advanced with recording options available with some research. If this is a preference, I suggest, also having an inexpensive notebook to write the messages given during readings. I find this to be a convenience when looking for specific information quickly, a backup for any recording issues and stands up to the fast-paced advancements of changing technology. Dedicated notebooks are appreciated later for remembering details thought unimportant at the time, to review all the readings collected and validating future messages.

More than a few times I've heard clients say they have great memory and by the end of the reading they already forgot significant details. So, write it down and be thorough. You will be glad you did.

PSYCHIC STUFF

ha ha, shouldn't psychics know why i'm contacting them?

Psychic jokes seem to make those telling them, feel clever. Sorry to rain on the punchline parade but why they are hilarious, is the breathtaking ignorance they're created from.

Vic Lee's (2012) cartoon is hilarious.

winning the lottery

Yeah, yeah...we've heard it a thousand times "*if you're so psychic, blah, blah... the lottery.*" And... don't think psychics haven't tried to, at least once. (grumble). Here's why winning the lottery has nothing to do with psychic legitimacy. **Questions** altering lifestyle significantly impact how people live, think, and decide that can affect the current incarnation's purpose. Wealth significantly influences all aspects of life and decided with the goal(s) chosen before re-entering the physical world (reincarnation). The life chosen may include affluence to overcome temptations of lust and power that we've seen positions with notoriety, publicly struggle with. For those thinking, "*geez, I only wanted a million dollars, for me, family and friends. Not rule the world!*" Ask the broke, bankrupt, scammed lottery winners that learned quickly having and managing wealth, aren't prepared for variety of con artists or expectations from family and friends.

Woman Who Won the Lottery –The quick version is, a woman has an impulse to splurge on a scratch-off ticket, that normally would be out of character. She asked for a $10 ticket but the cashier accidentally rang up a ticket for $20. To avoid any hassle, she paid the difference only to discover the cashier's error was worth $1,000,000.00. Her story was featured because she was close to financial ruins and the money came just in time.

do psychics give themselves readings?

Speaking for myself only, I don't give myself readings that often because when something is important, they let me know without asking. For the curious: emotions that influence objectivity seeks outside guidance, including family members (like serious health concerns) and psychics have the same rules, information that prevents or interferes with the outcome, is not given.

is receiving psychic messages tiring?

Readings demand a lot of energy even for experienced clairvoyant's able to tap into the universal life flow. From the observer's point of view, psychics look like they're having a regular conversation. It requires years of dedication to interact effortlessly without any affectation or pretense to keep the attention on assisting others.

Receiving and relaying information between the physical and spiritual worlds, as well as, working with the client's emotional state. On occasion, a surge of increased energy is felt working with the balanced mindset. Most seeking help come with a variety of intense stressors that can feel thick and heavy in their energy field. Deeper psi trance state awareness, is sometimes necessary. To prevent exhaustion, appointments are limited to a maximum number of readings (doesn't apply to training schedules). Giving one reading after another for eight hours, regardless of age, is more than unlikely. Hopefully, this adds additional clarity on the previous question.

in social settings

Reactions when discovering a psychic or medium at a social gathering can get interesting. Excited anticipation to presumed projections run the gamut shown as riveted curiosity, the whatever eye roll, or expectations to perform on-demand. I've been fortunate meeting mostly people respectful of my personal time but also on the receiving end of the exceptions. The friend's invitation to a BBQ with the nervous disclaimer; ...'*not everyone believes in what you do, so don't mention the psychic stuff.*' Other examples include the, *I don't believe in that stuff* and *can you answer just one question* people, the occasional *loiterer with focused concentration hoping to elicit a spontaneous vision from mind melding*, and the enthusiastic, *OMG! You can talk to the dead! Is anyone around me now!?* Curious people interested in understanding how psychic ability works is always welcomed. When I'm not working it isn't different than any other career that needs me time to unwind.

MEDIUM ABILITY QUESTIONS

This section continues with the most asked questions about spirit communication and the individuals who speak to them. Before we do, discussing linear versus heavenly time plays a major role when thinking about loved ones on the other side.

Linear time on Earth, is measured by clocks and calendars. The concept of time in alternate realities, is not a new concept but also, not understood. Dimensional planes follow its own set of logic. It's encouraged to read, near death experiences, or NDE, that comprise of stories that defy the definition of time. One story might be a person's heart stopped for one minute in the physical world and as several days, in Heaven. Linear time would hear this one story concluding shorter time in the physical, longer in the divine realms. Different rules, different outcomes. The newly departed soul might feel time as only a few minutes that would be months on Earth. Helpful for those concerned that several months have gone by without any visitation dreams or signs of contact.

the newly departed

The newly departed is when the soul releases the physical body and begins their transitioning back home or crossing over.

At the time of physical death, the veil of multiple dimensions lifts and greeted by a heavenly spirit; an angelic host, spirit guide or loved ones to escort the soul on their journey, by way of; a tunnel of white light, a bridge, door, etc. As we know, heaven includes the exceptions for the best outcome. In this case, illustrated when a newly departed soul chooses or the escort recommends, to temporarily not complete the transitioning. There isn't a set reason but understood to assist grieving by comforting family and friends feeling their presence. Although, not necessary to comprehend, some might find it fascinating what's involved with this decision. What's referred to as *soul realignment,* is necessary but a bit tricky to explain. The soul's natural state experiences time differently and begins adjusting during the journey back to the heavens. When decisions are to temporarily remain, the physical life's perceptions of linear time and their natural soul state, where time moves faster or slower, requires the finesse of the escort to adapt while experiencing multiple timelines. Meaning, the soul's recent association of linear time, adjusting to non-linear time, when remaining in.

The decision to offer comfort has been appreciated by millions of people who've shared stories about a loved one's undeniable presence, as a strong knowing, witnessing sightings or meaningful signs.

sudden departures

Unexpected trauma, illness or accidents are assigned an angelic host to escort souls to a sanctuary for healing. As previously discussed, realigning from the physical persona can take longer when sudden departure is involved. Their reality is partially aware of their death but still in their physical body. Like, people who feel their limb after it was amputated. These endings have a higher percentage for the soul to delay crossing over and might explain paranormal experiences. Delays are mostly short-term while the angelic host reassures and transitions. All sudden departures don't become ghosts temporarily, or, the reason for not feeling them or a visitation dream.

WHAT CLIENTS ASK

readings during the grieving process

When is the best time to reach out to a medium, depends on several factors. The overall recommendation is at least a month, and not the initial grieving stage. This gives your loved ones time while getting reacquainted.

did they suffer?

This question is asked frequently and every time, with few exceptions, the answer is the same. The death cycle is compared to the physical birth process. Some births are difficult for a tiny baby until the umbilical cord is cut and finally out. The same for death with one detail modified; when the soul is crossed over, any discomforts are replaced with sensations of love and lightness. A DLO's guide said to pass on this message to their loved one, *"The living asks for assurances. Be at peace, and know they are in God's hands."*

is my mom, dad here, did my dog jump on my bed last night!

Phew! Communicating with several loved, or having a family reunion from Heaven can be very exciting to think about. The same is true for loved ones eager to say hello and let you know how proud they are and miss you very much. When approved by the divine gatekeepers, the room can get crowded all wanting the opportunity to say hello.

who is who?

Speaking of reunions, when several DLO's come in, figuring out who is what to and where; a client's participation is appreciated, usually fun and sometimes, essential. Nina explains:

《 *Communion with spirits no longer incarnate, gather energetically and cohesively, requiring individual participation from the physical world to identify characteristics and distinguish. The souls in spirit are released from separateness, while remaining as one, dynamically. In a group setting, the energy overlaps, and joins.*

The physical body is finite as we have become accustomed to associating. Spirit is fluid energy merging with, no longer finite but back in the infinite self. The example shown was the Olympic Ring logo, as five interlaced circles to represent how multiple soul energy blends together.

why would a loved one not show up

The explanation isn't for paranormal reasons, or reincarnation, and discussed later. Loved ones might come in for a quick hello (with validation, it's them) to give reassurances they're safe, and leave. One reason, two examples: If the client would benefit from spiritual guidance or if a medium reading prolongs grieving from reconnecting with a loved one. Guides always have your best interest, even when it seems, otherwise. Communication, that heals, is never prevented.

the spirit of personality

Otherworldly personas, (including children) is the soul's most natural form reflecting the accumulated lifetimes of incarnations experienced. Medium communications with loved ones connect with memories how they were physically associated. What clients don't always include, are specifics, like, how they would respond to a stranger (medium) in situations. Private matters, as an example, they might not be forthcoming. Once the association is made, they open and usually followed by light-hearted laughter.

cryptic letters and rhymes

The header reminds me of a show, co-hosted by two men who debate what they believe to be nonsensical. The episode that caught my attention was their declaration all psychic ability is "bullshit." They pointed out practices that were fair and needed exposure. By midway, they lost my respect using a con artist as their expert witness and by the end of the show, quipped out sarcasm they believed logical and sounded like idiots. They seemed particularly proud mentioning when one letter is heard or given in rhymes: Jill, Will, Bill, Phil.

So, what's with messages needing a decoder ring? The answer is simple; most names are common. Imagine the medium standing before a live audience saying, "Anyone connected to Bob, Mike, Joe, Mary, Ann,

WHAT CLIENTS ASK

John, Jim, Susan, Lisa, Sarah, Paul, Charlie, Bill, Chris, Sam, Jack....? Let's play it out in an audience setting, the psychic medium says, "I'm hearing the name Sue." Four people anxious to hear from their DLO quickly stand-up before the medium can offer more information. Two have DLO's with the first name Sue, the third is a Chinese woman with a last name Su, the 4th is named Sue. The medium continues giving details and three of the four realize it isn't their DLO and hopeful anticipation becomes disappointment. As much as the answer still sounds like bullshit, grief in an audience setting comes with expectations, and sometimes fragile ones. An example of this was a client who believed concentrated focus was like a prayer sent and guaranteed a private audience with their loved one.

j, jah or m names

This topic was included after watching a video of short clips with mediums asking, *'who has the jah name?'* The skeptic felt like he was on to something, when his research discovered James and Mary are two of the most popular names in the United States. Yo, ding-a-ling, wouldn't these names also be the highest percentage of DLO's, too?

addicted to medium readings

People can become addicted to almost anything if associated with a reward. Excessive behavior alone doesn't measure an addiction rather the dependency being the way to improve their mood. Clients under this heading go from one medium (or psychic) to the next in a relatively short time period unaware frequency compromises received messages. Mediums may not immediately, but will eventually, know why connecting is arduous. The client may rationalize with closure or moving on is the same as forgetting about the DLO, not caring or similar, to justify. The spirit guide will explain to the medium the reason the DLO wasn't communicating.

SPIRIT GUIDE COLLABORATION

There are circumstances when communication is mediated through guides, such as **DLO's in the process of, or already reincarnated.** Keep in mind, when in soul state, capabilities are freed from physical restraints. Spirit guides, will then take the role of mediator relaying messages via the higher self or telepathically communicating with the transiting soul.

life challenges and emotional states...

afraid to let go, still too fragile from a recent loss or loss, possibly heightened from contact; are other conditions guides step-in. Expect they will explain the reason for their presence and when appropriate, messages from the DLO. When any of the reasons mentioned apply and direct contact is made with loved ones, the guide will instruct the DLO on non-advisable topics.

reincarnation

In cases where a DLO is preparing for next life, they are available for medium contact until their life review is settled with their guides. When a DLO is ready to embark into physical reality the universal guides divert thoughts away from scheduling with a medium. In rare occurrences, mental chatter from eager loved ones can be oblivious to the diversions sent. In this situation, the medium connects with the soul's personal guide to transfers the soul's memories directly. The clairvoyant is informed when this occurs but worth noting, communication received is identical as direct from the DLO. Last, is spirit guides connecting the medium to the higher self (or, soul twin) when a soul already reincarnated back into the physical world.

Notation from Nina: A twin souls (the higher self) is not permitted to represent their physical persona as a backdoor for permission, and presumed incorrectly by spiritualists and healers. Master guides have the authority to grant requests to the spiritualist or healer with the ability to directly communicate beyond clairsentience, empathic or similar feelings described as intuitive.

can all mediums connect with all dlo's?

The answer depends on two factors; how advanced the heavenly soul is and does the psychic medium's personal development align vibrationally. The easiest way to understand is to visualize vibrations as distance. The more advanced a soul is, the faster the vibration, the faster the vibration the higher the soul rises. Heaven isn't hierarchy based, as the physical world views status. The purpose for mentioning is specific to the question, and level of the medium matching, in situations where a DLO is more advanced. Typically, this isn't an issue. Guides tap into a seeker's natural intuition to find mediums with the skills and rapport most suitable, including advanced loved ones. Understandably, grief can distract the mind from noticing their guide's signals, choosing a medium unable or unqualified. The recommendation is to schedule appointments when the mind is quiet, without distractions.

ascending into higher realms and soul kingdoms

In the rare case where a medium's vibration doesn't align with departed souls on a higher frequency level, an intermediary assist in the communication exchange. When personal mastery is reached ascends to a soul kingdom. * In the very rare occasion, when a medium is asked to communicate directly with a soul residing at this vibration, and not vibrationally aligned, an intermediary gatekeeper steps-in to relay messages. I'd like to include additional clarifications to avoid any mistranslations. Not all challenging connections are because of vibrations connected to soul kingdoms. Advanced souls are 1% of the population. All souls are old souls – not all souls are old advanced souls. *Soul groups are not soul kingdoms but a level aspired to attain. A soul kingdom is the highest level of soul mastery with the next as returning to, or uniting with the Godhead.*

LOVE ! TO LOVE ?

"I would go to a psychic wanting to know, the future only; if the guy I was heartbroken over, was going to call me, and, be with me, again. They would answer my questions and I would feel better for a little while, hoping what was said was true. Very little, if any, validation was given during, because I only wanted them to answer my questions. After a few days, I wouldn't believe the reading because I didn't hear from them and didn't have validation, then call another psychic." **C.H.**

LOVE EXCHANGES 3

I'd like to know if a guy named John will contact me.

(What was received intuitively, including the reason for her question, is relayed to her) **Is this correct?**

I think so. Maybe.

What didn't make sense and I'll ask for more details.

Everything made sense.

I'm hearing John told you it wasn't working out and there wouldn't be future contact.

Are we getting back together?

I'm not sure I understand what you're asking.

I feel he will contact me. WE BOTH FELT THE SAME STRONG CONNECTION WHEN WE MET! He said he loved me.

Let me make sure I understand what you are asking for help with. Your question was will John contact you. My guide explained John was clear he did not want to continue the relationship. I know this is a hard time right now for you but knowing can really help with closure.

That isn't what I said. I asked when will we get back together.

(Nina lets me know her heartbreak is in denial and to expect strong emotional reaction). **You and John will continue going separate ways. Is there anything else you want to know?**

Another psychic said, WE ARE SUPPOSED TO BE TOGETHER and I FEEL LIKE THAT IS TRUE!

Would you like me to ask about future romance?

(tearfully) Wait…Is there really someone else? When?

LOVE TO ANSWER

It has the power to transform despair into elation, numbness to exhilaration, desperation into peaceful bliss. It is the purpose of life and why psychics are contacted to answer:

- How do they feel about me?
- Will I hear from (name)?
- WHEN, WHEN, WHen, WheN, when, when, when

Years before online dating apps, one of my mentors, a guru studied in Eastern philosophy, were discussing how everything is connected. This is going somewhere. She illustrated her point with the body's seven major chakras and how they also align with Earth chakras. Spiritual communities would include phrases like global shift, to describe its influence. She continued, saying the current cycle's vibration aligned with the heart chakra, (compassion, love and emotional power). The Mayan calendar was linked to more than one purpose, including when Earth's cycle would begin realigning with the throat chakra (communication and self-expressions of truth). Other than being interesting, I didn't see its relevance. That was until, dating apps became popular and ghosting became part of the vernacular, hearing her say, *'when the shift occurs, relationships will see many challenges connected to communication in ways not experienced previously.'*

re-paired

A real life example of single mindedness or selective hearing was when I hired a local handyman for a week's worth of basic repairs. I was already in the middle of a painting project and required working in the same room, part of the time. We engaged in casual conversation over the next few days, mostly about the tasks at-hand. Around the third day, his interactions began adding personal compliments but didn't come across as flirtation. By the fourth day, his interest was obvious and let him know I had no interest in pursuing anything beyond what I hired him for. His reply was unexpected saying, "*I don't believe you aren't interested,*" and cited instances assumed as reciprocal flirting. From what he said, dialog about the paint colors chosen interpreted as mutual attraction and saying I wasn't interested was playing hard to get.

Since the work was near completion, I reiterated feelings as strictly professional to circumvent any discomfort. He listened, acknowledged, finished the work, and left. The day after, we exchanged a few quick texts specific to the work done. Day two post-work, he texted if he could call to with a question, which I agreed to. When he did, he asked me out on a date, saying, "*You letting me call, shows mutual interest.*"

QUESTIONS ABOUT LOVE

what does he / she look like?

They have dark hair, brown or hazel eyes, average build, wear business suit attire to work, jeans on the weekends and have all their teeth. Good to go?

When it's simple curiosity, why would some clients be given specific details and, not others? Let's use the physical description above, adding the when and where. Next, are timing questions, inevitably asked. For this to happen, insert the crucial information, something like, in the next month or two, both will be asked to go somewhere, spontaneously. Watch for invitations or a compelling thought to hang out with a friend, and details to remove any ambiguity. The client is thrilled, and off they go. The month or two part is forgotten and the person who believes they'd never do this, activates the scrutinize-analyze phase, so they can conclude every thought is *spontaneous*. As we know, eager enthusiasm ignores that boring timing thing contingent on meeting a friend or invitation, because destiny awaits in the frozen food aisle sleuthing for their chance encounter (breath) from a sudden craving for ice cream. Who doesn't get the symbolism of ice cream, right? Now... insert, the part the real compelling thought occurs, and Ms. or Mr. *please tell me, I would never do that*, is at some random thing, in the opposite direction.

Anyone guess, what happens next? Correct, if the answer was, the psychic is contacted telling them the prediction was wrong.

Spirit guides include all of these behaviors, for what is and isn't given.

are we supposed to be together?

What the client really wants to know is; *are they my one and only*? The twin mate craze tripled, quadrupled this question adding to heartbreak's confusion and false hopes. Explained next, gives clarity with how differentiations work, and important to know. What if, the *supposed to be* part, was yes, but only for a temporary period? What if, the *supposed to be*, was yes because it led to an important future event?

The fates, coincidences and synchronicity, brings together for a purpose without any guarantees. Why the universe unites two people is usually as an opportunity for personal development. Challenges are inserted for the intense connection needed to shake up any unresolved emotions the, and why romance is chosen to reach life goals. The psychic won't receive a full download but likely sense, the relationship is important, but temporary. Human behavior doesn't need a psychic to know heart strings have a higher probability to dismiss anything not leading to Mr./Mrs. Right. But....staying in a one-sided relationship meant to be temporary, affects others and can have long term repercussions.

With the understanding of the above paragraph, how does the question change? The supposed to be, rephrased to discover the purpose for meeting. The future supposed to be example, as meeting three persons before getting married with the strong possibility, one of the three, is who. This way, the client has something to look forward to, without interfering with the desired outcome. If your someone, prone to pushing, like, which of the three, be careful because your guide might answer you.

are we getting back together?

Reuniting is a popular reason for contacting a psychic and understood it's not a, yes or no, replay. Hearing, yes, is rare, but does sometimes happen, make sure the psychic explains: 1) the motivation or what changed the circumstances 2) when, and if timing depends on other factors and 3) if reconnecting is temporary. The spirit guide will use discretion considering any reactions and behaviors that risk altering the outcome.

A word of caution: the individual asking is likely still vulnerable with the highest risk to impulsively contact hotlines and overshare. What desperation wants might be the bearer of false hopes and prolonged heartbreak. **Several chapters offer advice and give tips and strongly suggested.**

do i know them?

Or, another way of asking, *'are we getting back together?'* Exceptions: a secret admirer that sometimes a friend, a social/business contact not considered or colleague, yet to make their feelings known. Be open to any answer to avoid forcing conclusions to fit when the ex is still mentally lingering.

how do they feel about me?

Relationship experts who advise, *if you don't know –they don't care,* isn't always true and not so black and white. Sorrow swirls in the mind keeping attention on finding immediate relief, believing knowing is the solution.

If so, ask how will knowing give the peace of mind desperately wanted. Maybe they pop in and out of your life, when convenient, or stopped all communication. What answer, other than, the miraculous change of heart, will change giving them all the power? The mind believes it wants the truth but will deny it, when it doesn't fit the illusion. Ask if you already have the answer and its only waiting for you to see it.

THE INSTIGATORS

waiting and texting (wat?)

WAT is the major player why romance contact psychics. The intense connection felt is believed mutually reciprocated. From clients, there seems to be some consistencies leading up to, WAT: The first sign of future problems is obviously, erratic communication. But a lot is based on self-esteem view of being a nice reasonable person who doesn't over react, or, the benefit of the doubt period. Around the two week-ish time frame impatience sets in and the, *f*** it* stage ignites into a strong currency of emotions. Resisting the temptation to text becomes more difficult and lets loose after a friend's pep-talk or advice blogs confirm suspicions. The one hour text is carefully crafted and sent into the digital aethers with a feeling of resolute satisfaction, until the *ugh regrets* sets in. This means, a follow-up text is needed, that will be either, an extensive apology or detailed instructions on how they deserve to be treated. When the w.a.t. partner decides to finally text back, their reason is worse than the wait , like saving something adorable and fragile.

Nina suggests, a quick reversal of behaviors will give confusion the answer. No long overly detailed goodbye message hoping your words magically changes their feelings. The disappearing act works both ways. So, everyone is clear, the suggestion is for discovery and not to manipulate.

Important: Give yourself time to settle your mind before jumping too quickly back into the dating scene. It's understandable to want to feel normal again or find distraction to get over someone. When not healed, 1) the new person will be constantly compared 2) strong tendency to talk about the ex, a bit too often 3) past triggers heightened to behaviors resembling the ex.

is your phone haunted?

The word ghosting emerged when dating apps came with millennial conveniences of texting. We shouldn't be surprised, soon after, seeing social media posts with an angry emoji and the date suddenly going poof.

The ghoster's motto is, *no answer is the answer*, and don't think ghosting is insensitive because emotional effort wasn't invested…plus, everyone does it, so, what's the big deal?

Comment: Yes, a couple minutes to write one text can prevent months of hurt and wondering. Since we can't control anyone but ourselves – then, add a probation period until they earn your trust and any emotional intimacy. **See also:** love bombing, benching and gas lighting.

THE INVISIBLY REAL

when the smartphones are why's

The digital convenience smartphones revolutionized, not only communication, but how we communicate. The conveniences controlling decisions, have focused on the mystery hidden, not the truths revealing the character. Because of looking up, instead of down, contacting psychics increased to learn what wasn't given or can't be verified. There is a lot of advice on ghosting, so I'll skip over what most know, with advice most probably know, but forget. Clues for potential ghosting:

Majority of feelings expressed via emojis. Watch for any long gaps of time without a heads up. Stay out of nice person dialog, and pay attention to what your smartphone is telling you.

INFIDELITY

Not the happy hearts and poppy flowers part of romance but the icky deception, tears and betrayal and in the top three most emotionally charged topics, comparable to grief from loss and the effects of anti-social personality disorder. Because it's a fragile subject, be aware discussions might create initial reactions but eventually make sense.

is he/she cheating on me?

It will surprise most people to discover asking about cheating partners is unethical for a psychic to answer. As surprising, most clients asking, aren't married, or what happens after hearing the answer. What isn't surprising is a partner suspected of infidelity often denies it, leaving a nagging feeling.

Let's play it out what happens with intuitive help. One of two possibilities, is the dice roll. Hearing, yes, to cheating – what happens next? Is the partner confronted with how the information was given? If that detail is omitted, it's dismissed as paranoid, nonsense, insecure, etc. What about hearing no, to the cheating? Does the reason for having the suspicion go away? This becomes the quagmire who is given trust, the psychic or partner? Suspicions of unfaithful behavior, hire a private detective and get solid proof.

will they leave their spouse?

When affecting others choices and time, answers are provided. The spouse juggling two commitments may have honest communications and unaware unexpected family matters will arise in the future. A sudden change of heart from guilt, worried about a spouse's emotional health or other marital expectations to stay with the spouse – avoiding telling the one waiting.

the other man/woman

Nina provides insight on the responsibility the other man/woman has concerning infidelity… Fasten your seatbelts people because the answer may surprise, even anger.

"any morality, decisions positively or negatively affecting another with purpose or disregard, does not extend outside of the commitment made by two. The vows between the two is a verbal and loving agreement and energetically binds. It is beholden for the two. The commitment changes when one communicates to the other, even if the other agrees or disagrees to the decision."

Whether verbal or contractual, the honor to uphold burden of responsibility is limited to spouses, bound by commitment and doesn't extend to third party involvement. By no means is the language to be interpreted as condoning aspects of infidelity. Blaming the other man/woman is the expected reaction when hurt doesn't want to believe their spouse betrayed them. The other man or woman doesn't always know they're involved with someone married and, also deceived.

why infidelity isn't honest

As a long time, tarot reader some cards consistently appear for similar situations. The three of swords, on the previous page, is an iconic depiction of the pain felt from a love triangle. Why a partner chooses to cheat is often simple reasons connected to complex situations. The reasons most cheaters and the other man/woman give are: *(not in any particular order)*

- wants/waiting for the spouse to ask for a divorce
- both, or either, lost desire for sexual intimacy
- financial concerns: child support, alimony, health insurance, credit cards, separate living costs
- worried spouse will use kids in a custody battle
- doesn't want to leave while children are young
- support a spouse with mental or physical health issues
- emotional neglect or disconnect

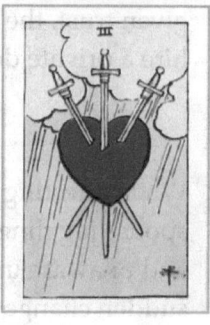

Rider-Waite's 3 of swords, (above)

The cheated on shouldn't assume they did anything wrong or beat up their self-esteem. Why it happens, might be fate to end one chapter for the next, experienced with another.

DECEPTION AND SERIAL CHEATING

The exceptions are serial cheaters having motivations purely based on self-gratification. Lying and manipulation is second nature with convincing performances of sincerity. This kind of deception, can be traumatizing for the cheated on who are aware something feels off but doubt and confusion overwhelm any rationale they had before the relationship.

Guidance: The devastation caused by serial cheaters is an exception and allowed to <u>psychically received help</u>. I think finding resources providing certainty, such as professional photos from a private investigator, is the better option to remove doubts and to confidently move forward. **If you suspect someone your dating is a serial cheater,** marriages are publicly registered and can be obtained online through verifiable websites in compliance with confidentiality laws.

SOUL MIRRORS

Any student chosen to learn the advanced psychic arts goes through stages of initiations for soul purification and tuning. Lessons from cosmic and heavenly masters are not experienced the same as a conventional classroom, rather life challenges, vivid dreaming, astral projection and ongoing synchronicities. My purpose for mentioning is to share a particular concept from my teacher, St. Germain, instilled from a psychic vision.

What the reader needs to know is: 1) psychic visions are experienced with the physical senses, just like conscious reality 2) the memory selected was to understand how truth is realized in soul state 3) when the recent life memories are reviewed.

The psychic vision Germain surfaced was twenty years passed when an eight month relationship was ending. The memory started when my boyfriend decided to stay home instead of joining me and commuter friends at a local bar. I was relieved because, John, a guy I was attracted to was also going and was pretty sure he felt the same.

Over the course of the evening, we were openly flirting with each other on the dance floor. A few hours later, we were saying goodbye in the parking lot before the group scattered to their vehicles. John followed me back to my car for the anticipated passionate goodnight kiss. Except, the memory, as I remembered, was modified, adding two details. In this version, St. Germain showed the memory with my boyfriend watching me kiss John, and he removed all the reasons I gave to justify it. To understand how our soul, no longer in the physical world, relives memories in absoluteness of truth. My boyfriend was standing a few feet away with eyes filled with hurt and betrayal. What I was shown was powerful shifting a paradigm that continues to still influence my actions and thinking.

"You can never lose anything that really belongs to you, and you can't keep that which belongs to someone else."

Edgar Cayce

LOVE TO LEAVE 4

Truth is incontrovertible. Panic may resent it. Ignorance may deride it. Malice may distort it. But there it is. **Winston Churchill**

A CHAPTER DEDICATED TO ASSHOLES? Wait, that doesn't sound like someone enlightened. Neither are twisted mind games from imposters of love. These parasites of chaos, don't present themselves with nervous tics, prescription bottles tucked in underwear, or spontaneous barking during a lunar cycle. Initially, they might up-lift and inspire, be unassuming and modest, amusing, awkwardly incapable, etc. Affection is a weapon front-loaded with slatherings of attention and captivating genuineness until their target is blinded by adorableness. The too good to be true, guy or gal, just can't be anything other than super cute with ulterior motives are also predictable. Early red flags can be to test the water's emotional tolerance. If charming allure easily convinces, it's the green light for the never ending pursuit of unrelenting uncertainties, diminished self-esteem, emotional devastation, built on the foundation of one more chance. If, this is you and straitjackets don't appeal to your fashion sense, help is on the way. First a mental chatter make-over:

- yes, one of your <u>many</u> soul mates, absolutely, not a twin ...
- the powerful connection does have a reason to...
- create self-awareness what is believed vs willing to accept on love
- yes, it's time to stop holding on to hope a love fairy will sprinkle them with, *honey, I'm ready to love you like a normal person,* dust.

psychological manipulation; a mental distortion for exploitative and devious methods, indirect, or underhanded tactics to benefit self-interests at another's expense. It is strongly urged to not ignore the signs of the **mind games** cited.

> **BENCHMARK:** If confusion is building, along with doubts, there is a straightforward method to gauge the situation. Remove the dialog and simply review their actions and non-actions, then add your emotional results. Is it balanced or one-sided? More anguish with only sprinkles of playful laughter? Yes, it's time for you to be the ghost.

why they do or don't, doesn't matter

Remember, deliberately hiding, can determine, right from wrong. This heading is when the imposters become an obsession intent on finding out why they do, how they became. Maybe if they really understand them and become their secret Santa therapist and magically fix them – they will become the fantasies imagined. Surely, there's some horrible story involving a bag of wet puppies why they cancel, aren't accountable, can't commit, scared to be alone and (sad face) lonely. Yo, opposite of sexy person; have you considered the possibility they want you to obsess? Here we go...*but, what if I'm wrong, I don't know them, they're different.* They always are.

So, Mr. Uncertainty dating Ms. Confusion needs a dead-line (ha, a pun!). No more than one month – then adios. Predictable is the here-and-there texts of, I miss you, hi, that pitters and thrills forgetting the usual look is Kleenex is stuffed into each nostril. Next, we present the douche wads.

benching

Benching is when someone is not exactly interested in dating you but at the same time, the person does not want to let you go. He or she tries to keep all the options open and would come back to you when they feel like it. Keeping a sexual or romantic partner on the hook as a perpetual Plan B until someone better comes along. It's essentially leading someone on, but for the express purpose of trading them in.

THE INVISIBLY REAL

gaslighting

Gaslighting strategies are used by abusers, dictators, narcissists, sociopaths and cult leaders by way of emotional manipulation for their target to question their reality over time. This type of mental distortion is somewhat complex and suggest further research.

captain hooked

Referred to as, *love bombing*, is misleading and decided on a more fitting expression. For those unfamiliar, the strategy used is overwhelming attention and affection to chum the emotional waters, hook and toss. This is a serious and depraved personality flaw with early warning signs of excessive and inappropriate displays of attention.

blubbing

Blubbing is a behavior everyone should be aware of because; 1) it can show up in every behavior category mentioned 2) and it's a behavior most are uncomfortable to question and they know it. The strategy is unique to emotional manipulation, to re-direct or overpower a situation, or person. The weapon is an excessive demonstration of tears fortified with tales of woes to induce sympathy, without question. Two's clues:

1) the observer's reaction to their tears is annoyance or neutrality that otherwise would illicit genuine sympathy 2) their behavior is unusually inappropriate for the situation.

REAL EXAMPLE: a sociopath spontaneously bursts into tears because his only son died from suicide. His theatrics was described as spontaneous hysterical sobbing, like flicking on a light switch. Once the desired result was achieved, tears gone. He killed his son two more times only to cancel previous commitments.

cherry pickers

The cherry picker follows suggested psychic guidance that is convenient, then confused the future prediction didn't happen. Another appointment is scheduled because the information was wrong and swear all the guidance was followed.

It's always interesting when a client's version is without any contributing details of blame, forgetting their audience, psychic not friend, right…they quickly add, *well, I did follow it, except for two things*. And, the two things suggested is blamed on their partner and the psychic, but keep returning to the psychic (eh hem). Exceptions allowing the same question is to help on prevailing issues creating the problem. Next, is an example of the chaos and advice for any relating personally.

A man calls for advice about the woman he's dating for two years wanting to know why she won't commit to the relationship. He's aware of a cycle resulting in the same conclusion but doesn't know why. Intuited, are some missing facts from his version, as *avoidant communication from her and anger from his impatience*. He's asks what's needed for change. Being one sided, ending the cycle relies on changes only he can control. Anger is a huge problem when he doesn't hear from her in a certain timeframe. The long response times, surface emotional triggers of impatience and hurt, built-up over two years, expressed in anger and lengthy text bombs.

His partner delayed responses might be to focus the blame on his reaction. Whatever the motivation is self-control is paramount to end the cycle from repeating. Cherry picker relationships can continue <u>for years</u> until silent, or the other ends the relationship.

energy vampires

A constant need of attention, in a constant state of conflict, and it's constantly never good enough. In a relationship, energy vampires are experts on what they need and how it should be given. At the same time, they give their partner's attention, are helpful and even offer support. And why there is the potential of devastation. Having a supportive partner creates doubt their ongoing needs are excessive, are the experts but always need help, and relationship conversations are what you aren't doing for them. They exhaust and take a toll most won't see it coming, until it's too late. There are early signs of needs that dominate conversations and plans.

narcissists and sociopaths (NaS)

Anti-personality disorders under this heading are symptomatically independent sharing common traits, including the distress felt by their victims. Psychopaths are omitted because of their far-reaching complexities that would be irresponsible to summarize in a few sentences. Condensing any of the three; psycho-sociopaths and narcissists, as *unable to empathize*, could mistranslate as unable to emotionally internalize. In the narcissists and sociopath's kingdom, pain and pleasure are processed only from their point of view; so, they feel more than everyone. So, the empathy isn't the big factor. Another mistranslation is NaS are super intelligent. Nope, they can be as dumb as a box of rocks. The single factor to be aware of is every breath, thought and desire is for self-gratifications for pleasure and deflecting pain, (praise and criticism). Meeting their needs requires a <u>convincing</u> persona that can be that normal, nice guy, overly emotional victim that's so vulnerable, charming with an easy laugh – that's why they're emotionally dangerous.

NaS generate a unique vibrational fingerprint natural intuition responds to (use common sense before jumping to conclusions). **A narcissist's** imprint is vague but compelling; a mental lingering, caution something about them is off. It would be strange for the situation or physical appearance. The energy **imprint** of a **sociopath,** is sensed as an alert or warning, to keep your distance. For example, an introduction and taking a step back suddenly, as an involuntary reflex. Queasiness or nausea is another intuitive response not limited to physical. I experienced while watching a documentary interviewing actual serial killers (not professional actors). This does not imply sociopaths or psychopaths are serial killers but all serial killers are psychopaths.

Nina explained the nausea experienced, as an affect from the sacral energy portal, called chakras, out of balance. **Sacral is the 2nd Chakra -** below the naval, links to how emotions are expressed.

sensed and sense-ability

To protect privacy and avoid irresponsible language containing psychiatric diagnostics, only generalized details are included. I had the unique opportunity to coach a *vulnerable narcissist*[1]. A likeable, unassuming guy who contacted me, as a condition given by his recent ex-girlfriend. Force by proxy, wasn't the strategy but trust and honesty. The thought behind it, was he needed my greenlight for any chance of speaking to her again. Because of my profession he admitted that he thought some nice guy charm would win me over. Fast forward past the failed attempts of cuteness, fits of rage, pouting, winning me over with compliments, back to pouting...shampoo, rinse, repeat. Eventually, our talks evolved into a genuine mutual understanding earned from transparency, honesty and no judgment for a glimpse into his inner sanctum. I told him it would be helpful to many people knowing how his minds processes as advice he would give someone romantically involved with NPD. This is what he said:

"We get away with doing what we want because we choose when we think there aren't risks. I know how my personality could be used to manipulate emotions - so [dating] *a confident woman I would back down from because it's too much work and won't buy it or won't need me. And... professional or education doesn't mean confidence. I look for someone that needs me, including financially.*

My advice? You must wrestle the control out of our hands because there are no consequences. Take control of the date like it's a chess match."

AUTHOR COMMENT: Say goodbye to the partner who takes advantage of your weak spots, and make you sleep on the wet spot.

Love is reverence, and worship, and glory, and the upward glance. Not a bandage for dirty sores.

Ayn Rand

---

[1] personality disturbance (or distortion) according to the fifth edition of The Diagnostic and Statistical Manuel of Mental Disorders (DSM-5)

THE PSYCHIC

THE SILVER CORD
5

Before the internet it was, "When the student is ready, the teacher will come." After, When the teacher comes, check their credentials. Michele Bigness

CAN ANYONE BE PSYCHIC? It was sometime during the New Age resurgence these four words were rearranged into; anyone can be psychic. Over the decades, the concept made its way into mainstream society and eventually filed into spiritualist's ideology. Understandably, no one questioned if it was psychically received, or, birthed into reality from a bong hit in the hot tub.

Psychic, like most professions, adopt nuggets of wisdom from experienced and respected peers. Yet, this misdirect, in particular was one with more weight that played a significant role in the current climate of mass-produced esotericism and seemingly overnight increase of psi services. The reinforcement effort for readers to not easily dismiss isn't in vain. Esoteric philosophy, without the deeper comprehension, will be translated from a desire or reward/punishment (twin mates, karma).

The human journey is not random. There is an equilibrium to the collective whole with every individual as one piece, part of its great design.

[Nina] *All humans are born with an invisible divine link directly connected to the internal soul, referred to as the silver cord. Not all are born destined to guide others intuitively. To guide other souls requires vast comprehension of its purpose and to know how, to be its purpose. A dedication that is not by whim, folly, fascination, or curiosity of divination. The journey is to recognize who are qualified to guide others towards self-enlightenment when seeking guidance from the universe.*

The explanation doesn't define limitation of human potential but extends a refinement allowing the implication:

- the natural intuitive body is inherent within all internally to guide our journey of life.
- a psychic experience is an internal communication to guide others journey in life.

PHYSICAL PERCEPTIONS

Natural intuition isn't the knock-off designer version of psychic ability, as some think. It's a divine link connected to prophetic, vivid and visitation dreams, alerts danger, provides hunches, can read people, sense other's emotions and when combined with practiced meditation can experience transcendental self-awareness. It guides, and allows guides to steer towards, away, stalls or quickens, subtly or obviously, for destiny or fate's arrival. The silver cord to the universe was designed as a Heavenly GPS, of sorts.

It's especially difficult when the five physical senses say one thing when the intuitive sense offers a dissenting opinion. Learning to trust your intuitive perceptions needs to appeal to the other five. How did you learn to identify single-channel impressions; hearing a single drop of water from another room? The burning smell of smoke with fire where action is taken knowing the sense is linked to a physical reality. There is no proof it happened yet we don't doubt it did. The bond our physical reality has with our intuitive body is naturally evident. Connecting associations of physical sensations to intuition, we can adopt into the rationale what logic requires as real. Clues are found in everyday language subconsciously linking to the 6th sense.

Sigmund Freud inducted the term, Freudian Slip as, *an unintentional truth from the unconscious awareness*. Applying his theory to the unconscious internal thoughts that relates to awareness of intuition, there are a significant number of subliminal examples.

Intuitive phrases and expressions: I feel like/had a feeling, I don't know, it's a gut feeling, had a hunch, I sensed you were coming, they seemed trustworthy, something about them, I don't know why…I just know it.

Intuitive physical responses: automatic reflexes such as, taking a step back meeting someone "normal" looking and smiling, spontaneous impulses resulting in a coincidence, feeling something is wrong/dangerous creating a heightened response, the parental and/or marital connection of intuitive response not connected to logic.

Sensations associated to the physical body upon initial introduction: in person, by phone or viewing a photo and felt instantaneously without logical explanation may emotionally connect energetically as – nausea, nervousness, alerted and heightened senses, and other spontaneous physical reaction.

SPIRIT GUIDING NATURAL INTUITION

[Nina] All souls are assigned guides. All guides have vast wisdom. Not all guides have vast access. Personal guides assist using natural intuition specific to the individuals Book of Life. Exceptions are vivid/prophetic dreams, where gates open specifically for the experience. Psi-medium guides are designated with various levels of access. One with sixth sense is capable of the highest plane within their gate.

There are four levels of natural intuition 1- vibrational syncing (I have a feeling) 2- prophecy dreams, feeling a global or significant event occurs 3- vivid dreaming connecting to DLOs. Higher intuitions temporary gate arranged by God. 4- higher self, channeling information relevant to the self, combined with interpretations of topics entwined with personal beliefs.

Divine Connection vibrations of psi energy links into emotional memory energy of the past present future. The higher (faster, lighter) psi energy, the external essence (aura) will merge with Christ Consciousness and internal-self to the super unconsciousness.

Being in-tune is someone who learned mental stillness within. Below, describes basic to advanced natural intuition.

Quick flashes of clairvoyant images or clairaudient thoughts, that manifest not long after. Connected to solar plexus chakra.

Gut feelings and a sense of knowing occurs sporadically to frequently depending on mental chatter.

Sensitivity to locations with paranormal activity felt mostly in sacral chakra combined with uneasy sensations, sometimes headaches.

Empathic transfer is feeling emotional output, in the environment that can be residual energy from the past or present, from an event or focused emotional energy. How in-tune, is the variable determining the intensity of transfer and how the emotional output disrupts energy flow. The experience can be an influx of short bursts or linger depending if residual and the event creating it. Transfer created by ongoing/magnified focused on a recipient(s) experiences as their own thought, and as a sudden interruption, replacing the current emotion. The key to recognize is, emotions quick shifting (non-diagnostically related). There isn't a need to protect yourself. Stand up and take a deep breath and smooth your auric field with your hands from your feet to crown chakra. Sacral chakra.

Premonitions related to health, big events, or serious situations with family, friends and close relationships.

Pattern recognition. Signs from the universe are recognized in synchronicities shown as repeating patterns or occurrences in the environment. Connected to the awakenings.

Nature signs. Nature responds to high vibration signatures to say hello, appearing in a way to get your attention. Connected to the crown chakra.

Nature messages let you know prayers were heard or from DLOs. Check with reputable sources for totems and its significance, when reoccurring.

Suggested guidance: Meditation and self-hypnosis helps with mental chatter to heighten intuitive reception.

Years ago, a psychic opened a world connected to a higher level of communication; an energy everyone is part of and can have with God. I didn't understand it but knew I wanted to be a part of it. **A.R.**

THE SIXTH SENSE
6

All humans have an intuitive body link called the soul within. The soul is spirit, the mind is the portal and the body is the vessel of matter. **Nina**

WHAT IS POSSIBLE BEYOND PHYSICAL REALITY? How can one predict the future before it's a thought? The unknowns of the supernatural have been pondered by parapsychologists and the occult for centuries. One of the great mysteries is how the mind receives signals from the unseen forces. The ability to communicate with the Universal Consciousness is referred to as 'a gift.' This implies a separateness of a divine connection as entitlement. Psychic abilities are encoded within the individual, not unlike a predisposition for a talent or interest, early in life. As is also true, competence of any talent is contingent to the state of mind's expression. The same is true for multi-dimensional insights and its relationship with the inner workings of the human, as a psychic. The context from higher dimensions relies on whether, when brought together associate through their resemblance to each other, or to what extent of disagreement. Principles and morality, formed early in life, are stored perceptions as facts and so, has greater risk of rationalized reinterpretation. The ability, when viewed as a separate entity, can then, determine the relationship with the psychic and how it regards its skill and commitment to the self.

Before grasping the finer concepts discussed in this section reviewing basic ESP phrases and terminology, is essential. Words like *clairvoyance* is a common term used frequently. Examples how the context is applied, might be: 1) referring to psychic sight, 2) a generalized designation of medium communication 3) a medium's formal title (Clairvoyant).

Metaphysical rhetoric can be intimidating but knowing a few basic key words explaining the different categories of abilities, on the following page and what the clairs are, next.

Clair, is French for *clear*. Used as a prefix, it associates to an **Extra-Sensory** communication, (suffix), identifying the heightened **Perception (ESP).**

clairvoyant (clear sight) – **clair**audient (clear hearing) – **clair**cognizant – (clear knowing) **clairs**entience (sensing) – **clair**gustance (clear taste).

PSYCHIC ABILITY CATEGORIES

Precognition	Retrocognition	Akashic Access
Past Life	Psychometry	Empathic Sensing
Medical Intuitive	Healing Touch	Seeing Auras
Psychic Art Channel	Animal Intuitive	Locate people/items
Remote Viewing	Telepathy	Telekinesis
Nature Empath	Astral Projection	Bilocation & Levitation

Mediumship – Paranormal, Channeling, and Celestial/Heavenly

The clairs are often included with the above, as separate abilities. This is not accurate and I'll explain why. Clairs and their relating suffix are sensory communication tools that work with all psi ability. For example, a medium (ability to connect with a spirit gateway) requires both *clairvoyance*, to see the spirit and *clairaudience*, to hear the spirit for effectively communicating messages. ESP mentioned above connect to usually more than one clair to receive, connect, and communicate.

tool; a natural ability necessary in the practice of a vocation or profession that activates and controls a particular function.

rare or elusive abilities; communicating with spirits with both the physical and psychic senses are born with senses aligned or merged. Meaning, it would not be a latent ability discovered later. Individuals can toggle between the psychic/physical independently or simultaneously.

READING CATEGORIES

Terminology confuses many clients when selecting a reading. Really, knowing the difference of psychic and medium is all you need.

THE PSYCHIC

References & Terminology: *Sixth sense* intuits the past, present, (*retrocognition*) and future (*precognition*) timelines about a person, place or object that was not known or experienced directly by the psychic.

All mediums are psychic but not all psychics are mediums. Psychic ability is a required to connect with disembodied spirits, heavenly or otherwise. Not all mediums give psychic readings.

Psychic: ability to connect into different timelines; past, present, and future. Methodology can be trance state awareness, connecting with a physical object or divination tools.

Medium communication is a direct vibrational channel connecting to astral and heavenly planes.

astral plane: a subtle state, level, or region of reality, each plane corresponding to some type, kind, or category of being or dimension of existence of the celestial spheres.

Psychic Medium: psychic = timelines and medium = spirit communication. Psychic medium, is a psychic and medium offering both categories of readings.

Medium: When defined as medium (without psychic preceding) is for the client to know readings are specific to spirit communication.

Paranormal Medium: the ability to communicate with ghosts, (earth-bound spirits). Deceased loved ones in the Heavenly quadrants vibrate on a different channel than the ghost plane. Reasons have to do with the differences in the density of each plane. DLO mediums can sense and can even communicate with earth bound but check to see if they include the paranormal as a service offered.

[Nina] Gaia psychics read the energy contained within Earth's auric fields, sensitive to denser energy imprints and able to psychically communicate with the holographic energy from the *transitory realm*.

AUTHOR'S COMMENT: Not all paranormal mediums are aware ghosts are not earth bound and on an astral dimension that is separate _and_ overlays with earth. Meaning, it is a duplicate plane separated by only a few seconds of time and why ghosts believe they are still on earth and people witnessing apparitions. *See the heavens section for more details.*

SCHEDULING & TIPS

- **Client responsibility:** Make sure all social media accounts are secured before scheduling.
- **Nevva, evva, evva!!!** Give your birthday or any personal details.
- **Reading choices:** psychic, medium and psychic medium. Select the service that best describes the outcome based on the type of communications offered. If a psychic reading is selected with a psychic medium, it's still a psychic reading. Psychic medium readings, 45 minutes is the suggested minimum, one hour is preferable. Include in the comment field if you want to split one hour with 30 minutes psychic and 30 minutes medium, if offered. This allows psychic mediums to connect before the appointment. Do not include details of the DLO.
- **Additional suggestion:** refrain from last minute requests nearing the end of your appointment, to communicate, or if the other side is coming in. Be assured, when a DLO wants to send a message, they will without inquiring.

For phone or video readings, find a quiet location without interruptions. This includes using the little boy's/girl's room and securing your fluffy loved ones with a penchant to bark at their own farts, paper bags or dangerous fuzz balls. Have a notebook and two pens even if you're recording, as a backup for technical issues.

SIGNS - PSYCHIC ABILITY

Identifying and recognizing the indicators of ability is an overview and may not include all the unique traits or experiences:

- People are immediately comfortable around you or when talking to.
- You hear comments, like you're looking inside or through them. Strangely, it doesn't contradict the first bullet point.
- God, is and always has been, an inherent part of you whether raised in a religious or non-religious upbringing, there is a natural connection you can't explain.

THE PSYCHIC

- There is a period of resistance/questioning God's existence during transformational periods of self-discovery.

- Curiosity or pull to the supernatural or questioning deeper life meanings of spirituality, since childhood.

- (When acknowledged later-dormant) Occurrences in life present an aspect of, or around, as reminders, until activated. To avoid mistranslation because of increased popularity, examples would be: someone giving you a tarot deck (or similar) connected to a coincidence, increased psychic-related flashes or vivid dreams about people, events, that aren't personally connected.

- ESP feels like it's part of you, impossible to ignore.

- Supernatural/paranormal coincidences occur frequently, consistently when developing/opening/ learning. A stage described as coo-coo for coco puffs that are difficult to describe or for others to believe. Over time, the mind adjusts, recognizing them as the universe talking to, and a way of life.

- I'm including hearing your name shouted when alone because of how frequently reported. These are experiences shared with natural intuition and psychic ability with more than one reason it occurs. Although many think it's a DLO, it can be a guide and even a ghost. It would be unlikely the intent was to prompt fear and usually heard with a neutral intonation.

Two questions will determine.

- How many <u>years</u> would you be willing to devote to learn your craft?
- How many years did you devote to your craft?

There are so many wonderful individuals sincerely wanting to help others, felt as their higher purpose and why they look to spirituality. Add, *'anyone can be psychic'* and it's easy to understand how someone would believe psychic development is the answer. For some, it would be true. But the same logic, if true, would apply to every skilled profession. *'Anyone can be a doctor.'* The same requirements of training and time to develop before working directly with patients, is not different. Psychics and mediums who excel in their field will develop faster, at the same time, don't focus on <u>their wants</u>, rather the time needed to offer people their very best.

PSI AND REINCARNATION

All humans are created with unrealized potential; realized in current timelines and accumulated over many lifetimes. Life is not random, or luck of the draw; it's organized, structured for life a destination found in both opportunities and challenges.

Psychics and mediums capabilities rely on the accrued tools of past lives needed to assist others. It's a point mentioned numerous times for seekers to identify competency over ambitions. Considering the impact psychic communication has on decisions the reincarnating soul has succeeded baseline keywords, connected to the ego. Without, is analogous to advancing an Elementary student into High School, skipping Middle School.

is having ability enough?

Proficient in the universal language meditation to control mental chatter and heighten reception and adhering to the rules of ethical practice, working with diverse personalities in distress, etc. All-important, but not the main factor. The ego defines sub-par abilities and one who has mastered their craft. I've met several peers too focused on fame, money and power. Achieving celebrity from recognized talent and using abilities to be famous is what differentiates motivations. The universe gauges truth by its vibrational signature that can't be persuaded, negotiated or disguised. The unbalanced ego is unable to ascend above the lower astral planes.

the art of questioning

There is some irony of the importance of how questions are presented. Conversations using the five physical senses relies on intuitive understanding, i.e., 'you know what I mean, right?' Of course, guides understand a client's frame of mind. Here's where it gets a bit sticky. Mental questions are like a prayer when confusion asks the question and answers it simultaneously. Meaning, a career question formed in the mind and concluding the desire or want. Other than love, to allow is a significant word.

Ask the divine for help, allow their guidance, remember why their guidance was sought. **Examples given below, when applicable:**

The question presented as asked. *"I interviewed for a higher position in my company and like to know the outcome."*

The question rephrased: *"What information is available on (the client's) upcoming promotion, including other career opportunities they aren't aware of, and guidance on the best option."*

Splitting timelines is a method Nina taught me, where I create a mental image (right) while presenting a question allowing multiple variables. For example, the center is home base presenting six decisions for the best option (the client); is promoted, takes the promotion, decides to wait for another position, employment prospects with other companies, etc. When applicable, it can be very helpful to assist client decide or discover unconsidered possibilities available.

knowledge

A psychic's mental data-base storing information and memories is essential for guides to relay messages. Intuitives who specialize, like a medical intuitive, being studied in anatomy. This allows guides to access related visuals and terminology, that would otherwise require more energy from the psychic and input from the client. Like trade professionals describing to someone who understands the industry and doesn't.

MIND MAPPING

Mind mapping is the human's inner guide creating conscious responses as reactive or heightened emotional triggers that can be the unresolved past or strongly held beliefs. Humans born with abilities, only indicates a raw potential to be a clear conduit dependent on how or if, refined. The example given below is obvious, yet not usually applied to the psychic's ability.

3 billion dollars is available for research.

- Where should the funds be distributed to benefit the global society?
- Who, or what group is the most capable to decide?

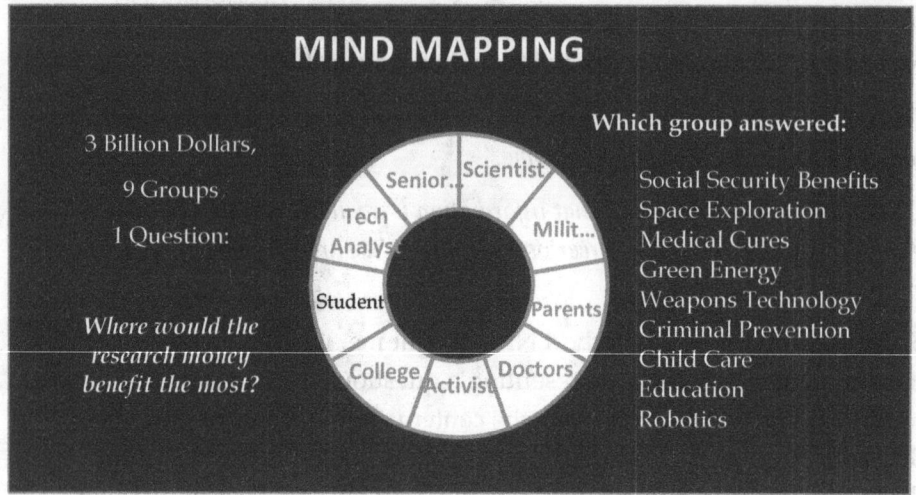

The above diagram, is an obvious illustration when self-interests are transparent and not difficult how the nine groups conclude. Overall, its understood personal and professional interests aren't as separate as people like to believe. As well, some occupational affiliations are difficult to separate the social and cultural viewpoints from the skill. This is especially true for a psychic's personal ideology connected to heightened emotions. Ascending the unresolved past and loosening beliefs will be mentioned throughout reinforcing its significance to data flow interruptions influencing interpretations. The ability, in-of-itself is the multi-dimensional gateway for messages to travel into the mind. Once received, the psychic's subconscious routes the information as presented or through the roads of beliefs resulting in intermittent disconnect, susceptible to retranslation. For instance, a client is worried her partner is being unfaithful and 1) talks to a psychic who will answer this question (first clue) 2) and has unresolved pain from a similar personal experience (undeveloped ascension). The psychic communication would intertwine sensory input with emotional output, meaning the unresolved blends with the intuition.

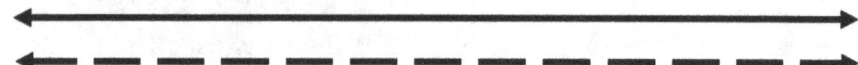

The Kindergarten depiction, with the solid line representing uninterrupted reception when receiving and dashed, disrupted from trigger(s).

indicators of interference

Two immediate indicators for clients to recognize is: 1) professional websites including religious affiliation like, Christian and 2) claiming abilities not matching experience, training and reviews. The issue isn't what faith a psychic is but the motivation to add their personal religious views, on a professional venue. I see this as a high risk of personal beliefs interfering when interpretating messages. Another indicator might be a neophyte with honest intentions that doesn't yet understand what they're claiming. If not this, the reason is likely a false confidence strategy to attract clients.

Another indicator is language to create dependency or over-power the seeker's choice; i.e., being told to leave a job, a relationship or similar life decisions. In a situation, involving abuse or threatening situations are considered exceptions for psychics to address directly. When this occurs, the spirit guides will explain why.

psi-ascension

Key phrasing repeated numerous times isn't to fill space on a page but to reinforce its importance, mentioned in the introduction. Personal development is one of these key phrases because of how it impacts data flow. The practicing psychic unable to surpass the personal conscious will not surpass the lower-level planes.

H.P. Blavatsky, gifted medium, master of the occult arts, founder of the Theosophical Movement and an instrumental role introducing Ascended Masters teachings. She was not known to be sparing in her views of individuals who would rather plunge into the psychic experiences than apply personal effort to spiritual progress saying,

"a psychic merely has the ability to see on a different plane of material density than the average person. But the level on which they are seeing and experiencing things is nevertheless still material and barely above the physical level, regardless of how wondrous and exciting it may all seem to the psychic themselves."

Blavatsky felt most psychics were impressed or infatuated with entry level ability, ignoring the divine connection altogether. It is the divine connection from which we derive divine guidance.

INTERPRETION

By now, it's understood intuitive language is more than streamline repeating. A psychic – medium's attention is focused on; listening, translating, and talking, often at the same time. There are some background sounds that are distracting and break the flow in any setting; the barking dog, texts-phone, baby crying, and restless toddlers.

Advanced or adept communicators demonstrate uncompromised dialog of conversational interchanges, accurately interpret symbols - metaphors, and have accumulated a comprehensive database of knowledge in a wide range of subjects for guides to access. This level of proficiency, is reached after years of practice to develop abilities and composure to manage clients in extreme stress, grief, or any number of difficult situations. Impartial objectivity is the key to preserving what is received, even when it's not what the client wants to hear, or personally disagrees with. This fact can be very challenging when strongly held beliefs interfere, from lack of self-ascension. An example is spiritual ideology confusing Christ Consciousness and Christian, as the same (or, any specific religion) and applies to all areas of ideology.

Ability is irrelevant when not properly cultivated. With absolute certainty, the ascended, the wise spiritual guides do not relay messages inciting fear and important to recognize those who divinely guide. Fear readings aren't from psychics, but fraud or undeveloped abilities. To clarify further, using an example of a reading involving energy not considered positive. Guides would not direct the client's mind or create awareness **to focus on** it, rather offer advice to inspire actions to re-direct current circumstances. More information on this topic is given in later chapters on recognizing the disingenuous.

THE SUBSCONSCIOUS MIND

The subconscious mind is where we imagine, dream, and remember.

The subconscious influences choices, (in)decisions, actions, and day-to-day life. It's the human database relaying signals, connected to memories, emotions affecting behaviors and then rationally processed in the active conscious. A separate awareness intertwined with the operational mind and gateway to higher mental capacity linking all lives experienced both, in physical and soul state. So, yeah, it's important.

Here's an easier way to understand is – the conscious mind holds short term memories, and where logic and rational thought is processed. The subconscious holds long term memories, and the emotions connected to each memory. It's also where habits are stored. How this plays out it, an emotional placeholder of memories. What is familiar is a habit, associated with beliefs, associations, that trigger emotions. Meditation quiets the chitters and chatters that otherwise run amok without learning mental control. Why personal ascension is mentioned often and how it relates to receiving psychic messages contradicting taught beliefs, and lower emotions (sad, worry) triggered from the unresolved past, that travel through the subconscious. Having control of your own mind is the difference of how messages are interpreted, not compromising accuracy.

CELEBRATING SPIRIT

I had my first conversation with (the medium) and was blown away. She connected with my brother, who passed away unexpectedly a little over a month ago. She provided details about his passing that could only have come from a first-hand point of view. I felt like I was actually speaking to my brother. She is a truly gifted woman, and I am so, grateful she chooses to share her gift with others.
C.G.

◆

(The medium) is on point! She helped me connect with my son who died unexpectedly. She knew things only me and God knew. I can stop grieving now because I know my son is alright.
C.F.

◆

Almost immediately, (the medium) started communicating with my husband. With only knowing my name, she related things to me only I knew and some things I didn't know. Her accuracy astounded me. Even when a validation didn't register, she insisted it was important and oh so right she was. I found peace through this extraordinary ability.
J.G.

◆

I scheduled as a skeptic after a sudden loss in my life. (The medium) new nothing of my background or family situation and what she told me was so on point, there is no doubt she was speaking to my loved ones. I left our session knowing we do live on and those we have lost remain with us and involved in our lives.
R.J.

◆

My daughter and I had a reading with (a psychic) and put us in touch with my son who we lost earlier in the year. The information passed on was private, and no way she could have known beforehand. She helped us in the healing process, and for that we will be eternally grateful!
K.D.

MEDIUMSHIP 7

YES, THERE IS AN AFTERLIFE. No ambiguity, presumably or tentative repudiations. I am a medium, not delusional or afflicted with hallucinations – maybe a little twitchy, sure. The evidence the soul continues has been established from the experiences of millions of people. It is the sole reason why, of all psi abilities, mediumship is the most sought with experiences that conclude with, wow. Mediums connecting to loved ones on the other side lets us know they are safe, no longer in pain, allows words never said and that life is not fleeting but truly everlasting. God knew we would need a way to connect with loved ones returning to Heaven and to know it exists.

So, why so much controversy? Because the ability is observed externally and mediumship is an internal experience. Of course, people understand spirit communication is more complex than repeating a dialog or describing mental imagery. How memories are prioritized also plays a role and so easy to do. Admittedly, I was guilty of almost everything that I tell my clients not to do when one of my students, a naturally gifted medium, felt my dad's presence. He would pop into readings from time to time but my medium friends or student could connect with him. Thus, I transformed into client headspace trudging through my memory data deciding what I believed he would tell me. Unlike psychic readings answering the unknowns, the client enters with a confident mindset established from memories experienced firsthand. What I'm saying is, yeah, I get it. What I hope to accomplish is creating the space needed for the client and medium to be a united team sharing this intensely personal and life changing experience.

SUMMARY

Mediums connecting to the Universal Collective Consciousness, adhere to the principles of all souls in unity. The gatekeepers consider the departed soul and physical soul requesting as what information can be given. Family and intimate relations hearing about the experience are also included as part of the decision, on what is answered, and how.

Medium communications charted in a seeker's soul book becomes aware of a strong urge, and/or re-occurring coincidences around a specific medium or online reference several weeks before. Once the intended DLO connects with the medium selected, spirit guides coordinate the arrival of the heavenly and supervise the interactions. The souls in spirit connect with the same sensory-telepathy transfer as spirit guide communication – with a few variables. When the soul journeys back to the Heavens, the memory and knowing blocked in the physical body, returns.

Physical and non-physical vibrations interacting is an intense energy based exchange. To sensory-transfer efficiently we access knowledge and memories. A few words or a symbol can ignite details of a memory that is five minutes or five days. What's obvious, isn't always obvious until ... Spirit communication to the medium don't fill their mind with entire memories. The senses see flashes of imagery, sometimes short movies, a grouping of words and other variables. Dialog can flow and be delivered the same as someone reliving the same memory. But mediums are relaying, not reliving, and without the beginning, middle and end of the memory that clients connect the messages to. For a medium, it's like opening a stranger's photo album to random pages and describing the people and events. The amount of focused energy involved is more demanding than appears.

PARTICIPATION

Mediums appreciate open, well-informed participation when contacting crossed over loved ones. Because the client plays an integral part a straight-forward approach will avoid the possibility of misinterpretations:

To connect with a DLO through a medium, the client, for all intents and purposes, is requesting indirect entry into the Heavenly gates.

Interactions are considered by the gatekeeper to assist the physical soul's intensions aligned with healing and will not interfere with life goals, in current or future timelines.

DLOs have a unique energy signature assigned, or accesses their multi-dimensional gateways. To communicate with the gateway, the medium, client(s) and DLO join energetically, like a three-way battery, strengthening the signal and prevents the medium from exhaustion during the exchange transfer. A quick example is being prepared with important key dates reduces time lapses that can interrupt or weaken the flow.

CLIENT PARTICIPATION

A student reminded me how easy it is to engage in the same thought process as a client when the tables turned and contacted my dad during training. My mind immediately began collecting cherished moments, funny catch phrases, quirky traits, private nicknames and last words. The mental dialog makes sense of the memories they should mention.

A regular coaching client lost her father years before and asked in one of our appointments if I would contact him. She was experiencing ongoing life challenges and hearing from her dad would help. Nina didn't support the request saying her current frame of mind wouldn't benefit from the connection. My client was understandably frustrated saying it was ridiculous, she loved her dad and saw contact as only beneficial. A few weeks later, she asked again with the same answer. Although Nina's guidance proved reliable the client was insistent hearing from her dad would help her heal. Typically, this type of persistence doesn't have any affect but Nina agreed. Her dad came with heartfelt memories he selected I wasn't aware of to know it was really him. Contact wasn't healing. His words reminded her of how much she missed him that turned into crushing grief and loneliness.

As the first paragraph pointed showed, it's completely reasonable for clients to have expectations that connect with intimate relationships. The heavenly assistants help with healing and, as my client discovered, see what we don't. Messages from loved ones not considered important don't always immediately make sense at the time but always have a reason. Selecting memories of the DLO include factoring in details, not considered.

It's necessary to know some basics about the subconscious first. Think of a storage room organized to access meaningful memories easily. Less accessible, less-significant; involve more concentrated thought. How this applies to messages without the exclamation points. One, some still associate psychic-medium abilities with telepathy, as the same. Remember, *that wasn't psychic, you're just reading my mind,* in chapter 1? Also, medium clients see themselves, rightfully, as the experts on the DLO and harder to please, regardless what the perception is. A mundane but specific memory, like that ducky wallpaper you almost forgot about, resolves any suspicions or doubts. Another reason is more strategic when DLOs are aware of mental gridlock requiring widening their reach with a less accessible memory. The last example is the most obvious. Memories shared in day-to-day life are part of intimate relationships and the most impactful.

deer in the headlights

Questions presented by the medium can result in deer in the headlight brain freeze. Watch any medium (authentic, preferably) speaking to someone in the audience immediately dismissing or when they don't immediately connect the information. Celebrity mediums, discussed later, receive a lot of information, very quickly, without the same luxury of time as a private reading. Yes, sometimes they get it wrong. The medium seeing brain freeze may decide to skip past it to relay other messages from the same DLO. This is also one of several situations where observation not educated on the internal workings would misinterpret.

It's expected clients preparing for the reading comes with a few oversights. When this happens, it's OK and suggested keep any unrecognized messages together so they can check afterwards. Numerous clients have emailed me saying, '*I have been playing connect the dots all day*' and, '*It's amazing how obvious it was later.*' My experience with people seeking medium readings is usually loving, and sometimes grief allows moments filled with laughter.

DLO PARTICIPATING

As mentioned, mediums aren't the decision makers on who or what is said, including when several DLOs come in at the same time. Logically, it's understood spirit energy isn't the same as physical, yet, clients will relate communication to what they know.

Communion with spirits gather energetically and cohesively, requiring individual participation from the physical world to identify characteristics to distinguish. The souls in spirit are released from separateness, while remaining as one, dynamically. When you apply this concept to a group setting, the collective energy overlaps.

Receiving messages from the other side will tap into various sensory perceptions in a continuous stream. Clairvoyance and clairaudience can be dominant but exchange with the other senses intermittently. Messages managed from the other side is based on what will benefit the client's healing the most – that is the least energy intensive to prevent exhausting the medium.

FUTURE VALIDATION

Other than deer in the headlight, a DLO with a sense of humor might show-off their new found psychic abilities on the other side. The way it plays out is, the client contacts flabbergasted the messages were exactly as told, <u>after</u> the reading. Just to be clear, it isn't that unusual for DLO to give messages that don't make sense during the reading. When this happens, usually I will suggest to ask others or see if it plays out later. The client later talks to family members discovering only they could have validated the experience. Timing might be the next day or a couple of months later, and always connected to a breathtakingly small but very noticeable detail described as being speechless and laughing out loud. DLO's may want to elicit joy or other family members to feel included in the experience.

Brain freeze comes with the aha! moment later with comments like this (actual quotes), *"I can't believe my mind was blank when you asked!"* or *"After talking to my family, they were stunned and felt like they shared in the experience."*

future validation from the dlo

Messages from loved ones can't always be validated during, but after the reading. Here are some examples of why:

- Validation only other family members know for relatives and friends to share the experience, indirectly.
- Remove any lingering doubts for the client and/or any family and friends who *'don't believe in that stuff.'*
- Depending on the message the DLO will give a message fitting to the known persona such as a playful joke for laughter or to know they are with at a needed time.

All of the above, is to let you know they witness you, love you, hear you. I always encourage clients to write down the messages received, even if recorded. Not only to safeguard from technical malfunctions. At the end of the appointment the client and I review the messages. There are readings where every message is validated and others where, the client experienced brain freeze able to verify as a result of post-prep. Future messages can be given the same way as a significant event memory where client thinks the medium just got it wrong – until, it isn't. Timing of message(s) can be the next day to several months (special occasions).

READING EXAMPLE 1

A woman scheduled an appointment with her step-mother to connect to her dad. When he came through, his communication reunited them with shared memories delivered with his personality. At the end of their appointment, there were three comments didn't make sense and I could feel him smiling when I pressed for more. Later, the daughter contacted me and told me a funny story when her step-mother finally remembered one of the statements. Two were still unaccounted for. A month later, on Thanksgiving Day the two unknowns happened in an unexpected way leaving them stunned and laughing, at the same time.

To conclude, participation is open to who comes in, what is said with a client's effort and attention to what is said.

literally, speaking

The literal personality type was mentioned in chapter one. The reading below is to provide a relatable benchmark on authenticating messages when information processing is logically particular.

READING EXAMPLE 2

A medium reading was purchased as a gift for Mother's Day from clients who were also brother and sister. I was looking forward to speaking with her knowing several family members, all with easy going, pleasant demeanors. When the mother called, I took her through my normal, here's what I do and you do, and began. Ten minutes of relaying what her DLO(s) were showing me, nothing clicked. Thirty minutes seeing European trips, farms, birthdays, and messages, nothing. I stopped the reading a few times to explain validation to make sure she understood. The hour scheduled wasn't important only figuring out why clear messages from her DLOs weren't registering and her energy felt open.

Fast Forward. Nina informs me to stay silent to allow the words to connect. A few minutes went by and finally she said, *'I did go on a trip to…. but my son or mother weren't with me. Do you think it could be what there mentioning?'* (cue the crickets). She did listen to what I said, but it wasn't logical, if she wanted to hear only from specific DLOs, why would anyone else want to say hello? And, why would DLOs tell her about her life if she already knew it. Good thing she was adorable, phew.

We reviewed the messages again, with her grandchild's exact date of a birth, the named location of her overseas vacation, the precise number of years and the year several significant events occurred; one by one, laughing every time no changed to a yes. Could anyone imagine the same reading in a live audience setting? The medium would be blasted for not knowing what they were doing.

DIRECT COMMUNICATIONS FROM A DLO

Loved one's will not communicate if there is any risk of creating fear or misinterpreted as not crossing over. Paranormal shows associate electronic disturbances, such as lights flickering or a television turning on or off, as signs of ghost phenomenon. They are not wrong but it's not always right.

There are no hard-fast rules when it comes to spirit communications, except one sign isn't enough to decide, nor is it ever only one sign. The most familiar type of direct communication reported are vivid dreams. People trust what's true when experienced through the five senses, specifically seeing, hearing, and smell. Loved ones can get creative to send a message, such as moving an object directly related to their physical life like a picture frame moved or a piece of jewelry, out in the open. A less obvious method is directly connecting with the subconscious mind. Interactions using 6th sense perception sensory is often dismissed into the imagination, unless you know what to look for. Influencing thoughts to change or turn on the T.V. or radio abruptly, associated with a coincidence. Feelings of sadness exchanged with memories to elicit a smile, joy, or laughter. Assurances a loved one is safe is part of the grieving process. Memories, thoughts and sometimes dreams causing worry are from an unquiet mind in grief, not from loved ones, as defined by Nina.

SHAGGY DOGS AND ZEST

My mom [from the others side] mentioned a shaggy dog my sister and I didn't understand]. I called my other sister after, and said before my mom met my dad, they had an English Sheepdog, just like the one in the movie! My younger sister and I had never even heard about it! She also mentioned someone who liked to bake, more specifically, making muffins with orange peel or zest, which we thought was strange but said I would get it later. When I talked to my sister, I didn't realize she had been dabbling in baking. Even more amazing, when I mentioned the muffins, she gasped! She makes muffins every week with real orange peel in the mix! My older sister's husband, who is a total non-believing skeptic, listened to the reading. He was blown away! He never, and I mean never, backs away from his beliefs, so to see him that intrigued was great and confirmed it even more for me!   S.T.

CELEBRITY MEDIUMS

8

Opinion is the medium between knowledge and ignorance. Plato

ARE CELEBRITY MEDIUMS MORE TALENTED? Public recognition comes with high visibility and even higher stakes. Considering the scrutiny of misperceptions combined with a medium's skill is the currency of their reputation, sub-par would be very risky. A medium's talent viewed publicly will inevitably conclude with disappointment.

"I never understood why mediums on television just don't give straightforward messages." My friend's question was straight to the point for the answer to respond, in kind. Psychic and medium ability is an internal experience that observation alone cannot understand. Case in point, is a true story about one of my favorite mediums.

MR. REE

Mr. Ree (for privacy) came onto the scene when my professional life was mainstream and psychic ability was still portrayed as an uncurable silly disorder. He wasn't the first medium on television but his rapid, precise communication style, relaying messages to the living from deceased loved ones captivated the nation; including me. I was thrilled people finally saw a conventional looking man in casual Friday attire, a simple name who talked extraordinarily, like a normal person. Watching spirit communication in khakis and a white button down without schtick or gimmicks was a halleluiah moment. It was the first time I saw someone embodying what genuine ability really looked like. By the end of the first show, I knew he was authentic and elated to watch him share his amazing abilities with the world. Of course, his popularity skyrocketed, alerting skeptics and predictably, cashed in on his fame. At the peak of his popularity, a popular primetime show took it to the next level mocking him with national attention as a cold reader and fraud. Recovering from the fallout seemed like impossible odds. Mr. Ree, didn't give up and neither did the people who believed in him. The beauty of truth; if he was a fraud, no one would have seen him again. Skeptics, even in their obvious defeat, struggle with this simple fact. They stooped to using animated characters to ridicule like playground bullies.

Around the same time when he debuted his televised show, my best friend; (pay attention here) a nudist Catholic-Jew-atheist, on-the-ready with a lightning-fast sarcastic wit, who never missed an opportunity to roll her eyes when anything psychic was mentioned, enters. How she's inserted into the story, needs a little background.

She was extremely close to her mom, who passed away not long after being diagnosed with cancer. The grief hit her hard. About two months later she invited me over for drinks. Over some wine, she casually mentioned that a co-worker gave her tickets to Mr. Ree's show. Of course, I sat up and gave her my full undivided attention. She continued with, 'you know I don't believe in this shit but I had the tickets and deciding to go, thinking it would be good for a laugh. Ok, so I'm sitting there watching people raise their hand crying thinking he's a fraud who probably paid his staff or actors who could start bawling on queue. You've seen his show where he says vague shit, like who has a B name and points in a general direction and only one person stands up hearing the most common letter in the alphabet. Well, he walks over to the area where I'm sitting and says, and I kid you not Michele, he said...there's someone named, does the tilted head thing like he's listening and shakes his head and says, alright...like he doesn't want to say what he's hearing. Wait...he says, there telling me their name is Alphonso and they died from cancer ...then says, I'm to let you know your mother is happy and misses you...then says my name. Holllleeee-ee sh*t! (She looks at me for dramatic pause) I just sat there dumbfounded, staring at him. I didn't stand up or raise my hand because my brain was trying to process what he said. Michele, that Is my grandfather's name. Not a B name, John or some other name millions of people have. No one, not even (fiancé's name) knows his name because he was the black sheep in the family. Seriously, it's not like the name is Rich or Billy...how can you guess Alphonso with cancer, and my mom's name? My friend told me the day it was aired on television she set her VCR to tape the show but it 'provably was edited out'. Her guess was because no one stood up. She still rolls her eyes when anything psychic is mentioned, because it's expected from her other friends. When she asks for psychic guidance from me, is our secret.

MEDIUMS GO PRIMETIME

The new millennium introduced the paranormal, UFO's, supernatural shows and mediums televised finding a niche in prime-time. Shows communicating with fathers with a *B name* could expect a sudden burst of tears, a look of astonished recognition to nodding contemplation. It was only a matter of time the media would want to capitalize on the most sought out psychic ability.

For any medium, maintaining a reputation for accuracy is extremely important. Clients look at testimonials for content, consistency and the number of people who shared their experience. I've talked to celebrities, have read for and trained with. Mostly, they are down to earth, sincere people who use their abilities to heal and help. They are not stupid and aware skeptic scrutiny is part of notoriety.

Have some fakers slipped through the public relations crack? Most likely. Does being a celebrity equal authentic? Absolutely not, but there are a few that are incredibly gifted that I'm a huge fan of. Celebrity is also a slippery slope with; editing, the public's assumptions of accuracy, deer in the headlights syndrome and other factors that make it harder to judge. This, being said, below, are four scenarios psychic celebrity has contributed to stigmas or misrepresented:

- Mediums with schtick and personality diverts attention away from the talent and, likeability becomes the factor. The medium may be very gifted, messages from the other side can be entertaining, but the ability isn't for entertainment.
- Viewers evaluating televised hits and misses can't factor in the information given when remembered later (discussed in this chapter).

- Magician debunkers offering money to pass their tests. With respect to James Randi, the once stage magician turned debunker's publicity stunt of one million dollars given to a psychic who could pass his test. He was a smart guy who wasn't luring celebrity mediums but to attract an audience. He would have known genuine psychics wouldn't take seriously. For the price of fame, he planted seeds of doubt into a massive zombie following not knowing they were part of his last act.

- Psychics participating in tabloid predictions about famous celebrities without permission. They do this for personal recognition and reckless. Celebrity doesn't give any person, including and especially psychics, the right to invade privacy. Imagine a stranger publicly posting a prediction with details when you're going to die, get a divorce or cheating or cheated on? Not only you, family and loved ones are affected.

Because of the above, false assumptions flood media forums with millions of participants (including people who *were* believers).

- Comments about the personality overriding credibility.
- Famous mediums representing the industry.
- Uninformed audiences with false perceptions and expectations.
- Viewers unaware information received that wasn't validated might be remembered later.
- Mediums not explaining techniques confused as cold readings.
- Tabloid prediction gossip presented as facts.

Increased awareness has certainly provided several positive gains but does it outweigh the risk? Televised mediums demonstrating spirit communication have an impressive number of fans with schedules booked out, sometimes for years. At the same time, the number of viewers doesn't represent only fans, there is always the element of limelighters looking to make a name for themselves. We all know by now; celebrity is targeted for air-play and technology has made it easier to appeal to the masses. Streaming news style videos is a great way for exposure when the right topic goes viral. Since talking cats don't fall in-line with serious broadcasters, plan b opts for controversial sensationalism to elicit a public response. The example chosen is from an up-and-coming digital talk show host deciding to capitalize on a popular medium soliciting approximately 1.3 million viewers. Using a countdown format presentation, her videomentary title was, clues when a medium is fake.

NEWS CLUES

CLUE – *Nothing Negative Is Said, or,* **messages from** the heavenly douche. (yes, really what she said) I tried to envision her version of the loved one back <u>in Heaven</u> telling a medium to forward <u>in front of a televised audience</u> something like; - hey, *you got really fat, wow!* or, *forget my husband that guy sitting behind him is super-hot!*

According to the journalist, messages from the dead are only authentic if the DLO is still a douche in Heaven. Who kicked this chick's cosmic puppy? It really isn't easy to dumbfound me into silence or freeze my brain with spontaneous jaw drop. After double checking if I heard her correctly, I concluded she would benefit from some therapy and maybe a hug. Since she put it out there, here's why souls in Heaven, who were mean, angry or a**holes, don't.

why do DLO's who weren't nice on earth, give loving messages?

If we go with, being the same in Heaven when alive - people who were jerks on Earth, tend to have a different public persona. Another, it's rare for people to seek a medium to connect with DLOs who they didn't like when living. This especially being obvious wanting to hear from them in an audience setting. The obvious answer is, once the soul leaves the physical world, the pain body sheds and returns to their true loving essence. DLOs keep their earth persona for the living to recognize and if the soul wasn't nice, they would acknowledge how they were instead of being how they were.

CLUE –*messages not revealing secrets.* The example given was telling a spouse about cheating (double the dumbfounded and yes, really). I've heard skeptics say the ridiculous, even with feisty fists but but but…. and she isn't special needs, needy probably BUT… explaining why a DLO wouldn't choose a televised reading in front of many people to reveal any secret, let alone while the wife is blowing out her birthday candles, Billy-Bob snuck into the chicken coop with his wife's cousin for the same. Wait, there's more. Several hundred people on the chat board were digitally high-fiving this clue as a gotcha. Where do we go from here, people? People's secrets, contrary to miss paparazzi and mister sensationalistic mindset, isn't for your entertainment.

Never has a client asked about a DLO cheating or vise-versa. Even questions pertaining to personal information, like non-disclosed legal documents or similar are viewed with discretion, alerting guide supervision on what information is allowed.

What about questions to find out perpetrators involved in murders or other assaults against the living? Same reason crime investigators are careful. Revenge or confrontations could result in tragedy, and jeopardize active investigations.

CLUE, '*Mediums misuse their power talking to grandparents on something insignificant like a BBQ when they could be using it to solve crimes.*' Doesn't 'mediums misuse their power' suggest they have power to misuse?

I'm not sure what the greater point is – her view of the soul in Heaven or the number of people ignorant to her ignorance.

TIMELINES 9

WHEN, IS WHAT'S PAST, WHY'S CURRENTLY AND WHAT'S FUTURE. When is asked more than any other question to know who, what, where and how. Asking a psychic when, is also one of the most complicated of all questions. Future timelines are comparable to a network of web ways steered by decisions until aligned. The universal guides will explain it from here, beginning with how a prophecy and prediction differ.

prophecy

A prophecy is a string timeline that prompt a series of events for a specific conclusion to happen. Depending on the scale of the event, a prophesy can be determined 500 years prior. Activating a prophesy will happen and always significant to create recognize or change group awareness. Destiny for one or two are powerful connections for multiple purposes, where prophesy are group collective events affecting the population, globally; equally unphased and unaltered by external influences.

predictions

Using the graphic; a prophecy would denote strings as thicker and predictions as delicate and transparent. Foretelling a future event, the string or prediction, represents the high probability of behavioral outcomes, or likely probabilities either, a person or population, will gravitate towards.

TIMELINES

ignoring intuition

Destiny, when connected to an actionable decision will prepare its arrival to ensure timelines are not stalled or longer than its original purpose. The soul(s) involved will be sent signals when approaching as feeling unbalanced, confused, intuition something is off/missing. If any involved in the decision continue to ignore, the Universe steps in and makes the decision or situation happen. Predictions are also affected when intuition is ignored or heighted emotions disrupting timelines.

- The employer who creates a position, waiting for "the candidate" to arrive. The predicted individual is still at other job, consumed by worry about leaving or focused on long-term security.
- The soul who feels a romantic loss or emptiness, while single – when the energetic imprint swirls around two people, both equally feeling a strong pull and deep connection; one of the two, have delayed, or remain in an unloving relationship.

In both situations, a free will variable is involved. The person, in either example, is given opportunities to triumph over a challenging situation. Timing is flexible, as a month to one – two years. Variable time slots allow all individuals time needed to succeed goals. Destiny timing is exact and any delays are circumvented with guides redirecting alternate outcomes to fulfill the timeline, such as; the same outcome with someone else. Alternate outcomes are not less than or to be considered experienced as.

every decision matters

Disposition and personality are considered, including intuitive inclinations and reactions. Pre-birth goals also consider these nuances, including reactive inclinations to determine the most likely result. If ignored, where the individual chooses to stay in a job, marriage, relationship, location that extends beyond allotted timelines can affect one or several, depending:

- Another candidate, is hired, less capable or doesn't spark inspiration to a co-worker or manager that leads to an important invention.
- The man or woman waiting, eventually moves on with another.

- The man/woman who stayed in a marriage, may feel a sense of remorse, or regret upon the discovery the destined mate is no longer waiting and in a committed relationship.

Psychic timelines energetically link into the highest probability, also feeling (when or if) anomalies of improbabilities and offer suggestions (when possible) to keep timelines concurrent.

EXAMPLES: suggestions to leave a relationship or employment and/or stay to extend time to realign timelines. The higher the probabilities of occurrences are to align, meaning both or all individuals' "planned paths" the more specific details can be provided. The responsibility of the psychic is providing the information received, including future variables contingent on changing the outcome.

AUTHOR COMMENT: Timing variables can be challenging for any client, especially when the reason for contacting a psychic is to gain a sense of certainty and direction. At the same time, when more than one timeline offered, it's always in the best interest of the seeker to help re-direct or prevent future outcomes. Experience shows, the more fear the client has, the less likely they will change behaviors or decisions, as guided.

PSYCHIC TIMELINES

Psychic timelines rely on a paradox, of sorts, static behaviors and achieving goals. Quite the conundrum. Accuracy, is also contingent on both. In other words, what has been predetermined before birth to achieve, are felt as motivations and desires from guides urging the direction. Many people struggle to break free of familiar patterns and by doing so, achieve goals and one of the purposes of reincarnation.

Fate and destiny are written in timelines. Free will is a variable, within a timeline, dependent on behavioral reluctance to change and how long. It isn't "we" or the psychic as wrong (but can be), rather layers of time holding their own timeline.

EXAMPLE: An agreement for employment success seems stalled. Several psychics are consulted and receive the same or similar information with the timeline continuously shifting. One reason for time delays; the individual is fearful to leave the job or exert an aspect of themselves to be noticed. The pre-birth goal slated both considerations; achieving the goal connected to leadership and behavioral complacency.

Why do some readings not happen? Why say anything if the outcome is contingent on something/one else, or, at least what it's contingent on? why describe with words like soon and years go by?

Reasons for psychic timing, vary from one altering the outcome as discussed; staying in a marriage, one focused on another not noticing any other, one interfering with many others, such as, an employer's jealousy or control resulting in poor leadership for others to succeed.

Words given as now, today, are significant and true as written in the Book of Life. When one alters, interferes... we adjust for another opportunity. When [the same individual is] continuously interfering, God steps in directly for the results as written to be. Divine intervention comes in many ways and God sees every individual as important, as the collective whole. When interference is by a group representing one voice or action, the group is removed of all power, negatively affecting God's purpose and for the words in the Book of Life to remain as truth.

Why do future predictions not happen for some individuals as described, when behaviors aren't a factor? Maybe offer variables how it could change, or, not give the answer and say, not allowed to know?

Many times, what is given as described, or answered, is the actuality of events yet to be known. When not, a constant statistical set of variables are altered. We, (as the ones who answer), called divine guides, are aware of the proclivities presented in accumulated timelines, as to which path. The unconsidered, we see and understand. What alters futures, are the fear-thought to be resolved, instantly re-directing the forward movement to slow, stop and turn, or (the fear) becomes blind to opportunities in the present affecting the emotional sight. These instances are not pre-recorded, they are created and inserted into. Timeline agreements coincide with personal goals, set forth. Spiritualists describe planetary shifts and this has some elements of truth. The purpose for, does not. Exchange the word shift, with segmented time allotments and in each segment, there are individual and collective goals slated to acquire.

We prefer expressions defined as *"The Age of"* astrological or chakras or any language used in the universe or divinely, to avoid creating any more confusion. Individual goals, the first shift or segmented period, occurred gradually over the course of several years from 2006 lasting until 2011's third term. A transition of relationships experiences was heightened in each category; family, work, romantic, friends and including brief acquaintance. How every individual related, relied on, responded to, when prompting strong reactions. The recognition of ongoing behavioral patterns, re-cycling, from one to the next very few ascended above.

predestined timing

We've established a soul's incarnations are pre-written in their book of life before entering the physical 3-D world. Before re-entry into the body, fate and destined occurrences are pre-set, or programmed, into the DNA. The circumstances meant to activate can be experienced as sudden impulses, inspirations, and thoughts considered peculiar creating a series of events to unfold for fate and/or destiny to occur. Silent helpers create instances as signs in the environment or found in synchronicity to navigate direct to the same location. In the timeline illustration (above-right) the lines representing fate and destiny points are brighter indicating significance. Varying lengths are the allotted segments of time that can be a selected day, month or longer. An important factor are the external influences to simultaneously converge for the who, where and when to connect. There are destiny/fates events that begin the aligning process in childhood or several years before. These points are linked to impactful romantic partners, birth, and death but destiny or fate is any life changing situation.

The story about the woman winning the lottery, in chapter one, is a perfect example of a destiny point. Stories, such as hers, is usually followed with hearing, *'my prayers were answered.'* Yes, but sometimes prayers are part of the pre-written destiny points when faith was needed as much as the financial relief. Think about the number of people involved before and leading up to the employee handing her the wrong ticket, and the woman paying the extra money when already monetarily stressed.

Psychics won't receive destined/fate timelines if they somehow interfere. Guides consider the seeker's emotional disposition on information given.

Knowing the future can prevent or alter outcomes. As the opposite is also true, like an impulse to schedule a psychic reading, to prompt one.

vertex points

Vertex points are two or more lines or curves, that aligns on timelines as a chance meeting for the purpose of setting an important course in motion. Encounters that eventualize as a destined life event directly affecting: birth, health, death, employment, marriage or any significant connection resulting in. Vertex destiny points are not influenced by free will or life goals.

sliding destiny

Longer periods of time are slated to allow destined occurrences to align and synchronize with a group and/or person. Free will allows individuals time to choose and choice can be a few days, up to two years.

EXAMPLES: strong urges to change employment begin entering your mind. It continues to grow, getting louder until almost constant. You see or hear about a new job opportunity that seems perfectly timed. Now, let's add one of the life goals you came in to experience and conclude; fear of change. Fear and anger are two powerful emotions and louder than intuition. Fear of change begins to rationalize the reasons, heard as logic; "*I have good job security, benefits….*" This results in staying in your job that might be affecting another's destiny as your replacement, stalling destiny, until another opportunity opens.

The Universe begins to create louder signals, perhaps becoming uncomfortable at your work – creating various scenarios to assist reaching the life goal, until concluded. In the same setting, adding a vertex point, where the inclinations to leave was not contingent on a karmic goal, a situation is orchestrated and the decision is made for you, such as department downsizing, getting fired, etc. When responding to strong inclinations, the destined segment allows the shortest amount of time for all involved to meet. The example given, as discussed previously, can be applied to many circumstances creating profound change. Very rarely, are urges ignored when linked to destiny and considered very serious. The Creator is directly aware of any anomalous timeline fluctuations, including destiny affecting a soul to experience and will rewrite your soul map for the same result with another, personally overseeing until concluded.

fate and destiny

Fate is an event pre-ordained in a soul's mapping designed to do one thing – trigger emotions. Destiny is pre-ordained as an equal exchange without conflict, and not temporary. Fated occurrences are relationships impacting one, more than the other, that lingers in the mind triggering emotional confusion linked to self-worth and/or temperament. Fated moments are purposed to create awareness of reactions to achieve reincarnated goals. An exception can be meeting someone briefly but with long lasting impacts, such as pregnancy, introductions that affect career, home or important decisions.

will a psychic let us know when it's destiny?

Abilities connecting to the lower astral planes, not in tune with destined timelines. When this happens, the universe begins creating a new timeline for the destined event. Two question may come to mind: Why give the psychic information that would interfere? And, why isn't the seeker redirected to another psychic? The individual incarnating with psi is given opportunities to develop responsibly. Not all choose to. Seekers connecting to undeveloped psychics are guided, as well, more likely to either, ignore or unable to hear our intuitive guidance, cues or signs.

ADVICE: ask the consulting psychic if they will answer infidelity questions. Yes, is a clue (without the exceptions mentions).

AUTHOR COMMENT: In my earlier development period, I believed if a question was answered meant the client could receive the message. This stopped when Nina explained in a meditation, ability used irresponsibly have consequences, especially when interfering or altering another's timeline. Why she didn't offer her advice earlier was part of the learning process and purpose of connecting through meditation. Her council didn't compromise clients, nor wouldn't. We established a partnership agreement for information assisting the highest good and never to interfere with life choices. Nina does inform me on current or approaching destiny events, when it benefits seekers.

DIVINATION

DIVINING INSTRUMENTS TO HARNESS SUPERNATURAL POWERS from God, or a god. From the earliest days, man has called upon the Heavens for secret or prophetic knowledge. Evidence of ancient civilizations around the globe practiced the occults by means of an aid Babylonian augury (flight patterns of birds), scyphomancy[2] Egypt, Oracles of Greece, haruspicy (the inspection of animal entrails) in Rome and bone casting in ancient China.

Modernized divination has removed the superstitions and animal sacrifices opting for pre-packaged instruments and book sets. The more popular methods of divination, included in this section are only a few of a sizeable list, to introduce the reader to basic concepts.

DIVINATION AND THE DIVINER

Future predictions, secrets of the unknown or reveal hidden truths is the general idea for divination. Nostradamus' prophecies preferred, scrying, using a reflective surface, like the fortune teller's crystal ball or water gazing, and a divination method still strongly associated with psychics and prophecy. Over the years, a few popular divining tools have made their way into mass-production, honoring the mystic's language of universal symbols and metaphors. For readers just learning divination, I'll address a common misperception finding its roots in superstition. The physical divining object

---

[2] considered one of the oldest methods of divining by means of crystalline reflection, using a cup or goblet of water.

isn't the actual source of hidden or magical power on its own. Divination draws from the energetic intention of the diviner and may assign their own meanings, in turn, generate a new static vibrational frequency. In other words, let's say a skilled diviner creates her own tarot cards. He or she assign a meaning to each card on par with other decks, or dissimilar. The reading would be as accurate with this deck, as the other decks they used. In this case, divination tool is fluid, working with the rules of the diviner.

Palmistry or chiromancy, and astrology, are not fluid, following the commonality of obtained knowledge to interpret and established guidelines to decipher details specific to birth and life maps of the individual. A good Palm Reader can see more than meets the eye, able to recognize the subtle complex patterns of each hand; the left as the original path we are born with and the right, as the path taken. Unfortunately, charlatans have abused this method to where it practice is synonymous with fraud. My understanding isn't comprehensive but after a personal experience with a very gifted Palm Reader, I was astounded at the details she knew… that could not be guessed. Psychics aren't always easy when sitting on the other side of the reading table. We are hard to impress with the tendency to mentally micro-manage (or, that's just me). If you can find someone to refer you to a reputable and ethical Palm Reader, I highly recommend the experience.

TAROT HISTORY

Tarot, pronounced (tar-oh, ta-roh) was originally designed in the 15th Century for the purpose of playing games. Countries throughout Europe came up with their own versions and rules but no one is certain how it became synonymous with the occult and divination. The earliest evidence of a tarot deck used for cartomancy, (card reading divination), is from an anonymous manuscript from around 1750. The popularization of esoteric tarot started with Antoine Court and Jean-Baptiste Alliette (Etteilla) in Paris during the 1780s, using the Tarot of Marseilles. After French tarot players abandoned the Marseilles tarot in favor of the Tarot Nouveau around 1900, Marseilles is now used mostly by cartomancers.

DIVINATION

(above) The Rider-Waite Deck uses symbolism to depict the relationship of meaning to each card. The first three cards (left to right) The Fool (0), Wheel of Fortune (10) and Magician (1), Major Arcana's or the 22 cards of the Fool's Journey. The Queen of Cups, 3 of Pentacles and 4 of Wands, represented 3 of the 56 Minor Arcana or Pips

RIDER-WAITE TAROT DECK

Illustrations have changed dramatically since the tarot of Marseilles, found in occult, spiritual stores and mainstream bookstores lining shelves with beautifully depicted artwork. The Rider-Waite deck was originally published 1910 and one of the most popular tarot decks used for divination in the English-speaking world. The cards were drawn by illustrator Pamela Colman Smith with heavy symbolism to provide the subtle and obvious interpretation each card represented from the instructions of academic and mystic A. E. Waite (Published by the Rider Company). Tarot deck cards include the following:

major arcana - 22 of the 78 Tarot cards represent the Archetypes in the Fool's journeys referred to as; the greater secrets, the major arcana, or trump cards. The first card, the Fool, represented by zero (0) and The World, as card 21.

minor arcana - following the same format as playing cards the remaining 56 cards are organized into four suits with 14 cards within each; referred to as the lesser secrets, minor arcana or pips:

ten numbered cards - Ace to 10 and four court cards. King, Queen, Knight/Jack and the Page (the 4 added, not in playing cards)

the four suits - Hearts/Cups, Diamonds/Rods or Wands, Clover/Pentacles and Spades/Swords.

TAROT MYTHS

The supernatural is not a stranger to myths, many originating hundreds of years ago from superstitions derived from Christian Crusades and practices of a few misguided occultists. Moving forward to the two mid-twentieth century events: University Books (1959) made tarot accessible to the general public the *Waite Smith* deck and *The Pictorial Key to Tarot* and a year later, Eden Gray published her first book, *Tarot Revealed: A Modern Guide to Reading the Tarot Cards.* The combination offered the public a straightforward, user-friendly format that has since been considered the popular standard. By the early twenty-first century, Tarot decks were no longer found only in spirituality stores. New Agers had their own dedicated aisles at stores like Barnes and Noble and Books-a-Million.

The old myths come from the days of the Crusade or recently created from untrained enthusiasts (who will undoubtedly disagree in their blog with a long list on why I'm wrong).

myth #1 the inverted pentacle

One, a pentagram (magical symbol) can include a pentacle (five-points) in it but, not always and they are not the same. Two, Wicca religion use the pentacle as a symbol of faith.

The inverted pentacle is still widely thought to be a symbol of evil, satan cults, etc. Its origins came from the occultist Éliphas Lévi attempts to interpret the pentagram. and continued with French occultist Stanislas De Guaita (1861–1897), who created the first ever "goat pentagram," found in La Clef de la Magie Noire (1897). Nothing like a place called the Church of Satan to use the symbol as their logo, to lock it in as the Christian devil.

myth #2 tarot's death card

The Death card is a Hollywood favorite for chilling plot twists to create suspense showing up mysteriously, as a literal omen. The entertainment world plays a significant role for spiritual concepts with exaggerated artistic license contributing to stigmas and inaccurate clichés.

From the popularity of tarot, it is understood the card doesn't indicate literal death. It's one of the 22 major arcana as an archetype representation of endings allowing new growth, like winter to spring. It can also be a release of illusions or an idea. Literal translations should only be interpreted from an experienced reader and with psychic ability. They would be able to determine, knowing the circumstances for the exception. Amateurs card readers are strongly discouraged to ask serious life questions not understood.

myth #3 tarot's devil card

The Devil card, number 15 in the tarot deck uses a chilling depiction of a nude male and female bound by a chain as a horned beast towers over them, adorned with the inverted pentacle. None-the-less, it's another Archetype representation of temptations and fears that manifest these two words into obsessions, materialism, vanity, addictions, infidelity/sex, abusive relationships, as the one giving or receiving. Ironically, a tarot reading about Christianity's methods forcing the people how to worship and those who did not obey were accused of heresy and devily stuff. The horned and sometimes horny mythical creature has been a 'scapegoat' for lack of self-control and perhaps the Rider-Waite depicts through symbolism and metaphors, the male and female, or human lust is the chain of reincarnation.

…" The rest, whom we adjudge demented and insane, shall sustain the infamy of heretical dogmas, their meeting places shall not receive the name of churches, and they shall be smitten first by divine vengeance and secondly by the retribution of Our own initiative" (CTh. XVI.1.2)."

myth #4 rituals

Don't let anyone touch your cards, wrap cards in silk, cards must be presented as a gift or memorized before reading… None of this is true and how it started doesn't matter. What's important is this; if you want to read tarot cards, go out and buy a deck that appeals to you, allow others to hold them and keep them in the box or under your pillow case. The choice is yours and the intentions you give them. Memorizing the cards isn't necessary but practice, practice, practice, to familiarize yourself while establishing a relationship with your guides. Before you do a reading, an elaborate protection ritual isn't necessary to keep bad juju away –ask for your personal guides to help is the only ritual you need.

myth #5 tarot readings and psychic ability

Do you have to be psychic to read cards? Change psychic to enhanced natural intuition, and the answer is YES. I respectfully disagree with advice offered from experienced 'non-psychic' tarot readers ignoring the very definition of:

divine: of, or pertaining to a god. **diviner:** *one who divines*

divination: [1] from Latin divinare "to foresee, to foretell, to predict, to prophesy", [2] related to divinus, divine), or "to be inspired by a god", [3] to gain insight into a question or situation

When training new students, for psychic development or heightened natural intuition I recommend a method of divination to exercise the psychic muscle. It also helps with strengthening spirit guide connections, as well as, gauging accuracy to build confidence.

TAROT READINGS

Myth #5 ties into the popularity of tarot cards offered in a wide array of stylized illustrations and mass-production. The fascination to consult directly with the Heavens continues to intrigue the mainstream population. Why wouldn't it? Of course, it does help to know the basics such as what happens when the emotional wreck with tissues sticking out of their nostrils ask questions on the reason, they need tissue. And, must be followed up with - just sayen. Professional readings given by the novice to mid-level is a worthwhile topic to address. Hiring a tarot reader will assume they are experienced and an expert. Let's focus on what this will imply to the client. An expert in divination is associated as someone also with psychic abilities. For any disagreeing, advertise as, *'non-psychic Tarot Reader'* for how clients respond.

tarot seems so random. how does tarot work?

How can 78 cards, shuffled and cut into three piles and organized with established placeholders be so accurate? I wanted to know, too, and St. Germain offered his wisdom. He did not disappoint.

❰ A diviner uses the divination tool to create a visual aligning with the vibrations simultaneously tapping into a greater psychic. Nostradamus is an example of a diviner using a method called scrying entering a trance-state awareness creating clairvoyant impressions, resulting in prophecy. With any form of objective divination taps into the mystical forces of alchemy purposed with physical matter. In the hands of one capable, sense the vibrational energy of each card psychically. The arrangement is less random then perceived when considering the hands as tuning forks detecting imperceptible expressions felt subtly. As the unconscious veil lifts, shuffling is intuitively engaged until arrangement matches the sequence, for the desired result. Not unlike the actuality of exchanges energetically when the inner mind doorways are known, bypassing swirls of all known thoughts of the past, present, and future, stored within the mental landscapes of the human brain. Along the way, other doorways present themselves in moderation variables. Meaning, see part of the physical brain as a gateway of many gateways.

To access *The Gateway* into the Multiverse of all answers known; the route to the neural-pathways is cleared from obstacles, called beliefs, interfering emotional factors creating the belief and without the logical sector overriding the stillness within, to detour. When not, other gateways, considered as The Gateway, is entered, and depending on the belief and/or logical inferences is detoured, is what door opens. When the gateway is opened, the hand's vibrations align with the vibrations of the divine universe, can hear each sound. The considered impossible, (hands) listening to every card instantly, until arranged (shuffled) and divided (cut) in the timelines of three. So, you see, the human capability reveals beyond its known potential, each, and every day.

The purpose for all humans is to journey through the mind, capture the illusion and free it, not be imprisoned by, even one. To achieve this, one is to recognize what holds them prisoner. All are born with the keys to free the falsities layered in time and every decision is the individual map to choose the door opened.

St. Germain's answer blew me away explaining when using tarot cards, our hands become vibrationally in-tune at the unconscious level sensing how long to shuffle and where each cut of the deck should be. His comment about human potential was referring to the imperceptible at the conscious level unaware of the subtleties from within.

Several years ago, I picked my cards up again and gave myself and friends some readings. They're always within reach and my fascination with them will always be, perhaps because of the role they played in my journey to be a full-time psychic medium. It doesn't matter how many times or the length in-between, the accuracy has amazed me, each, and every time. I don't have a problem making fun of myself to admit my imagination considered the cards were somehow transmuting one by one, as they were laid down in the Celtic Cross, as the reason for the exquisiteness of how perfect each card placement was. In a weird way, my imagination's explanation seems easier to believe than the human potential we are unconsciously, unaware of. The implications are enormous if you think about it beyond tarot cards it may explain so much.

The **Ouija** (*top, right*) divines' answers using only fingertips lightly touching a **Planchette** (*top, middle*) to navigate in a sliding motion over letters or numbers. **Divining Chart** (*below, left*) with a **Pendulum** (*top, left*) vibrationally responding in a swinging back and forth motion over the answer to the question posed.

DIVINATION

I-Ching Coins *(top left)* and **Rune Stones** *(middle left)* are divination tools for prediction or divining guidance. **Tea Leaves** *(top, right)* symbols and shapes are used explore the past, present, and future based on proximity to cup handle (not shown). **Palmistry** *(bottom, right)* examine the major/minor lines and structure of the hand, as a past-present-future life map. The infamous **Crystal Ball**, associated with fortune teller's gazing is a form of scrying. Nostradamus' quatrains are a result of water scrying.

Astrology Wheel or Natal Chart (right) is divided into 12 houses or aspects of life with 12 Zodiac signs within each house.

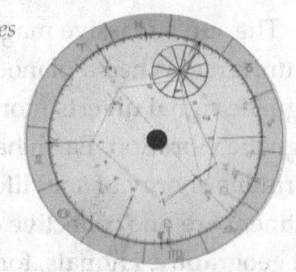

ASTROLOGY

St. Michael volunteered his wisdom on how and why natal charts are so freaky accurate.

[*St. Michael*] The astral plane is designed and not random; each planet, star, sun, and moon have specificity for placement, size, and detail. The molecular inhabitants, meaning, the embodiment individually carry its own signal of force vibrations. The vibrations interact with its environment, also having a vibratory signature, independent and within its own grouping. In other words, Jupiter's signature interacting with its mated moons – the mated moons vibrational fingerprint, independently and collectively creating one combined energy vibration, overall.

The sun in the Milky Way, is a vibratory hub aligned, not only to provide life for Earth but a magnetic core each planet and their mated moons specifically interact with, as one unit. Now, we have Jupiter's and its adjoining moons with independent and combined vibration as one, interacting with the sun, thus, creating another independent signature. Add in another variable layer - Every rotation in every second maintains an overall vibration, and simultaneously and distinctly changes within. For example, a soul in the body begins as a baby and continues to grow and age. During the individual soul's life, they are always the same essence at the core and each day they change and every year, individual or group interactions and experiences add, change or integrate into their vibratory signature, and so on.

Vibrations carry specific signals or frequencies. There is an infinite number of individual vibrations, every one defined, comparable to musical notes. Individually, two musical notes can sound very similar, and are, yet to a skilled composure, one note can make a significant difference.

Vibrational energy exists individually/collectively in all energy and is energy. For instance, Jupiter's location in the solar system interacting with its, hub or sun, will generate an overall "personality", if you will, creating a dynamic imprint with every rotational spin (using Earth time), each 24 hour day, as a vibrational frequency or communication back and forth with the sun. The sun's massive magnetic field re-transmits the signals back out into the universe. When a planet has fragmental soul energy, (humans) the magnetic signal diverts more signals and vibratory energy to each fragmental magnetic vibration. Earth has its own specific signature because it carries enormous energy of soul life, independently/collectively. Souls on each continent are one collective energy overall as each country, state. The land and geography, animals, forestry, mountains, waters, and elements...you getting the picture? The exact minute a soul is born (in astrology) can have one significant change but rarely. Birth charts are important to distinguish planetary/cosmic influence if birth was morning, midday, or evening (sun, sun-moon, moon). Specifics are necessary when birthdays align between two planetary vibrations, what astrologers refer to as cusp. The solar system sectored into individual signs during time of birth and the influence of the sun, being the hub provides what vibration signature – the personality of the sign independently and its vibratory personality alignment with the sun. Planets and their moons do not specifically affect souls on Earth. The interaction they have with the sun retransmitting energy magnetically back into the solar system is what affects overall/individually.

Very skilled astrologers learn to read the behaviors and interactions of the solar system with birth charts. Within the individual soul chart will indicate additional patterns, again, each having an individual behavioral/personality vibrational signature they interpret for the soul's overall energy, down to specific influences each year, month, day. Astronomers or stargazers from Earth's ancient times knew this as a science and relied on, somewhat like the Farmer's Almanac. There are many on Earth knowing the simple complexity of this ancient art or tool, and as many that do not. The influences of the solar system and sun affecting individuals is significant. If an "expert" miscalculates or is not skilled to accurately interpret a soul's chart, "challenges" may be described to feel like free will is given to the planets or to proceed with caution. The perceived challenge to the skilled Astrologer is an opportunity for growth to create specific awareness. The universe functions systematically within a structure of vibrational sustenance magnetically ebbing and allowing, repelling, or attracting the same energy, called timing. One influence of many affecting souls as tools for life, independently and collectively.

CELEBRATING SPIRIT

I called a psychic about a misplaced Amethyst ring. They told me the ring was tucked away in a jewelry bag at the bottom of a moving box with kitchen items and papers. I went through boxes in my shed and sure enough, came across a box as he described and found my ring. K.G.

I awakened in 2009 and have avidly pursued spiritual knowledge since then. I have received many readings. (The psychic) is top of the list. Her channel is so amazingly clear, and like the other reviews you read of her, I can confirm, her accuracy is breath taking. Her predictions materialized even sooner than I thought, but most importantly she understands and clearly conveys the spiritual energies involved to guide me to my highest and best good. Deepest gratitude. R.B.

I spoke to a couple of psychic mediums before I found (psychic). Their amazing gift to see precisely what has been long buried was life changing. Through intuitive coaching with her I have become aware of what's held me back while rediscovering my true self. Her ability to uncover unspoken thoughts has been pivotal in my journey to healing and growth. S.H.

(The psychic) mentioned a shift that I experienced when "inside a metal container, and I couldn't get out". I didn't recall it--we moved on. That night, when calling my mother to ask about reading topics, she mentioned that I was a different person ever since I was "7 YOA and was trapped in an abandoned dishwasher and I was able to finally kick open the door and avoid suffocating TO DEATH". I DID NOT remember it until that very second. The psychic was the real deal, no doubt about it! T.L.

THE ABILITY

*Do not several sorts of rays make vibrations of several bignesses, which according to their **bigness** excite sensations of several colours, much after the manner that the vibrations of the air, according to their several **bignesses** excite sensations of several sounds? (grin)*

Isaac Newton

THE INVISIBLY FORCES

11

Every individual is a unique essence and answers received are to be heard with the psychic energy received for any answer to flow through the conduit clearly, without fear or comprised translation. My brain is only a receiver, in the universe there is a core from which we obtain knowledge, strength and inspiration. **Nikola Tesla**

INTUITIVE ENERGY IS AN INVISIBLE FORCE of mental waves traveling across worlds or connecting with the person receiving. The concept becomes simple once you understand the basic laws of physics which see all solid objects as a manifestation of a vibrating energy. Imperceptible waves such as sound, radio, electricity, light, television waves, microwaves, x-rays, gamma rays and psychic energy waves are vibrating energy. The same principle applies for the human mind, like an energy station, which creates, transmits, and receives energy. The fact the mind has a will of its own adds an interesting dimension to the concept of psychic energy when we think the output can be gaged as brainwaves transmitted to and from the human mind from within the earth plane. Communicating with entities in the afterlife relies on this psychic energy connection, received clearly, and connected to the Universal Consciousness. For the exchange to extend the senses beyond the veil, **psychic** energy is encoded within the causal body creating a unique **signature.** *This chapter is channeled information, with noted exceptions.*

the veil

***the veil**;* when the soul merges with the body, in-utero, a veil shrouds DNA strands blocking spiritual sight; energy existing at individual vibrations. When returning to the Heavens, it isn't loved ones come; the veil lifts seeing life forms already present. As each life advances, what is referred to as psychic is a soul having various abilities based on how in tune or how transparent their veil is. Individuals with the ability to hear and see under the veil are appointed mediators between two vibrational planes of existential awareness to deliver messages.

energy - advanced

[*The Universal Timestream*] Energy's core, what is unseen, solidified, what matters, as the matrix definable and inconceivable. We use this word to express movements of life as emotional, thermal, nuclear, the fuel of the body and transportation, as the key and is. But what is it? The protons undiscovered in sub-atomic fusion's nuclei. It is a responsive element existent, dispersed atmospherically, living in hydrogenic carbonates. The expression energy cannot be destroyed only transmuted is true because it is already a universal component waiting for thoughts to shape it, substances colliding to reform or creational activity to command it.

holographic energy - advanced

Holographic energy is *parsed intelligence* reconnecting into radiation light waves dimensionally. Psychic energy transmutes holographic energy into a vibrational circumference allowing multiverse transmissions between dimensions. *process of analyzing a string of symbols, as a natural language*

Psychic thoughts travels at the speed of sound, not light. Direct communication is a telepathically received interchange between the sender and receiver, stationed Earthly and Heavenly. The two opposite vibrational frequencies, measured in megahertz for the output and quadrophonic input, are synchronized for communication occurs.

Psychic ability is a human who captures the energy signature traveling through the mind portal and the mind portal is the access achieved from the vibrational sequence aligning to the door that opens – or matching the soul's energy signature as the key.

Higher vibrations can lower to open the intension but lower cannot rise, unless the internal causal is pre-designed and achieves oneness, to by-pass base level, mid-level illusions that respond to corresponding frequencies. For example, the individual born with medium ability capability; some may have early age experiences, whereas others choose a journey to develop incrementally or later in life. Both scenarios require development to craft the ability and, ascend personally. Either, neglected affects the energetic signature and the key to which door opens.

energy – simplified

The translation is a loose interpretation that may not be 100% accurate.

Vibrational frequencies capture energy signatures to communicate with the 5th dimension. The psychic's vibration acts as the door key that opens to the other side, and connected to the psychic functioning established pre-birth, encoded into the DNA. Souls reincarnating to psychically guide in physical form completed halfway of mid-level and higher to prevent negatively influencing other souls, that would add, not reduce, incarnated lives.

how does the mind travel by thought to other worldly places?

❰ (received information continues) Is it the same when reminiscing about a beautiful place traveled or forming any visual memory transporting you back in time? Remarkably, the powerhouse we call the unconscious knows exactly how to locate each memory instantly. Ideas, form several memories into one, are regarded more significant giving it curiosity's attention. Add the complexity of the imagination to a new thought and it's called a revelation, epiphany, invention and sometimes prophetic. The brain physically, is not extraordinary visually, when considering the mysteries, it holds. Neurons, pathways and regions, specifically organized to

---

The Central Nervous System is the integration and command center of the body. It consists of the brain, spinal cord and the retinas of the eyes.

Æther is the visual equivalent of EMF fields (electro-magnetic fields) within the body and the external force shield, known as the auric. Meridians follow invisible lines externally, called ley lines, as a geometric grid partitioning geographically sectioned points of concentrated energy. As this is the same concept within the body, independently and interactively aligned atmospherically. This is æther, and extends as the universal cohesive element.

communicate with its companion called the Central Nervous System connected to every aspect of human function.

THE MENTAL MATRIX

The mental matrix is the human mind's three states of soul level awareness; what influences decisions/non-decision, what nourished the soul in the past, and what knowledge and beliefs formed morality, deciding the future.

- that which is tangibly defines the reality of logic - conscious,
- that which was remembered defines the subliminal emotional reality – subconscious,
- that which transcends the ego perceives the universal existence as one concurrent reality - super unconscious psyche (sie-kee).

The essence of individuality is an energetic signature unique to its essence in time. As energy matters what is quantumly definable –the soul is not soluble but an ethereal essence that transcends the super- unconscious beyond space and time. The mental matrix are the three minds co-existing at the soul level defined by the individual's experiences creating perceptions of reality formed in the conscious and subconscious. The super unconscious is a gateway into the universal mind is the physical world ego released of what is and should be.

Returning to the question: How does the mind travel to other dimensions?

To perceive the external forces divinely guiding the wisdom internally communicated, is within the individual from birth as a vibrational frequency aligning with the universe, (*like a transmitter*). Invisible signals radiate, like binary megahertz – as a string of code that interplays with the 5th dimension.

ESP intuited at lower astral planes is lower plane intuition influenced by unharmonious beliefs. ESP communicating with the 5th dimension transcends into the radiant body for higher truths.

Trance-dimensional communication is not linear or with the physical senses. See it as a three-dimensional cube accessing an array of multiple sensory perceptions to dynamically provide expression. The mental landscape receiving information of another is also dissimilar. Conversations exploring the imagination or logical conclusions pull stored thoughts, known and understood. Whereas, intuited experiences of others, isn't known or understood, articulated 3-dimensionally.

Communication in the physical world, is the conscious mind relating to memories from the unconscious to describe words, images and sensations. Information from the 5th dimension or the super-unconscious transmits another's memory as; images, sound, emotions and knowing concurrently or in various combinations.

PSYCHIC INTELLIGENCE - PI/Q

The general principles, provided above, ties into the Psychic Intelligent Quotient or Pi/Q. Using IQ as a relatable model, each sense is identified to a range of numbers and gate accessing the ability. The range of each, represents the lowest (undeveloped) to the maximum potential (personal ascension) of each skill level. *Numbers don't follow IQ standards.*

ESP	PI-Q RANGE	DOORWAYS AND CONNECTED ABILITIES
6th	50 - 100	Material Planes, Psychic Timelines
7th	101-150	Medium Communications; Discarnate Energy Connected to The Human
8th	151-200	Advanced Communication. Telepathic Reception from the All Universe, Super Conscious, Heavenly, Cosmic, Akashic
9th	201-400	Light. Shape Shifting, Bilocation, Levitation, Energy/Light Manipulation
10th	400+	The Human Potential

Pi/Q range represents rudimentary to expert level specific to the designated sensory perception. For example, the 6th gate, with a 50 Pi/Q is an individual capable of psychic ability but hasn't the experienced or experience without personal development. Maximum Pi/Q of 100 is transcends the ego, to hear the divine uncompromised.

Personal development is mentioned frequently because of the role it plays. Think of psychic abilities having, two vibrational signatures: the ability and the individual, and when combined, becomes one base frequency. This says every psychic has a unique vibration and the vibration is the translator. Maximum range is unaffected, given as received. The lowest range is affected by the physical world's ego, suspect to bias interruptions.

A rule of thumb when it comes to vibrations – higher can go lower, lower can't go higher. This keeps it simple knowing each sense has a frequency and this frequency is the key to which gate opens. The 7th gate travels through the 6th, the 8th through 6th - 7th and the 9th sense through the 6 – 8th gates; or until the gate that aligns with matching frequency.

Because the 6th and 7th senses, psychic and medium ability, are explained throughout the book, I'll skip ahead and emphasize a point important to understand. Lower and higher ranges are not measured by years of experience rather the stage of personal ascension. The individual decides to persist at the novice vibration indefinitely or incrementally advance.

8TH SENSE aligns with channeling Universal Energy or Godhead's stream of consciousness, Ascended Master Guides, Angelic realm, Sages, and high-level advisors.

9TH SENSE, notice how the range changes from 50 increments to 200? One sense higher connects to very advanced capabilities very few people on Earth are known to have achieved. Shape shifting, bilocation, levitation is all connected to the ability of kinetically manipulating light matter.

10TH SENSE is the human potential. Details of what the human is potential of, is restricted knowledge. My guides would not tell me why and any incarnated, including Master Souls, are not permitted the memory, during this time of our evolution.

pi/q feedback

Introducing the new concept of Pi/Q was exciting and even more so when my research found supporting data in *The Holographic Universe*, that coincided with Pi/Q.

Valerie Hunt, a physical therapist and professor at UCLA, performed kinesiology experimental studies of a person's energy field with an electromyograph (used to measure the electrical activity in muscles). Hunt discovered the electrodes and electromyograph could pick up subtle frequencies related to the physical energy fields, specifically the auras and chakras. The most astounding discovery was recognizing how cps (cycles per second) frequencies coincided to thoughts and/or talents. For instance, when a person's consciously is focused on the material world, energy fields were at a lower range of 250 cps, close to normal levels of biological frequencies. But people who are psychic or have healing ability tend to range 400 - 800 cps. Those capable of going into a trance, channeling information from other sources skip these frequencies and operate in their own narrow band or field, between 800 - 900 cps. Above 900 cps are what Hunt categorizes as mystical personalities, where the psychics or trance mediums are conduits of information, the mystical level knowing what to do with the information. A few individuals measured as high as 200,000 cps with an awareness of the cosmic interrelatedness in touch with every level of human experience.

The frequency ranges of cps line up with Pi/Q gate levels of access as well as the three soul level categories discussed earlier in Michael Newton's book. Overall, it offers an interesting perspective relating to human potential and how it connects to capability.

THE GATE KEEPERS

A brief overview of soul guides:

- Our ethereal friends in the Heavens referred to as spirit guides assist all souls while in the physical body.
- Spirit guides achieved higher levels of vast knowledge and skills.
- Guides can be the same from birth or change when soul mapping exceeds beyond the pre-designed goal(s).

THE INVISIBLY FORCES

Being that a medium's guide needs to facilitate on a broader scale of communication, access is more expansive. Below, is a general overview of what access guides require, grouped by sensory perception:

THE 5 PHYSICAL SENSES are guides accessing the soul's Book of Life.

6TH GATE PSYCHICS require information to assist many souls and assigned guides with access to the Akashic Records.

7TH GATE MEDIUMS are assigned guides having entrance to the Akashic Records and *The Key of Souls* to coordinate DLO communications.

THE KEY OF SOULS – Soul books contain all chapters of life, but not all chapters are accessible. When speaking of psychic or medium, here is where the fundamental difference is. Guides tending to the medium, gain access to all chapters for all souls, heavenly and embodied.

8TH GATE CHANNELS, in addition to the 6th and 7th guide access, and navigate independently with the universal time stream and super unconscious. Guides assigned are teaching level (Sage or higher) to assist their students during their developmental stages and interact directly when needed.

9TH AND 10TH GATE are spirit guides when not in the physical body. Reincarnation is a choice and always has a specific reason. Heavenly guidance is given, as needed.

EXCEPTIONS: Heavenly teachers are alerted to individuals achieving goals earlier than anticipated or their pre-established soul mapping. Anomalies alert high-level guides to map out an addendum into the soul's chart. Because of the rarity, the same high-level guides resume as their main guide(s) to oversee the new plan charted.

THE UNIVERSAL TIMESTREAM

By now, you have a better understanding communicating beyond the physical senses isn't a Magik 8-Ball and requires dedication and diligence. The Universal Timestream explains the journey necessary when individuals claim advanced connections. Sanat Kumara, a greatly appreciated teacher and ancient overseer, volunteered his wisdom.

❲ The Universal Timestream is unlike the 6th sense of timelines or spirit communication in the 7th. It is the doorway to the super unconscious; the recent consciousness population was inspired by. It is the concept of the universal mind. Human potential is beyond the most fantastic imagination and, as the masters who walked this Earth taught, is the earnest journey of self-discovery. Modernization has provided conveniences and the same mindset presented to spiritual seekers of transcendental enlightenment. There are millions of individuals around the world declaring a channel receiving arcane wisdom of the ancient beings or directly from the Book of Life (Akashic Records). Understanding the abilities is to shed light on what it means to claim such qualifications. A number greatly exaggerated.

Universal knowledge is a formation of layered light sectors, as lower astral planes, to the purest light of the God Head, as all knowing. The brighter the light, the faster colors refract and multiply; colors not known in the physical worlds. The Universal Timestream is a communication level able to retrieve arcane[3] knowledge. It is not a literal location rather a vibrational consciousness. Some may refer to it as universal wisdom, the super unconsciousness and mistakenly, as the Akashic. It holds all knowledge of the Universe and life in it, the collective thoughts of past, present, future, what has and is happening from all life.

Accessing these dimensional gates to the multiple realities simultaneously occurring, when unprepared, is restricted to prevent psychotic overload.

PSYCHIC MENTORING

Sanat Kumara's explaining are a perfect segue, not only for budding psychics but for clients to understand skill the difference of developing from trial and error versus guided from experience. All psi requires transcending self-awareness and control of the mental chitter chatters.

---

[3] occult is "knowledge of the hidden", arcane or esoteric knowledge of the paranormal meant for certain people; the study of a deeper spiritual reality that extends beyond pure reason; supernatural practices of phenomena involving mysticism, spirituality, extra-sensory perception and parapsychology.

At some point during the neophyte stage finding a mentor is beneficial. I haven't surveyed all psychics and mediums that have worked with mentors but those at the top of their field have or an equal equivalent.

A mentor takes on the role of an entrusted advisor with mastered expertise able to apply their experience, crucial for the trainee to build on natural strengths. Finding a spiritual teacher aligned with their student's goals is described as life changing. My mentor was a guru of eastern philosophy, mastered in the healing arts. Her wisdom and experience taught me at the fundamental level but explained from experience how to work within the various levels of communication scenarios, a trainee wouldn't consider. The recommendations are when selecting a mentor:

Promises focused on fast results. A guarantee before assessing a student's abilities is not language from a qualified teacher. There are, of course, general principals taught in a group setting (when applicable). An experienced mentor also recognizes individualized learning is a choice of how much time and effort is given. It isn't unusual for students to discover latent abilities to surface or not aware of.

Conclusion before evaluation. There are numerous psychic and divination classes anyone can participate in. Mentoring introduces basics suitable for a classroom environment as well as one-on-one to assist with what's unique to the individual. If the motivation is purely for money the individual will be less discerning. As a mentor, my students are evaluated to determine psychic abilities present.

Code of ethics. Mentors teach ethical standards as part of the training. Ethics involve moral practices, laws as they apply to medical advice, and privacy infringement is necessary.

The **mentor's abilities are demonstratable, not** intellectual knowledge – and psychic, medium and empathic as the qualification suggestion. Training exercises may surface unaware abilities for other communication connections. A psychic-medium can assist with psi and communications with discarnate beings, whereas. psi will not have the direct experience to relate beyond the 6th sense. Most, if not all, mediums are empaths at some level and very useful to interpret emotional blocks.

Word of mouth with proven results is always the preferred choice. When this isn't available, schedule an appointment before signing up to witness ability, communication style, rapport and ask questions.

recommendations

Meditation: A healing touch practitioner I know made an off-the-cuff comment why his hourly fee was high, *"People are paying for my twenty years of daily meditation."* He wasn't wrong.

Meditation, is the art of training the mind into stillness. When thoughts are running the show (can't turn my brain off) it's like an unsupervised group of unruly children running amok. How many kids depends on the intensity of focus resulting in worry, anxiety and/or nervousness. Meditation is key to controlling personal opinions to override or invade psychic communication. If you're a beginner, patience and practice starting with three to five minutes daily to avoid giving up. Do this every day and gradually increase the time until comfortable with 10 – 15 minutes. Quality is more important than quantity.

My hypnosis background helped me a lot. What was even more effective was walking to a large secluded field near my house. I would stand with my eyes closed with my face towards the sun. The setting is important. Not everyone can find a secluded field but this can be sunshine from a window, back deck or balcony. Most important find a quiet location without the risk of the phone ringing, doorbell, your cute dog playing with a squeaky toy, adoring kitties rubbing against you affectionately, kids, spouse, etc.

Spirit Guides: When born with psi, think of your guides waiting for you to acknowledge them. They hear you telepathically and if you're like me, includes mumbling to yourself out loud. If you are presently offering readings or just beginning, establish with your guide to receive guidance and information that will not interfere with another's journey.

Divination: Using a divination tool, is fun, and helps exercise ESP muscles. Review the chapter on divination for more information.

Stage Fright: When you go from practicing on willing friends to paying customers, some neophytes get nervous, like an actor before going on stage.

It's normal. Remind yourself of all the training, practice and validation your guinea pigs gave you.

Client Feedback: Clients are a great resource to assess your ability, and if your communication was relayed clearly. Friends and family are not always reliable when it comes to honest feedback, if uncomfortable with being direct or feel like they HAVE TO find something to criticize. It's impossible to make all clients happy. Our job is forwarding the guidance they need to know, not what they want to hear.

psychic elitism

The views we have about ourself is shaped by how the personality processes perceptions and expectations. Humans place a value on what is unique, rare and uncommon. Explaining private exchanges with the Universe without coming across as exaggerated or far-fetched, would be difficult. When initially developing or in full stride, at some point most feel like they're privy to secrets few are aware of or relate to. The divine Universe sending signs, coincidences and synchronized timing are experiences that can't be explained without sounding like a fruitcake. It's difficult not to translate through the ego and why I dubbed it the psychic elite stage that lasts until self-realized. Some may translate as being biblically important in a past life. I have witnessed these wonders from students, as well as, parents about their children who consider the possibility. Perhaps true, but this stage shouldn't be the only basis. Consider the possibility, the purpose is to balance the ego.

psi population

Nina's percentage of psi in the current population statistics, less the groups below (guided estimations}:

- haven't achieved the soul level to incarnate with abilities - *60%
- choose to not use abilities for the public *10%
- under 18, over 70 (too young or no longer practicing) - approx. 30%
- not developing abilities or transcending the self *5%

Percentage of the population is an approximation. disabilities and Psychiatric diagnosis that interfere would not incarnate with abilities.

6th sense (2%)   7th sense (4%)   8th sense (1.7%)   9th sense (.05%)

10th sense unknown

The statistics appear to align with the concept of universal balance, equally distributing all skills and/or careers globally. In addition, it provides a more accurate representation of people claiming abilities versus genuine capability. Deception may not be the only motive, nor does it discount motivations for self-interest.

OVERVIEW

Natural intuition within all, is the universal guidance connection for personal life direction. People with heightened natural intuition,(referring to themselves as psychic) looking to access another person's Life Book are restricted to lower astral planes.

Psychics are born into life instilled with a vibrational frequency capable of capturing the energy signature to communicate with the 5th dimension. The psychic's vibration acts as the door key accessing the mental doorways to the other side.

The vibrational key connected to psychic functioning is encoded into the DNA of the soul, pre-birth. The souls selected to psychically guide others on the earth plane have completed base level and at least halfway through the mid-level key sectors. As is also true, not all heavenly souls have achieved the status required to guide the earth plane, not all people are capable to be a divine intermediary.

Of the millions claiming to have abilities, the greater number are unable to reach the 5th dimension. The universe is balanced and incarnate souls with psychic ability, incrementally, never to exceed 7% of the population [souls, mid-level or above]. Of the 7%, not all will choose to be a professional psychic, demonstrating their ability in other capacities.

THE HEAVENS

REINCARNATION
12

I BELIEVE, YOU BELIEVE. A statement similar to a cheese doodle - has no nutritious value, filled with air, and requires more. Words my friend and hypnotist uttered when the topic of reincarnation was broached. Since our opinions differed, our talks remained mostly on clinical hypnosis. To my surprise and delight his viewpoint drastically changed when a woman asked for help with her eight-year-old boy who was having strange dreams. The mother explained she would hear him shouting in one or quietly dialoging in others but had no idea what he was saying because it sounded like gibberish. Recounting the details, he stopped for a dramatic pause to let me know the next part transformed his thinking. The child easily entered a deep state of hypnosis, called somnambulism[4], before regressing him back to the dream state memories. As he began re-experiencing the dreams, the gibberish reported sounded like a foreign language. The next appointment, a camera was setup to videotape the session. My friend was certain what he was hearing was a language based on the speech patterns.

Linguistic experts were given copies of the hypnosis session to translate. Several days later, he was contacted with an analysis, *"not only is the boy speaking another language, the boy is speaking an ancient dialect that is obsolete"*. My friend interjected that he'd heard similar stories from his peers but thought they exaggerated facts or made them up. He eventually met with an ancient languages Professor able to translate the vernacular to ancient

---

[4] somnambulism is a condition associated with sleepwalking. In Hypnosis, the word is used to describe a depth of trance where the mind goes into nothingness.

Macedonian[5] but what was even more exciting was what the boy was saying. The Professor confirmed with one his colleague the child was accurately describing the environment, garments worn and lesser-known details that occurred during the time period. In the deeper recesses of the child's subconscious surfaced a past life over two thousand year before. Eventually, the dreams recessed back into the memory's filing cabinet and my friend updated his cheesy poof statement to, *'I believe now, I believe.'*

The Heaven's reviews soul incarnations and enlightens us on the one word asked the most – why? why did …why don't…why haven't.

LIGHTS, DHARMA, ACTION!

A question asked regularly about reincarnation is, why don't we remember our past selves? The second most frequently asked is, why is knowing who we were even relevant to our current life? Consider, if you will, the karmic journey as a series of short stories with you and your heavenly family choosing various characters, like seeing famous actors in different roles and storylines. In this analogy, you are the actor with members from your soul group (soulmates) together, deciding the timing and role (that aligns with their goals, too) joining the cast. Most likely they have played a part in some of your past movies, maybe as the co-star, in several scenes, a few lines or an extra in the background.

Universal Pictures is the big boss, angelic healers are the producers, and main guide(s), are the director assisting the story line. The script writers for each movie depends on the budget; beginner souls require more supervision, time, cast members and strongly affects people (block buster), mid-levels would be equivalent to a documentary (instructional, teaching) and advanced as an indie film. All the movies chosen are written for your character to explore the variety of locations and countries, ethnicities, religious themes, the tragic hero to the simple life of a farmer. Certainly, some roles have a stronger impact found in natural inclination, unusual

---

[5] **ancient Macedonian** was spoken during the 1st millennium BC and belongs to the Indo-European language family. By the 4th century BC, it was replaced with Attic Greek that became the basis of Koine Greek, the lingua franca of the Hellenistic period.

fascinations and strong dislikes. The collection of the past selves is stored in our mental matrix remembered at the unconscious level as these anomalous proclivities and emotional responses. Considering we have portrayed thousands of characters, one or several, will experience a life of notoriety. It isn't unusual for people to research historical subjects having a sense of déjà vu. People worry about ego in past life readings upon hearing mention they were a prominent figure. As also true, depending on who, it may not be revealed if knowing interferes with the current life. The point is, there is a divine balance without any hierarchy. The nerdy guy or awkward gal behind you in the grocery store may have once been a monarch, famous artist or philosopher. Our stories are connected to a much bigger picture with each life as a cog of opportunity to experience ourselves.

what is reincarnation and its purpose?

Reincarnation is time slotted for soul perfection to create individualized stories, each unique, combined with all souls as the clue to the vastness of The Creator, as all and every is. Every soul is a key to unlock the mind for personal progress and achieve soul re-generational experiences to conclude.
– **God** Reincarnation is the physical incarnation of individualized personas to experience the self-diverse. Every lifetime completed is stored in the collective higher self-memory. Simply put, beautiful, wealthy, gifted, is an experience, as is the opposite. The wealthy were poor, Christian a Muslim, servants and served. It isn't unusual for ongoing strife thought to be punishment or rewards, instead of an opportunity to ascend above it. Goal oriented challenges are more obvious than the lives many people envy. For example, we know beauty and fame attracts a large percentage of the population wanting their attention. New and old friends, romantic liaisons, even family; trusting sincere or insincere motivations is a very specific challenge not understood unless directly experienced. Ego plays a significant role in reincarnation, connected to temptation, power, self-worth (inflated or deflated), righteousness, and more. What about how some create self-worth from their bloodlines and heritage?

Accomplishments of individuals in the family tree are there's alone and blood lines don't carry over from one incarnation to the next.

THE INCARNATED SOUL

Overview of souls preparing for their journey into physical life. The duration of time varies for each soul:

- the soul reviews the recent incarnation with their main guide (see weight stations)
- re-unites with soul groups
- partakes in activities/education specific to strengthening previous life goals
- meets intermittently with group leaders for next life objectives
- agreements with the soul group members joining are discussed, such as; relationship roles, available opportunities geographically, environmentally, and physically that best fit the desired outcome
- a holographic trial run is experienced before re-entry to determine likelihood of success of the chosen lesson(s). This includes choices discussed for soul members repeating one goal without success over many lifetimes. In the likelihood, the souls involved are aware and have the option for multiple lifetime goals.
- the incarnated journey is reviewed to decide if the opportunities match the selected goals and experiences from past lifetimes match the tools needed for the soul to rise above the challenges.
- when a soul agreement, or contract is approved by the guide and soul preparing for incarnation...
- DNA coding is given to the heavenly developers the genetic markers contributing to the life goals; physical attributes, gender, personality traits, natural talents and proclivities
- A main soul guide is assigned to assist (see soul guide chapter).

BEHIND THE SCENES

My heavenly teachers help me grasp complex ideas as a bystander in various simulation created environments, comparable to a vivid dream. Each, impacted my paradigms differently as I'm hoping will for you. The experience shared was an observational representation of souls preparing for reincarnation.

I was in a bustling dressing room of a theatre observing men and woman, preparing for their selected role. After a few minutes, any individual focused on, I saw and felt, as them and regardless of the role they readied for, all exuded a pure joy of friendship. Mates who were fated to meet with challenges were embraced lovingly for offering to create awareness. One-by-one, I could see their radiant body transform as each changed into the selected costume. The visual shifted where I was no longer the observer but as one preparing to experience how it felt to put the costume on. My radiant body was light and wispy. I stepped into what looked like one of those full body suits and became consumed by the density's weight. The costume didn't look like a heavy person but once on felt like it weighed 300 lbs. As time went by, my memory faded of the dressing room, believing the costume was who I really was.

THE SOUL

1. The soul is within the physical body on Earth.
2. The soul leaves the physical body and goes to Heaven.
3. The exceptions are souls, called ghosts.
4. The two emphasis being Earth and Heaven.
5. The Universe has planets and sentient beings.
6. Earth, Heaven, Beings.

When introducing sophisticated concepts of sentient life existing in the Universe, it's effective to begin with over simplistic ideas to build on. human evolution will eventually insist on releasing rigid beliefs to allow what isn't known. It's ridiculous to use conviction on what is true or isn't when it's an ongoing discovery. A mindset, anything is possible, comes across as fluffy motivational speakers, no one know what to do with. Consider transcendence as allowing unity by releasing or adhering to the bylaws of segregations. Our infinite God is much more interesting than given credit for and human actions are much less evolved they give credit to. Our potential is vast and to reach it, first we are to understand...we were created already evolved and reincarnating to be as we were created. As magnificent creatures, know nothing until you can be anything. This is how you will learn and be the potential within you.

THE EXPERIENCE OF DEATH

Death arouses a wide range of reactions. The inevitability of it, isn't the fear most have, but how it happens. One of the benefits of being a medium is the certainty of the immortal soul and the indescribable love in the Heavens. The journey of the death isn't to be feared. St. Germain explains.

At the exact instance of physical death there is one single moment of complete darkness. Heavenly beings seen in the transitional stage moments before, begin to guide the departing soul during synaptic nerve degeneration. This is experienced biologically as a visual explosion of white light mistakenly associated as part of a spiritual transition. All of this happens rather quickly before continuing towards the prearranged passage. Some travel over bridges, highways, in translucent bubbles, vector scopes, swim through water, or climb mountains. There are numerous travel routes depending on the destination. Traveling towards the Heavenly gates is not difficult but rather pleasant. Tunnels and low bridges are two examples specific to Near Death Experiences, but only a glimpse of. **Guides continue escorting souls to the destination....**

The information on the following pages is necessary before remaining message continues in the next chapter.

ROLES AND STAGES

This section is fundamental to understand why you are and how you are. What I received directly on soul levels were not included, after some consideration, I believe readers will benefit from the expert on this subject. Dr. Michael Newton's *Journey of Souls* is bar none the go-to on soul levels and have recommended his book to hundreds of clients and every reader.

Dr. Newton compiled years of recorded hypnosis regressions using a technique to take his client's consciousness in-between lives, or in Heaven. I was particularly impressed with his exceptional ability to dialog impromptu on topics he was learning simultaneously. Newton's years of regressing people from different parts of the world, diverse occupations, and all ethnic and environmental backgrounds discovered a soul's extent of knowledge of the other side was directly related to goal completed when incarnated. Newton appealed to the younger soul's spirit guides for permission on advanced topic questions and when approved, the guide would directly answer, channeling through the patient.

JOURNEY OF SOULS

Newton organized his book into three soul level groups, based on awareness and directly from the regressed souls not affected by ego. Next is a no frills general over view of each soul level with the highest percentage being, *The Beginner Soul*[6], *(roughly 73% of the population)* currently reincarnating to achieve base-line goals. Examples, not limited to:

> blame, envy, materialistic, self-centered, arrogance, violence, prejudice/bigotry, ungenerous, unsympathetic, rage, bitterness, deception, self-denial, insensitive, rigid beliefs, impatient and power (over power, to allow being over-powered)

Keep in mind, the above gives a basic idea of beginner level goals and don't imply overall personality traits. Impatient or insensitive, when not the general demeanor would apply to specific situations, or category (career, parenting, etc.). Blame, connected to personal accountability is another situation based example, when compared to narcissistic tendencies are personality pervasive.

THE INTERMEDIATE SOUL (*26% of the population*) has concluded base level behaviors, able to work with soul guides as assistants and assessed as potential teachers. Not all mid-level souls are meant to be teachers and will discover areas of talents and skills best suited. A few characteristics of a mid-level is their modesty in respect to

> An old soul is not one having more lives or older than others. It is a soul with more God essence achieving mastery during physical lifetimes. St. Michael

---

[6] percentages are an approximation from case studies and may have slight variations.

achievements, an astute attention on morality with a trusting, confident presence.

ADVANCED SOUL OVERVIEW - The ascended soul has concluded most of the fundamental lessons and incarnates to assist others while specific self-actualization is finessed. Absolute truth is the final layer peeled away and out of presumptive learning grasping a greater reality in the matricidal universe, adapting the flexibility of belief systems. Meeting an advanced soul can feel like meeting a familiar soulmate sensing their high vibrations. Their demeanor emanates a sense of quiet knowing. In conversations, intuitively, trust is given almost immediately. Physically, they emanate a sense of composure, expressive loving eyes that penetrate the soul, combined with a melodic or soothing voice. Personalities can be contemplative, playfully witty, smile easy, serious to intense. They blend into society, may have prominence or live simple lives with an almost otherworldly presence, peaceful disposition combined with an intense sense of intelligence and in-tune with life and nature. The following was received from Nina <u>before</u> reading the excerpt from Journey of Souls:

When an advanced soul (approximately 1 - 7% of the population) incarnates with the purpose to guide in spirit will assist, to improve and/or enhance the values of physical lives. The choice to reside quietly in modest abodes or in the cultural mainstream depends on different factors.

Special thanks to Dr. Newton. His knowledge in *Journey of Souls* happily endorsed as a transformative book to many of my clients; each contacting me letting me know the content impacted how they view the other side, significantly.

THE CENTURIONS ON ADVANCED BEINGS

"We no longer learn from extreme contrasting environments, cannot be swayed by other's pain or negativity, do not follow untruths, and know untruths. We are independent in our own personal journey and respect others to find theirs – even if dissimilar. Dissimilar is not represented by hostility, and have succeeded past severe actions. We accept and encourage differences, as we see each other beautiful for what is found in unique statures.

We are a collective group, cohesive in unity, individually contributing and encourage thoughts. For soul life to be the same; follow tradition or forced life styles, is primitive. We cannot understand the behaviors on Earth insistent in judgment or value, to determine. When the human soul no longer resides in the shell of their physical body holding the voices and pain experiences defining limitations of existence, this simple notion is remembered, again. Advanced beings simply know this when in the physical or soul state, without distinction."

KEY WORD SECTORS

PREJUDICE	EMOTIONS
racism,	fear
ethnicity,	anger
sexism,	stress
religion	dismissive
anti-Semitism	deviant
ageism	arrogant
homophobia	bitter
nationalism	disgusted
vanity	conceit
political	spiteful
academic,	envy
wealth	abusive
status	superiority
disability	inferior

A key word sector example, is prejudice (not preference). And for illustration purpose, think of lower emotions (*left*) as subcategories associated as *being better than* or *less than others*, or, those who discriminate and those discriminated.

A key word sector represents the themes of life experiences in the reincarnated purpose. Each key word sector has inter-relating sub-categories being the identifying goals to succeed, meaning any circumstance it could apply. The key word sector and subcategories create a unique singular vibration of goals succeeded and yet to be **All souls have the same key words with variables such as different order and how many lifetimes to succeed.**

Beginner souls are recognized by wants of the individualized self, called base level goals. Its feasible incarnations beginning 30- 70,000 years ago required 300 lifetimes to complete one sector, as it is also true, souls have completed entire levels under 5000 Earth years. In other words, we are the captains of our journey deciding how long or short we don't see ourselves are better, or less than others.

Another key word – power, *the illusion of being more than, or less than;* control, manipulation, arrogance, self-worth, pride, dominance, supremacy, temptation, deception, greed, etc.

Key words for mid-level souls are in-line with the progression of increased responsibilities to assist younger souls. **They** work closely with soul guides to determine their path and given duties commensurate with their aptitude. On the other side, mid-level vibrations qualify as junior guides or function in similar functions.

Advanced soul level no longer reincarnates with key words, independently capable of progressing the spiritual self.

Key word sectors provide another layer of clarity physical embodiment isn't random and part of the natural design in the afterlife, understood when the soul returns to their true form.

WEIGH STATIONS

Near-death experience (NDE), is when the heart stops for a short time (minutes) and the soul is transported and witness a glimpse of heaven. Testaments of the afterlife share one commonality; the experience was transformative and life altering. Are NDEs the same experience when physical life ends and isn't temporary?

Knowing the Universe isn't random says it's safe to assume NDEs are choreographed awareness experiences, not only to benefit the individual but with the understanding of later testaments to the public. Timing would be considered when heavenly accounts included assistants from star systems. Perceptions of Heaven separates heavenly beings from life in the universe. Certainly, NDEs would have been dismissed at the very idea aliens assist the celestial realms. That's just silly even for those thought bubbles, "I believe in this stuff."

According to St. Germain and other advanced intelligent spheres, the cosmic world, play an integral role in human evolution. St. Germain explains:

When the incarnated life completes, the first destination is not always Heaven. An interim location, called a way/weigh station located on another planet is not unusual and likely, the first stop. To avoid confusion, not all planets are weigh-stations and not all weigh stations are only for this purpose. One such ancient civilization are the Arcturians and assigned guardians to assist Earth.

ARCTURIAN WEIGH STATION - SOUL DEVELOPMENT

[continuing with St. Germain] Let's continue answering the remaining part of the question, what happens at the time of death, a few pages back, leaving off at, "*Guides continue escorting souls to the destination...*" accessing an intricate webwork of portals or dimensional doors to what we refer to as a way station. It's crucial to not see the Heavens as a location apart from life in the universe. Existing, are ancient civilizations as old as the universe assigned by God, as heavenly assistants.

Weigh stations were designed for soul re-generation, to rejuvenate the essence from trauma, review recent life and map out physical reincarnations before re-joining with heavenly mates in their group. When the soul transfers from the physical into its most natural form, it will travel through our gates. Some continue to the Heavenly realm and some reside at the weight station for a duration of time, depending on several factors. The Arcturians resolve for souls to advance in future incarnations by "weighing" life decisions, outcomes and achievements by evaluating previous struggles and progress. Soul teachers are present when it's time for the soul to continue their journey to their core group.

Longer durations involve souls benefitting in a contrast education method used to reinforce opposition. Souls selected have resisted higher vibration achievements over several lifetimes such as; acts resulting in extreme physical/psychological harm, self-interest deception and disregard for life. The soul is isolated in a chamber to contemplate as they review all previous lives from the perspective of the souls affected by their actions and decisions.

Overview from St. Germain (an Arcturian): All souls (with few exceptions) were birthed simultaneously. All levels of personal growth experience the same challenges, collectively. Ascension is designed for all souls having time as the choice, to when. A soul choosing actions resulting in harm to others personally, intimately, by group, or executive order, the soul is instructed to review each action in every life. In soul state, justification defenses are negated to experience each decision, as felt, to every soul. This is not punishment, retribution, or karma. We have mastered ourselves beyond rudimentary teachings. Our method was to develop the tools necessary and reinforce the empathetic nature stored within the subtle unconscious.

The Arcturian way station is for all souls to benefit from our ancient wisdom. All souls during the incarnation journey will travel here to review their Book of Life. We are entrusted with the Akashic Records, as the Parliament to God's White House.

AUTHOR'S COMMENT: Initially, I wrote as weigh, until it dawned on me later the word chosen can be cleverly used interchangeably as a play on words, equally expressing; I am the way or weighing, as balanced justice scales.

way; thoroughfare for travel or transportation from place to place; an opening for passage; the course traveled from one place to another: route. method of accomplishing, regular, or habitual manner or mode of being, behaving, or happening; movement or progress along a course; the means taken or procedure followed in achieving an end.

weigh; to measure the weight of: to consider carefully especially by balancing opposing factors or aspects in order to reach a choice or conclusion: evaluate.

JUPITER?

Initially, I was hesitant hearing this message about Jupiter, wondering if a generic title would be more acceptable concept. The reason wasn't my disbelief. My experiences have shown me time, and again, what is true is subjective to the knowledge of the beholder. The concern was how far the reader's mind could bend out of their mental comfort zone until the goofy alarm goes off met with eye rolling and spontaneous mumbling. As I considered a mentally non-threatening replacement, Edgar Cayce suddenly popped into my head. Curious to know why, I searched if any of his readings mentioned Jupiter. Not only did our sleepy friend mention, it aligned with Germain's words, "*In Jupiter we find one having a great influence upon the lives, the experiences of others – by choices made by the entity.*" (Reading 2834-1)

Germain continues explaining Jupiter's role.

Jupiter may be surprising when considering what is suitable or not suitable in the physical world. From this viewpoint, it is irrelevant. What is known from telescopes or NASA's technology doesn't represent the actuality. Human thinking is still in its infancy determining what's true and real only to satisfy what's already known. Sentient beings are capable to manipulate technological imagery, shield atmospheres or disguise atmospheres. The purpose is knowing the decisions that would be, when viewing planets seen as green and lush in the Milky Way. The result would distract evolution's progress becoming too eager, too soon. When science and technology is capable to directly experience this landscape, it coincides simultaneously with evolutionary progression.

SOUL LEVEL ADVANCEMENT

When souls shift into another light level the teachers assigned to Jupiter assist the transiting map for next stage awareness

Jupiter's way station souls go upon the completion of key words and ready to advance to either a higher level sector in the same grouping, or next level. For additional clarity, the Arcturians assist with *key word development* to advance where Jupiter assists with *advancing souls in next vibration levels*, when successful. An example is a beginner soul preparing for mid-level or mid-level to advanced.

WAY STATION WITH THE ELDERS

Cassiopeia, Andromeda, Pegasus are designated interims explicit to soul review. How these locations differ from the Arcturians is specific to mid-levels to advanced soul achievement, reviewed by group council, known as the ancient overseers. Ancients, or the elders are the highest level of teaching guides and responsible for modifications to soul timelines, other than God. (These are the guides discussed in the Book of Life when a soul completes slated life goals early.)

Advanced souls meet one-on-one with The Elders to re-review original soul mapping for modifications, insert change or alter original goals. The soul being reviewed also participates, having the experiential mindset and capable to be more involved in deciding their future lifetimes, including lives in-between.

ADDITIONAL INFORMATION

Souls traveling directly to Heaven do so when soul guides determine uniting with their soul group is the best course of action. Reasons can be to replenish energy after trauma, prepare for future reincarnations or similar.

Mediums (depending on the DLO's journey) will connect to loved ones at weigh stations with the higher probability of initiating communication before 3 to 6 months from physical departure. The medium will not be informed or be able to differentiate, nor will it be offered voluntarily. Weigh stations are part of the heavenly system and why enlightening the seeker or medium is viewed as inconsequential.

BEGINNER LEVEL souls meet privately with their guardian or soul group teacher at a weigh station.

MID-LEVEL souls who were previously prepared for advanced level sectors (Jupiter) are guided directly to the Heavenly gates to review achievements with soul masters, bypassing weigh stations.

ADVANCED souls incarnate less frequently and when they do, it's either to fine tune or re-experience Earth conditions for in between life guidance. Upon departure, advanced souls are met by the Heavenly Host, welcoming them back home. It's not unusual for an advance soul to review on their own or with their group for further development as a teacher.

SOULMATES

When the concept of soulmates was introduced, it sparked a word-of-mouth phenomenon. Romanticism, and the search for the perfect mate was modified in the public exchange until soulmate became synonymous with one half completing the other. Over the years, those adept in the spiritual arts adjusted the definition back to the truer meaning; one soul (soulmate) of many in the same group (soul group) sharing multiple lifetimes for the karmic journey of experiences.

A word or phrase exemplifying the love penetrating deep within our being representing the ultimate expression of emotion is more than likely how soul mate was redefined. Even though soulmates aren't the one and only, it isn't completely wrong, bearing in mind members of our soul group have shared intense and intimate relationships in various roles over many lifetimes. Add the possibility that souls have reincarnating for 30 - 70,000 years; recognition is an understatement meeting a soul mate who shared many of lives together. The lifelong partnership or relationships wrought with strife are reasons to reincarnate together.

When I was introduced to the idea, *we are part of the decision-making when selecting our family in our physical incarnations,* it wasn't easy to accept. This meant I couldn't blame anyone for all those crap-ass moments. Thoughts went to working as a child development worker helping severely abused kids and the horrendous, evil they endured. The idea wasn't reasonable and wanted to reject the idea. Why would anyone knowingly choose an environment filled with such loathing and suffering?

While writing *Planting Seeds on Concrete*, I asked God to help me understand, not seeing how His answer could possibly satisfy, or, even be answered, at all. Well, it was answered, including multiple scenarios provided and, it made sense. Please keep in mind, these are only a few examples:

- Life goals of a soul never include any physical, emotional, sexual violations to another. These acts are disconnected from their grace.
- Before reincarnating, the probability a soul will disconnect from their slated path is reviewed with guides and the souls involved.
- Soul advancement is the primary reason the recipient souls will agree to experience the possibility of harm. Soul advancement can be equal to an acceleration of multiple lifetimes (receiving additional preparedness in spirit to ascend the traumatic experiences) and/or as the beacon of hope to assist others and create awareness on humanitarian issues avoided.

Again, I'm remiss to introduce as a finite concept and would like to reinforce the point; the representation provided does not encompass situations more complex.

IDENTIFYING THE SOULMATE

soulmate; a separate entity one has spent many lifetimes as a friend, lover, co-worker or partner, or drawn to fulfill a specific undertaking.

The soulmate is one part of an entirety, called a soul group. Shared reincarnation experiences can elicit a great attraction, bond marriages, union of hearts, for a temporary period or over a lifetime. Soul group clusters represent the varying relationships shared.

OUTER RINGS, souls infrequently reincarnating with, or the least number of times. They are the acquaintances, brief relationships; elementary school teacher, a childhood friend or neighbors who move and don't stay in contact with. Outer rings are mutual endings, fade away or grow out of; endings without intense emotional reactions.

MIDDLE RING: abundance of lifetimes together with the likelihood of familiar a relationship; family, longtime friends or co-workers. Upon introduction there is a soul recognition that may feel easy, comfortable or a strong dislike (not because of low vibration energy). Middle ring soulmates are fated relationships to occur with variable intensity levels, depending on the purpose. The ring signifying the highest number.

INNER CIRCLE: Meeting an inner circle soulmate is an immediate, powerful connection with the fewest of souls we experience thousands of years of reincarnations with. Roles can be intimate romantic partners, the best friend from childhood until old age, family members with close union, or any relationship creating an instant impact. When romantic the intense connection has been erringly defined as twin mates. Connections felt from one without matching intensity, is to ignite reactions most likely a key word goal. When mutual (not temporarily), can be a lifelong relationship.

"And when one of them meets with his other half, the actual half of himself ... the pair are lost in an amazement of love and friendship and intimacy, and one will not be out of the other's sight, as I may say, even for a moment." Aristophanes on the transcendent experience of two soulmates reuniting.

experts on twin souls

A friend offered his viewpoint after reading this chapter. His focus wasn't on the specific topic rather the unqualified claiming expertise (and a later chapter) being rampant and felt I didn't emphasize the seriousness of the point enough. As a frequent traveler, he compared it to his encounters with novice yoga teacher's negligent instructions and how they could easily result in irreparable muscle damage. Surprisingly, his experiences weren't cottage industries but brand name gyms. He said, *because the gym is a corporate franchise, members are confident instructors are vetted*. It wasn't until overhearing a Yoga instructor's reckless nutritional advice, he decided to ask the club about her credentials.

Wannabes playing expert can be dangerous and devastating, as the woman in the following true story discovered.

THE WOMAN WHO WAITED AND WAITED

A new client, I'll call Jesse, scheduled a psychic consultation by telephone, on matters of romance. When she called, I could feel a wave of her nervous energy rush through the phone that was more intense than most. A couple minutes to say hello usually helps and when it didn't, I let Jesse know what was felt empathically. She verified quickly, as if waiting for me to verify. Before I could say anything else, Jesse added that she knew validation was important for me to give her but her friend met with me several times and she wanted to explain the reason for contacting me. It was unusual but agreed to her story.

Three years ago, several strange coincidences occurred that led her to a function, at a local church. After a few minutes passed, a man she was standing next to, said hello and started a casual conversation. They discovered knowing several of the same people and visiting the same places. Both agreed the likelihood was more than strange. At the same time, Jesse explained having an instant romantic attraction that isn't typical for her. The man's demeanor appeared to share the same attraction.

As Jesse talked, my intuition was telling me something different, and telepathically asked Nina, what she wanted me to know. She advised to continue listening and remain calm when I hear what she says next. When Jesse's backstory concluded, she was ready to elaborate on the anxiety as a result when consulting with a psychic. She told the psychic the reason for the appointment and continued to give details and wasn't told to stop. Since it was her first time, Jesse assumed that's how it worked ending the information with, no one, in her life, has affected her like this man.

'You met your twin flame and this is a powerful union. The coincidences say to wait for him, he will return to you." She repeated the words, I could hear a glint of hope in her voice I would tell her it was true.

To help, I gave her the time needed (free of charge) to untangle her mind and heart from the devastation caused by the wannabe psychic. The referral eased trust concerns but personal validation is always important, especially for first time clients with this type of experience. Because of the information provided Jesse's validation focused on the areas of her life her friend wasn't aware of and topics unrelated to romance. When satisfied, I said, 'Jesse, I don't see him around you. It looks like he moved. Do you know if this is true?" Another bombshell came when she told me he moved a few months after meeting him, to live with another woman and… in another country… three years ago! My heart continued to sink for the softly spoken, gentle woman and asked, "you are still waiting for him after knowing this?" Jesse replied, "Yes but it's also the reason I called you. My friend who referred me insisted I set up an appointment with you".

Nina helped her with guidance, answers for her life to begin moving again, **AND CONCLUDED WITH,** "the soul giving guidance, doesn't consult with spirit guides. She confuses emotional ideas as intuitive, affected by her own self-esteem. Referencing twin mates is one of several passionate conclusions offered as psychically resonated believed in her mind as true".

Jesse has a doctorate and articulate, aware of people pretending to be psychic for greed but not of the new category, just as dangerous. How do you put a price on three years?

TWIN FLAME

At the time, I wasn't aware this sacred union was a trend, or a possibility people wanting to be liked? could be this reckless and decided to check. Entering twin mate in my search engine the number of cut and paste websites flooding my screen was disturbing and rivaled the journalist's ignorance in News Clues.

Our Yin to the Yang, divine soul who guides the other half from the Heavens was reduced into inane bullet points barely recognizable as a soulmate, let alone twin. For anyone misled, *God explains*.

The Twin Mate is a conjoining of two physical embodiments matching at the cellular level that activates upon initial meeting. The encoding has both identical and complimentary traits for the profound relationship, similar to the birth of twins sharing the same womb.

The Twin Mate, romantically in union, **is not found disharmonious in any circumstance, reason or purpose**. When incarnated, it is significant, immediate, mutual, recognized and rare. The term from spiritualists have confused powerful soulmates; two souls from their primary soul group having many incarnations together, with the soul twin. The crucial and identifying difference is never found disharmonious and **not distinguished by how powerful the connection**, as the only reason. This includes, two soulmates immediately recognizing, and perhaps, feeling love immediately. Nor will the rare occurrence of incarnating on Earth, at the same time – find each other, falling in love and conclude, in an early death (during their prime of life). This would be unbearable and inconsolable, beyond words. It would not be, in any condition, for any reason, have a purpose to be. This includes, if a partner returns to Heaven and their living partner, ends their own life or living life, described as "never recovered from". This is a first level soul experiencing, young level strengthening, as described.

Twin Mates incarnating together – Reviews are with soul group teachers, first, then, approved from Me, the Creator directly, and, why rare. When approved by the Creator, for a romantic union, the reason is:

- for one to inspire the other and/or, each other, affecting many
- or the union witnessed by many, for the purest definition of love, inspires and affects many, to understand the contrast, of what most accept, as love.
- **as a friend, relatives, or co-working partners** – when reincarnated in this role is to create an important invention, a discovery occurs, or, simply a collaboration bringing joy to many. Romantic partnerships,
- are not found disharmonious, in any circumstance, reason or purpose as the crucial identifier.
- Birth signs (astrology) find 180° opposite, in both Sun and Rising sign. Together as 360°, circle of life.
- Can meet early or later, in life. When too young for romantic unions, the reasons vary, to why, and revealed when re-connected.
- Both are advanced souls (end ☾)

Rising signs can be found on astrology websites with charting software. You'll will need to know time of birth and city, state born of any involved.

opposite signs (sun _and_ rising sign):

Aries is opposite to Libra   Taurus is opposite to Scorpio
Gemini is opposite to Sagittarius   Cancer is opposite to Capricorn
Leo is opposite to Aquarius   Virgo is opposite to Pisces

For instance, a Libra sun sign, Gemini rising sign with an Aries sun sign and Sagittarius rising sign. To summarize; twins fits the given descriptions, the astrology signs, AND, both in the advanced 1% of the population.

HEAVENLY WORDS
AKASHIC RECORDS (A.R.)

The Hall of Records, or Akashic, is a vast consortium of knowledge, not unlike a library. To explain briefly, every soul book and chronicled event is catalogued embracing several doors to the spirit planes: Book of Life (akashic), Universal (Timestream) and the Key of Souls.

❨ "The Akashic Records, is the soul library one could describe as a literal location in the Golden City's Parliament. Reviewing a soul record in the great library is possible for the physical soul. Access into the Heavenly gates can travel one of two ways – a channeler with advanced level guides relaying indirectly or entering a deep trance meditation communication to access directly. Of the Psychics living on earth in current time, 7% of all claiming, are genuine. Abilities to [directly] read soul records, as Edgar Cayce, finds 20 individuals worldwide capable of such."

AUTHOR'S COMMENT: Calculating 7% includes 8th gates approximation and PSI Population statistics, at the end of this chapter.

BOOK OF LIFE

"Upon time and space is written the thoughts, the deeds, the activities of an entity – as in relationships to its environs, its hereditary influence; as directed – or judgment drawn by or according to what the entity's ideal is. Hence, as it has been oft called, the record is God's book of remembrance; and each entity, each soul – as the activities of a single day of an entity in the material world – either makes same good or bad or indifferent, depending upon the entity's application of self ..."

"The record, is that [which] the individual entity itself writes upon the skein of time and space through patience and is opened when self has attuned to the infinite and may be read by those attuning to that consciousness..."

Above quotes from Edgar Cayce's Area for Research and Enlightenment, (A.R.E.)

[*The Universal Guides explain*] The Book of Souls are the heavenly recordings of every soul life that lived and living. Parental birth choices to evolve the karmic journey are previewed for the environmental influences affecting mental capacity, behavioral tendencies, and physical attributes best suited for the desired outcome. Pages provide the details of participating soul group members, core soulmates, fated or destined to a participating role.

Blank spaces represent variables of behavioral possibilities, not pre-written, and specific to attaining goals in purpose and anomalous paths. Variables are not permissible to psychically access without the consent of an Elder or Sage. A reference would be a soul incarnating to experience challenges in early childhood thus affecting aspects of the personality. Physical or psychological harm, are not written in soul books, nor related to previous lives, referred to as karma, rather the soul who harms, unresolved path. Potential outcomes of harm are recognized as a percentage of probability where the soul is aware of the probability when deciding the future incarnation. When or if, the probability occurs, a recurrent timeline appears to adjust the purpose for vast soul growth for the one harmed. Alternate timelines reveal awareness challenges to occur [and] to ignite the emotional memory mind.

In segmented stages during the adult years, reoccurrences continue until the new decisions are made changing the outcome, also written in the Book of Souls. Variables can also occur when a soul accelerates timelines [that results in] achieving goals in half the time slated. Although the variable or blank space is a known possibility, it is considered rare or an anomalous timeline, to succeed earlier than slated. In cases where goal(s) conclude earlier, participating soulmate(s) for the current or alternate timeline, are reviewed that may require adjustments, for each soul book affected, including enhancing DNA, as necessary. The soul reviews the alternate timeline with high level guides in dream state. [end]

The above was received with intuitive knowing that doesn't translate in the words alone, and added here. Soul books record all lifetimes, past to current incarnations with details of childhood environments, the soul group members joining and how significant their role is, and vice-versa. Fate and destiny points are marked into timelines with occurrences leading up to, as well as, vital data concerning; proclivities, future probabilities, potential for success, temptations struggled with, opportunities, and so on. Timelines with blank areas not recorded, are variables. In the rare instance, where a soul surpasses the original purpose, timelines significantly alter. Here's what needs to be explained. This means, decisions in the original timeline didn't happen, affect others – subtle or significant. The new chart is reviewed with the original interactions of soul group members and adjusts all timelines involved, without interfering with the goal's objective. Which apparently, they know how to do, because their smart and thinking about it hurts my brain. Last mentions are, souls can incarnate with the intension to achieve in an accelerated time but it's rare to accelerate when not pre-established. When an anomaly occurs, Elders and Sages are alerted to meet with the soul in their dream state (not-remembered) to review the adjusted timeline and continue as their spirit guide for the remaining life duration.

SOUL CONTRACTS

A close friend shared his experience with a gifted psychic who specialized in soul contracts; removing obsolete programming affecting current life, influencing thoughts, personality, or inclinations, creating resistant or preventing personal joy and prosperity. (wow, right?) It requires the ability for their spirit to commune with an elder council on behalf of the client and request a review all life contracts before, deciding if/what to remove or keep. Of course, this was completely fascinating to me, hearing one of my closest friends saying that he felt a tangible physiological and spiritually uplifting change. A statement not heard from him, often, for sure. Personally, I find it inspiring to hear about gifted healers who truly understand the art and their skills. Since this was uncharted waters, the following day I asked the universe to elaborate so I could share with you.

[from Sanat Kumara] A soul contract is a spiritual term to define goal agreements in one or several past incarnations. These cannot be removed, as this would remove the benefit to achieve the goal – and the memory storing the experiences necessary to reach the conclusion. What your friend experienced with the metaphysician, yes, a very specialized psychic gift in tune with elder soul energy. When the elders review past lives, we see where a former personality or indelible influence was necessary to re-emerge, triggered to assist with a current life path. The memory of concluded lives, in a scenario such as this, re-surfaces into conscious time becoming intertwined with the past-present. For example, your friend described a warrior personality re-experienced; a persona counter-intuitive to his present being. When he joined the military's structured group dynamic with imposed rituals a remnant of his former life re-assembled from the memory matrix to assist with a specific discipline that his current life opposed. This is one of millions upon millions of reasons for a past life personality to re-emerge. When no longer needed, or more specifically, when your friend's current life personality was once again dominant, the warrior life went dormant.

Previous lifetimes of the persona and the associated experiences lay deep within the soul. Any re-activation drives the lifetimes from the unconscious to the subconscious, creating influence on the conscious mind. Understand, it isn't the removal of a contract, we replace specific signatures deeper or back into the unconscious, not as accessible for the conscious mind to readily remember. Soul Contract Psychics or Life Path Psychic, as the truer term. One is to be selected, pre-birth, as any affecting great soul change. Those selected to assist are born with inclinations within, gravitating towards the study of, for years or events creating the motivation to self-study required for the meditative self-surpassing into all consciousness, capable of direct communication with the elder council. This is not to be practiced, unless, a soul is led into a profound knowing; not by whim's curiosity.

WALK-INS

The walk-in[7] being/individual retains the memories of the original personality, but does not have emotions associated with the memories. As they integrate, they bring their own mental, emotional, spiritual consciousness and evolve the life to resonate with their purpose and intentions. Incarnating into a fully grown body allows the walk-in soul to

---

[7] Bjorling, Joel. Reincarnation: A Bibliography. Taylor & Francis, 1996. pp. 141-142
Partridge, Christopher. *UFO Religions*. Routledge, 2012. pp. 114-115.

engage in embodiment without having to go through the two decades of maturation that humans need to reach adulthood. A walk-in soul also does not experience the conditioning of childhood and has a different relationship to life because they were not born.

The concept (see footnote) of walk-ins comes with several defining variations creating confusion exactly what is going on. I asked **God explains what walk-ins are:**

Energies as numerous spiritual lights formed from the God Spark created, as independent disembodied assistants are direct creations not currently defined or understood, as a category known of. They are the arbiters, the time keepers and have ability to create. Their essence is a collective soul force to keep Divine Law orderly and record Divine Law for every universe and life creation.

Manifesting into the physical body, referred to as *"walk-ins,"* although extremely rare, is part of their role. They can bond with a physical body presence when directed by Me (Source), to "cleanse" a soul. Cleansing a soul is to eradicate dark energy creating illusions influencing the mind strongly, affecting the encoding where the soul's original purpose can no longer be intuited. The dark energy surrounding the auric field or within, are the influenced thoughts of negative energy. The cleansing ritual performed is subtle, as the slight touch from a stranger bumping into them or [in] proximity to negate the mind and free it. They do not need to be called, I will always send when the mind is ready to release their burdens of the past and not invest as their own perpetual victim.

Thought forms connected to dark energy influences decisions made from false beliefs creating fear. In turn, directly influences the process of reincarnation. It was explained to me worry and fear within, correlates to the root words of the beginner soul. Key word sectors, is a new concept from the universal guides explaining goals of the soul journey.

CELEBRATING SPIRIT

A profound experience with a psychic, wasn't from their guidance but specific details that happened exactly, as described. They told me a friend, by name, would contact me in a few days and suddenly offer advice that would be extremely helpful. Three days later, I was sitting in a park and my friend, the psychic mentioned by name showed up, unexpectedly. He sat down and said hello and out of nowhere offered me advice on a project I was working on. It WAS very helpful and never told him what the psychic said. *R G*

... question about a misplaced Amethyst ring. [the psychic] told me the ring was tucked away in a jewelry bag at the bottom of a moving box with kitchen items and papers, I went through boxes in my shed and sure enough, came across a box as he described and found my ring. *K.G.*

(A psychic) helped me believe in myself and understand who I am as a person. She doesn't use her gifts for financial gain, but to genuinely help others and make sure they have the tools to continue their life journey towards happiness. Personally, she has become an important figure in my life and helped me in numerous ways unimaginable. I am blessed to have met such a wonderful person and she became more than a friend to me, but an inspiration. *C.H.*

(The psychic) continues to blow me away with her incredible insight & laser accuracy. I ABSOLUTELY love watching everything she says play out, & smile to myself as I see it happen. *D.H.*

I hoped to hear from my dad. Within 30 minutes of talking to me and how to move forward she realized that my dad had been sending her messages for almost six months. I only found her three weeks ago. One session helped me see that everything I had interpreted all these years was wrong. I left feeling lighter and happier than I have in years. *N.A.*

SPIRIT GUIDES

'Who are you speaking to?'

'My spirit guides and people on the other side. They give me messages to help the living.'

'They're here? ... right now? ... these invisible.... spirit people?"

'My spirit guide is, yes. You have spirit guides, too.'

I see. What are my guides telling you? The Psychologist writes in her notes: *I believe Michele suffers from delusional hallucinations creating a complex fantasy world made up of invisible beings she refers to as shadow people.*

Spirit guides. You wrote shadow people.

How did ...? Wait...I really have a spirit guide...what are they saying?

The idea of people having a spirit guide isn't a new concept. They are an elusive group not understood beyond being invisible assistants to the physical world. As you know, Nina, is my confident and loving friend helping behind the scenes. I wanted to redirect the attention and learn more about her and the community of spirit guides. She does not disappoint.

INTERVIEW WITH NINA – PART 1

Hi Nina. I'd like to begin with clarifying the higher self and the role of spirit guides; are these the same or separate?

The higher self, also referred to as the twin soul does not act as a guide. It is to be understood, the higher self retains the heavenly knowledge but also retains the level of the soul journey; a beginner soul on Earth, a beginner higher self in Heaven. The higher self reflects the Yin/Yang, the vastness and duality – as The Creator, as created from.

Heavenly and Earthly selves are connected to the silver cord's 'natural intuited body.' Spirit guides will, using the closest word to associate, borrow this link as an alternative to project into the mind directly.

Thank you, that's the first time explained like this. Refocusing to the spirit guide community, are their indicators or physical signs?

We appear in dreams, reflect and project our wisdom, compel thoughts, to do or remain. Even the busiest, loudest minds settle into quiet, eventually. We use these fractions of time to offer suggestions and re-direct compulsory thoughts.

Explain the spirit guide community as simply as possible.

The physical soul and the soul in spirit, when part of a group cluster have one main teaching guide. When the soul is ready to embark into the physical life, their teaching guide oversees their life map. Variables and additional guidance are not unusual for the youngest or transitional advanced souls.

Meaning?

Meaning, young-beginner stage of human evolution has difficulty surpassing, what we refer to as, base-line keywords. The goal is for all to succeed, as a collective whole. Additional guidance helps prevent falling behind where Earth can no longer provide the environment to advance.

I've heard it suggested very young souls aren't assigned guides.

The youngest of souls struggling with their personal evolution receive concentrated efforts from several guides, with the hope our influence generates a signal louder than the lower vibrations covering their magnificent self. It isn't they do not have guides, young-beginner souls are not assigned one guide, rather a collective force. We would not leave the youngest children unattended to wreak more havoc, already demonstrated.

Is it accurate, 1% of the population are advanced souls and qualify spirit guide level? And, does this imply assistance is no longer required?

Transitional advanced souls incarnate for specific reasons to benefit humanity on a wide scale or one individual, for the same result. It isn't necessarily the advanced soul requires guidance, what's involved to align the multitude of shifting fluctuations, for either situation, is a series of complex timing segments not suitable for one guide.

Are there indicators to recognize the young-beginner souls?

- Preoccupied thoughts of the self with little to no regard for human or animal life. Taking another's life (directly or giving a commanded order), is the most serious, when for pleasure, self-interest or game.
- Preoccupied thoughts for monetary gain, at the expense of others.
- Acts in the name of divine council, for personal gain, is a direct confrontation to Our Creator. Any one of these acts is impossible to fathom for the advanced soul.

Acts in the name of divine council, **can you elaborate?**

Any acting in the name of The Supreme Creator, heavenly enriched beings on behalf of, or said communication. Theological reverence or claims of ability, for notoriety, ego or monetary influence.

What happens if young souls don't succeed even with the guidance?

Their energy will be reworked back to its pure state and begin the reincarnation process on another Earth like system.

The population currently, what percentage are young-beginner souls?

Approximately 70% are beginner souls, of which, 55% are working hard to raise their vibrations and attain a higher level within the beginner group, with the remaining 15%, at risk of falling behind.

A significant number when considering the total population.

Indeed. Without, civilization would look very different and why our help and other beings of light have joined to assist.

Is there additional information to add, I didn't consider?

The three levels, as described, are more intricate than suggested. Beginner level, from the youngest to the highest, or near intermediary would recognize significant evolution advancement. In other words, the highest level of beginner and the beginning of the intermediate level would see little difference with only slight vibratory fluctuations.

INTERVIEW WITH NINA- PART 2

I'm often asked about knowing what a guide's name is. Any advice?

The recommendation is developing a relationship with their main guide. To learn our name is not difficult. Ask the spirit guide, out loud or mentally, as we are all telepaths, to reveal their name. When difficult to pronounce, we will offer a simplified version or one suitable for relatability. Within a short period of time, or, over several weeks, our name will begin to be revealed through repetition by coincidence's synchronicity.

Can you give the readers an example?

The easiest method is technology; compelling the mind to watch a movie, listen to music and other media venues, finding one name heard consistently. Another sign is hearing one name within a short period of time that is out of the ordinary. Someone introducing themselves at a public store, a vanity license plate and a friend with the urge to call and mention the same name in conversation. If the mind is receptive, we will introduce ourselves in dream states, visually or heard.

How would you define the energy of a spirit guide?

Guides are advanced beings that have or near completion of the reincarnation process. The realm of light. We are a completed essence, in servitude to mankind's future possibility, the potential yet to be.

'Completed essence;' as the reincarnation process or one stage within?

The level of a spirit guide, the soul has accomplished a vibrational level within the reincarnation process. The absolute completion is Source, the transcendence of light, knowing and love. Spirit guides have attained the upper tier vibration of the advanced level, tier 5 and 6.

Are their higher tiers?

The Sages are tier 8 and higher. Tier 7 is reserved for the Teaching Master Guides, no longer working with incarnated souls, to provide council for spirit guides.

What tier are you, if I'm allowed to ask.

My tier level is 8, Sage or Ascended Master Guide.

How would you describe the experience from a spirit guide's point of view?

To guide one soul or several is an honor, comparable to a parent joyfully witnessing her child's first steps.

What capabilities have spirit guides attained?

Our capabilities cannot be associated with the perceptions of man, currently. A soul, a light being or sentient energy understood as a completed essence, is one with the Christ Consciousness, you call God. Within this realm of light, souls guiding physical life forms are many, in the variety: 1) humans who have surpassed contrasting life experiences from several Earth like teaching planets, 2) beings referred to as highly evolved from other star systems, 3) the Angelic Choir (assigned) and 4) the Sages, known as The Ancient of Ancients.

As much as I would love to elaborate on your answer, following up will need to be addressed at another time. For now, questions will focus on questions creating awareness for seekers of higher wisdom. How would you describe the personality of spirit guides?

Different classifications have unique personifications. Guides who lived as human may choose a persona to reflect a previous lifetime found enjoyable.

Are their guides without physical life experiences?

Light energy, without physical life incarnations have been mistaken for angelic. They are not. Light energy guides were created by God specifically to endow the universe with extremely high vibratory sensations, as their purpose. They can be assigned to a human soul achieved in advanced awareness and capable to endure their presence while assisting their remaining journey.

The spiritual community is fascinated with Ascended Masters and Angels. I understand it's rare to be assigned either as a direct guide. When they are, how would you describe their essence?

Joyfully, wise and playful. Planetary resources are the Ascended select, known in the human spiritual circles and unknown. Personalities are diverse, specific to the star system. Generally, more matter of fact and gentle.

The Angelic Choir; when a soul is honored for their life assistance, as the Seraphim, Archangel or Principles to name, will know them as beautifully perfect, for no other description. When upon the chosen, it is to carry the soul through trials set upon them to endure a greater purpose.

The Ancients of ancients, called Sages or the Elders, are granted to oversee selected souls for the same reasons as the angelic choir. Both, are given the command from Source directly to watch over, for wisdom to impart, to protect and guard. Angelic and the Ancients are equally commanding, direct, observant and always respectful.

I think basic terminology with descriptions will prevent confusion for readers. What is the contactee, psychic or psychic medium called?

We don't use formal titles. To answer the question for clarity; initiates, mediators, adepts, any of these words are sufficient. When abilities are within, yet to be fully developed, the student is assigned a spirit guide in-training, and very capable. The level of soul ascension within must reach a level of vibration to alert a master guide the soul is ready for their higher-level assistance.

How are guides assigned to physical souls, including soul levels.

First level assistants guide, is assigned to the non-intuitive population, student vibrations of the 6th gate and empaths.

Second level assistants guide, student level vibrations for medium communications. The student medium does communicate with deceased souls but relies on the assistant guide's communication. In other words, the medium will sense, see and hear (DLOs), but haven't yet achieved sustained communication endurance. Meaning, intermittently connecting with the DLO and their own mind. Second level guides try to fill in the gaps with intuitive relay. The medium at this level is one becoming aware of spirit communication and not in the professional sector.

Spirit Guides, for psychics and mediums are teacher level, to accommodate the abilities, in various capacities, including *gatekeeper*. A gatekeeper accesses the Books of life of all souls, escorts, and monitors souls from one plane Heavenly to the midways, for communication.

Ascended Masters are the highest vibration within the human tier level of advanced souls. Master Jesus is an example, who since transcended as one with The Godhead. Most Ascended Masters known, are this or Universal Guides, allowing the title for simplicity. Few names' spiritualists associate as, are well known, yet with capabilities beyond human understanding. Universal Guides, such as myself, attained full consciousness and work as part of a Godhead. We are assigned at birth or later, depending on several factors pertaining to the soul's choice. Our mission, if you will, is to work with 8th gate initiates to assist humans evolve. Sage, another name we have been referred to, confused with both Ascended Masters and Ancients. Ascended Master are not part of the Godhead.

Elders or Ancients, are the highest-level vibration as one with The Godhead, The All Creator and can individualize into a self-consciousness and assume any form. Although a separate category, the Ancients and the Angelic force are equal in the energy frequency.

INTERVIEW WITH NINA – PART 3

Clients seeking guidance is what most associate spirit guides to. Timing questions are discussed in another chapter but would like additional clarity on any variables involved with precognitive guidance. Does the client's mindset affect the future? And, I'd like you include when psychic error and misinterpretation is involved.

The behavior of every individual plays a significant role, sometimes very subtle where the psychic would not see as relevant. It isn't the psychic ignores irresponsibly, rather considered redundant.

Why would the information be given in this manner?

The information is given exactly as it needs to be. Our efforts to, highlight or not emphasize, has reason. This will be a difficult answer for select readers to accept. Seeking divine guidance was part of the Creator's plan to assist souls truly seeking change and reassured from the answers given. We honor behaviors based on the mindset asking. When the seeker's mental dialog *'won't believe until it comes true'* or disputes answers contradicting the desire, our role is diminished to accommodate fantasies, without basis.

You established previously; clients are essentially interacting with spirit guides directly. How do emotions affect future predictions?

The stronger the emotion, the greater the future probabilities shift, towards or away. When precognition involves others, which most do, all pertaining influence the potential outcome. There are numerous precipitating factors for two people to align. Timing given, occurs as initially given, when attention is elsewhere, letting it happen.

Seeking answers under extreme duress, become absorbed on wanting and getting with little. Consideration is without any other or the other as the desired. Attitude's such as this, are demanding mentally to the psychic, when, how and who. This, is the reason a percentage experience the information, as said, and others with heightened emotions result in questioning a psychic's skill.

I'm not following since most people looking for guidance are distraught.

Emotions of worry, or sadness, isn't the factor. When the emotional mindset is in a persistent, fixated state, obsessed thoughts cycling fear-desire, desire-fear. From this, an energetic wave of disruption occurs.

When applied to the category of relationships as the inquiry – with two people, John and Jane are slated to meet and still unaware of each other. Add in another factor; both intensely focused on the same desire. John seeks psychic guidance, Jane doesn't. Both, are equally fixated on being in a relationship – the timelines disruption intensifies.

Guides have fewer opportunities to ease the natural intuition with thoughts overwhelming the mental dialog. The mindset, becomes rigid from desperation and anguish, with the very desire as the hinderance, disrupting the original timing.

If I'm hearing this correctly, the subtleties aren't explained (to the psychic) to pass on to the client because their emotional mindset would not be open. Is this accurate?

At times, yes. The state of mind would internalize the reason into a form of blame, either to the psychic or to them. Constant thoughts of worry, fear, anger creates a paradox of duality without personal accountability to review their behaviors.

How does John or Jane's future translate in their Book of Life?

Emotions controlling the mind, body and spirit – ignoring the intuitive impulses programmed in the soul code to meet what is fated and slated outcomes – appear as blank areas, the variables, in their Book of Life. When connected to resolving goals, one or both are vulnerable to higher probabilities of faltering.

One or more purposed goals (John and/or Jane) established pre-birth could be; the timeline selected to align was projected as completed and, one or both failed to leave or move towards a situation. It is not to assume, the goal(s) chosen to conclude, were same (for John and Jane) when goals involve both. John and/or Jane may have experienced thousands of lifetimes to conclude one key word, with fears redirecting their course of action.

Thank you, Nina. Last question, for now; it might be comforting for people who are emotionally distraught to know they are not alone. Are their physical signs when spirit guides are present?

We make our presence known 1) when our charge is cognizant of spirit guides, 2) when asked 3) and can recognize the signs. Individuals, yet to recognize their spiritual path or would benefit from, are sent numerous and sometimes, ongoingly universal signs to alert their awareness.

WHO IS NINA

Nina is short for Ea-It-hanna, Ithanna, Inanna. How she made her presence known to me isn't typical and probably difficult for some to believe.

When Nina first appeared to me, I was completely submerged in spiritual and psychic development, focusing on the subconscious with self-hypnosis and daily meditation. The intensity of effort, I believe led to experiencing spontaneous waking state visions and where Nina chose to introduce herself in a physical form. She was a beautiful woman approximately 30 years old with long thick black hair and caramel color skin. We were inside a rustic chalet sitting at a round wooden table and looking at each other, quietly. Who she was, wasn't so much as an instant recognition rather a silently knowing we were connected somehow. After a minute or so, she telepathically told me she was my teaching guide but didn't say her name. There was a deep feeling of love exchanged and we hugged each other before returning to my conscious waking state.

About a month later, I was in my upstairs bedroom with my door shut and noticed something hanging on the doorknob. It was a baby bracelet with four little white cubes linked together with thin twine, with the name Nina. My first, second or fiftieth thought wasn't, *oh, this must be my spirit guide*, and no, it didn't occur to me to tap in and psychically ask. I did what any mother would and assumed it belonged to one of my neighbor's daughter who played with my son. When they didn't claim it, anyone who visited, were asked, eventually, left as an unsolved mystery.

Another month-ish later, Nina came to me in another vision, her long black hair was white, retaining the youthful appearance. We stood in the center of a two-lane empty road like you'd imagine the deserts in New Mexico or Arizona. The baby bracelet mystery, resolved placing it in my right hand, covering her hands over mine radiating immense love, hoping she felt mine, too. Telepathically, I asked why her hair was white and she smiled saying it was symbolic of her wisdom she would bestow on me in this life; as in many lifetimes of the past. It was the last time she appeared in physical form, and decades later before Nina would reveal (in our interview) being an ancient guide. As far as the baby bracelet physically manifested into reality (apport), my ancient guide showing-off (grin).

THE ANCIENTS

(*The Creator explains*) They are called The Ancients, the gods of myths and lore, watchers in the sky. As the Universe is infinite, we can assume life proceeded long before the days Earth was erected. In this vast cosmic space are sentient beings created into existence with ascension's wisdom, in multiple timelines. Written in history books as the pantheistic gods worshipped in every culture. Words evoking philosophical debates, secular divisions, archeological theories and psychological divides. Sentiments aside, the ancients exist. The parameters to define sentient existence in the Universe exceed capabilities known to man, but a glimpse of the human potential's future goals, God classifies as:

ADVANCED SOULS will impress the curious mind, having information beyond the human memory, as experience and wisdom.

VERY ADVANCED SOULS access the deeper knowledge of the *universal infrastructure*, partial creational history and limited references of details, specific to other sentient life in the multiplied fabric of space time allotments.

MID-LEVEL ADVANCED SOULS-UNIVERSAL, are extraordinary to the utilization of soul-body reformation and creating life forms, already existing; not by proxy of new categorizations.

ASCENDED TEACHERS are main guides assigned to souls with natural intuition with humanitarian goals affecting many people. When working with Intuitives, can assist any gate.

ASCENDED MASTERS completed karmic experience incarnations. In history, these are the souls written about in theology, but not limited to.

THE ELDERS, ANCIENTS, born into life with advanced knowledge and wisdom expressly to assist soul life; the completed essence of all cyclical life experiences, direct Godhead access, universal, creational, time awareness. Historical–present-futuristically. Capable of assimilation, creators of new life existing or new, when approved by Me, as it is Divine Law. The majority of experiences categorically; human, other planetary life forms, the gods of once were, in time as the angelic pure, also for the experience. They are overseers for humanity and sometimes individually when assigned. Top echelon of the 8th gate and higher.

DIMENSIONS WITHIN THE MULTI-VERSE

[As explained, by Source] The astral plane, also called the astral realm or the astral world, is a plane of existence hypothesized by philosophies and mystery religions. It is the world of the celestial spheres, crossed by the soul in its astral body on the way to being born and after death, generally believed to be populated by angels, spirits or other immaterial beings. The astral planes may be analogous with dimensional overlapping existence containing variations of matter, helium, carbonates affecting the vibrational denseness, that affects perspective of time the consciousness exists in. Ancient life exists in the highest vibrations, no longer requiring sequenced propulsions of waves. Their essence is dense, comparatively, because vibrations are occurring as a singularity.

The Mental plane – Soul Body School, Material and Immaterial

The Astral Etheric/Æther Plane – Soul Transitioning

The Material Existential Plane – Astral Body Travel

The Cosmic Reality Plane – Connecting Dimensional Time Sectors

The Alternative and Parallel Co-Existent Universal Plane - Multiverse

The Lower Heavens – Dimensions Existing in the Astral & Material

The Regional Heavens – Soul group matrix relating to higher/lower transitional levels for soul development. Midplanes for advancing soul regeneration, the embodiment of the astral planes, interdimensional photon sphere transmutable energy directives relayed within the stratospheres.

Kingdoms of Heavens – Unity of souls within the Godhead. Near Death Experiences travel here for the God experience, as messengers to deliver truth of the eternal soul. The kingdom of Heaven communing with the Creator, when the soul vibrations attain resonance to sustain.

Celestial Schools Heavenly – the Heavenly magistrates for souls preparing to join the zenith of lights, the interstellar universe assisting life to evolve

Higher Awareness, Plane of Supreme Consciousness – The Ultraverse connection to the super unconscious' esoteric wisdom of celestials, creational, of what will be. Souls entering this trance dimensional multiplex consciousness are selected and guided to knowledge attainable, as given, with purpose and never random. What is received is not ahead of evolutions timelines, received to advance, incrementally.

Creational Matrix of Existence – The Architects of Life, Worlds, the cosmic platform of time – concluding with God Supreme.

HEAVENLY HELLOS

SYNCHRONICITY AND COINCIDENCES ARE NEVER RANDOM, always significant, planned with a purpose and have a reason for noticing. Maybe to simply know a request or thought was heard, will be answered or, make their presence known. Signs sent frequently indicates an important event, situation or meeting is coming up, or guide towards. Signs perk up the senses resulting in curiosity and to pay attention. Significant life events, will receive signs for a length of time, at the same time, are associated with the word spontaneous or sudden - prompting a spontaneous, sudden interaction, not expected, or considered.

Timing – multiple occurrences, strong urge to go somewhere and obstacles stalling or re-directing; are the signals the universe is navigating timing. Positive life altering events or to prevent an outcome not immediately known. The same with **feeling observed** (not associated with psychiatric conditions) connected to a cosmic or celestial, is always light, not dense and heavy. Feel honored, there is a reason they would go from the quiet assistant to a noticeable presence. When struggling within from ongoing challenges –know you are not alone and very loved. when the master's guide

The Angelic realm has been a fascination for people around the world. Devotees call upon them for healing. Religions, as the most influential depicting a divided group creating fear and the other being the champion.

In the Heavens, their songs are heard to ease the new souls returning, healing vibrationally as a chorus of melodic notes. On Earth, they can appear in human or angelic form, briefly or durationally to: prevent danger, ease mental torment and heal. Their love is immense, powerful and answers any who beckon their assistance.

THE ANGELIC REALM FROM ARCHANGEL MICHAEL

> *Our divine presence is magistrate with God and as one with. We are the light bearers brought to humanity for love, healing, and harmony. To know our light is to know yours within. To be in our holy presence for a healing touch or words pure for others to know, is found in the Holy Trinity for all life created from. We are an extension of the Most Holy representing God's grace, never fallen or divided. To believe words that begat from man for God's grace impure in sacrament's divisions, believes this for Our Father and Holy Mother's will of creation.*

We answer all. Love is given for any who call and those who do not. We are fierce, strong, beautiful, gentle and cannot be conquered or banished. We are the messengers serving only One. The One Creator of All for all unconditionally, is our purpose. We are the holy spirit in union's trinity. Our healing energy is generous and gracious. Our words are few, given to those knowing Our Grace without darkness divided, as God – as created from. To know Him only is to know man. To know We, knows God. We are male, female, neither and both, beautiful or unnoticed. Find us upon you and know We are. ***

When Archangels are assigned to guide a soul throughout a lifetime, why is unknown and deemed by the All Creator. Signs Archangels or Seraphim are near to assist in times of hardship or to rejoice in their light is provided next.

Many of the signs found on the internet are accurate, like seeing numbers 44, 444, 4444 connected to the angelic vibration. The following expands on existing and adds some unknowns. Quick review: 44 seen ongoingly is to let you know they are around. 444 and 4444 is sent to get your attention something important is happening or going to. When it is a warning, you will be influenced in thoughts to change direction, go, or not go somewhere, abruptly, and compellingly. Listen to your intuition, there is a reason when this suddenness of redirection and/or motivation occurs.

HEAVENLY HELLOS

ANGELIC PRESENCE WHEN NEAR AND ASSISTING

Music – Songs that "pop into your head suddenly." Turning the radio on to a song with lyrics significant to a current situation, or heard in your mind.

Birds – in, close-proximity, flying into your home (alive) and feathers Situations to catch your attention. Doves and Eagles are significant indicators that an important change is approaching.

Four's – 44, 444, 4444 seen on clocks, randomly pausing a move/show with time segment, waking up at 4:44, are some examples. Coins with 4's or dropped suddenly on the floor.

The number 167 signifies the presence of the eternal flame guided by the angelic trinity.

Flashes or sparks seen in peripheral vision, various colors.

Cloud formations of wings and/or angelic

Temperature Changes – feeling a warm or heat glow sensation, like wings being wrapped around you. When cool or suddenly cold, (not an uncomfortable chill)

Mental images or dreams seeing large wings wrapped around you.

Smells that are sweet and/or earthy.

AUTHOR COMMENT: *descriptions were intuitively received) *the eternal flame* represents Our Lord of the Most High (God's) infinite love delivered by the Seraphim personally, as a gesture you are very loved and appreciated, during times when encouragement is needed.

SERAPHIM (Seraph - singular); messengers of the Creator. Celestials of the highest order, directly in the presence of God carrying out assignments, given from. There are no hierarchies in the Heavens, rather, varying vibrational essences; The Powers, Principals and Seraphim are one, and the same, as Archangels with different roles of service.

ARCHANGELS AND SERAPHIM

When assigned to guide a soul in their physical journey, the signs mentioned are present, in addition to the following identifiers, <u>seen consistently,</u> but not necessarily continuously. Assigned as personal guides, you would feel a special affinity for this realm, not associated with religion or taught to call forth for healings. All humans are loved and having an angelic guide, yes, is an honor but also comes with many life challenges, and one of the reasons, when assigned. People who work with the Angelic realm, may become healers, as a result of their strong influence. Readers who suspect they are divinely or cosmically connected, the signs and clues will be important to help determine. Most, or all, of the following signs are present.

Birth – birthdays may align with repeating fours. such as: April 4, 1944, born at 4:44, or astrological mapping.

Visions of, and vivid dreaming of angels. These signs may begin in childhood depending on the environment. When later, there would be a strong feeling that directs the mind, or drawn to know, study and research.

Incidents of miraculous rescue may occur to create awareness of their presence.

Meeting (or befriending) people with various Archangel names, or your Angelic Guide. This can include meeting numerous people with stories about angelic occurrences, combined with other signs around the same time.

Feeling compelled to watch a movie, read a book directly relating to personal life experiences. Because this is one of the signs that overlaps with other categories, watch for number patterns to distinguish between.

A strong sense of your life purpose is to assist people, in some capacity (with other signs).

Visuals of colorful orbs, including finding them in photos (in color).

Rare occasions, angels may appear in physical form to speak directly to you. When this occurs, it's to guide/assist you, deliver a message or personally encourage. They will introduce themselves as, demonstrate a profound ability or implant knowing within. In other words, when you meet an angel in person, there would not be wondering, speculating or any association with maybe. You'll know.

Orb categories: First, what <u>are not</u> angelic white or semi-translucent opaque are loved ones on the other side. Ghost orbs are solid white, fragmented around the edges. Large bursts of translucent but vivid pastels, are cosmic celestials, referred to as Elders. Ascended Masters do not come as orbs, nor do, cosmic beings (planetary). The angelic realm form as brilliant white shapes that can be small figures with traditional wings, star elements or wispy colored strings. Size depends on the environment.

INTUITIVE EMERGENCIES OR WARNINGS

Warnings signs from Heavenly guides, angels, spirit guides and Source are sent to safeguard our personal safety. Fears from news, impending weather, caring friends or family; isn't intuitive but doesn't mean ignoring or dismissing. Use common sense. Anyone suffering from paranoia and/or over dramatic tendencies; pay attention to keywords underlined important to the interpretation to avoid unnecessary panic:

> A <u>sudden and urgent</u> feeling to leave your current location or stay. The body intuitive will not question, when felt. When danger is the reason, it's very <u>powerful with an immediate response</u>.
>
> You may <u>audibly hear</u> a word shouted in your head, such as "leave now", "stay", "hide" if impending danger is near.
>
> Watch for obstacles preventing you from going somewhere or created to leave – combined with a nagging feeling something doesn't feel right.
>
> Signs sent to create awareness, that can include preparing for an upcoming situation, often experienced with nature anomalies suddenly appearing. Research for the meaning.
>
> Prophetic vivid dreaming experiencing a future event (discussed in later chapters).

NOTE: Signs sent as a warning or emergency won't create wondering and will leave no doubt to catch your attention.

WHEN GOD IS GUIDING

During specific times in our life, His presence may be more noticeable and She will bring signs so you feel like the most special human soul on the planet. The Creator presence is unmistakable, clear, often and mind boggling. Often, initial reactions will continuously question until the signs happen so frequently, you're left with no other conclusion. The following are signs to look for:

Environmental coincidences (detours, electrical anomalies) combined with a compelling urge to go somewhere or do something. God is creating a path leading you to meet someone or be somewhere, important to experience, understood immediately or in the future.

Synchronicity defying logic, timing precisely aligns, responding to thinking, a prayer or current challenges with an answer or relief.

Deja vu and occurrences coinciding with a situation, event, prayers.

Hearing the names of loved ones on the other side, ongoingly to catch your attention. This is God choreographing timing to let you know they are (if crossed over) happy and safe or thinking about you, too.

Vivid dreams of departed loved ones are always orchestrated by God as a gesture of love to reunite, offering solace in a temporary reunion.

Seeing flashes of blue, gold and pinks,

The number 777 multiple times in a short time period.

Triplicity - 3 cars with the same name on a license plate, talking to. or hearing from 3 people in a short time, hearing the same name, place, book that has personal meaning.

Car mileage coincidences

God, as a lifelong guide or durations in life comes to those, simply, to know Him and Her. Prayers are tributes and requests from a distance.

ASCENDED MASTERS

The Ascended Masters are the spirit guide's-guide providing council, when needed. For this reason, rarely does an ascended master choose a soul to directly guide. Exceptions are; to assist a soul temporarily during a re-written life journey, that may include drastic and/or severe turn-of-events interrupting free-will and destiny points. When a soul calls upon an ascended master for help during a difficult time or provide inspiration is answered seeing the first sign, below for as long as they are present. In the rare situation, an ascended master is assigned as a life guide the purpose is to guide souls reincarnating to globally contribute in areas concerning the environment, humanitarian awareness or inventions (affecting either). Signs are seen over a lifetime when chosen as a life guide.

Repeating or Sequential Numbers in triplicity (000, 111, 222) sequential (12345) or 333, 3333. When seeing numbers 11, 22, 33, this is a sign specific to the vibration of the single number amplified and seen until life goals, lessons, etc. are achieved into mastery (example, 11 to 111, 22 changing into 222, 33 to 333). Find reliable sources available to discover the significant of the number. Numbers 4 and higher are messages from the heavenly groups associated (God - 7's, Angels - 4) with other numbers or physical signs. For example, if you see 555, first discover if Ascended Master or Cosmic (Pleiadean/Arcturian, etc.) signs that might be overlooked or dismissed. The 555 is from who and the second sign is the message. Note: 6's, 66, 666 is NOT demonic.

Five. For those who have a direct relationship with Ascended Masters (or Cosmic), know this number is fifth-dimensional awareness. It vibrates as a swing in duality as the dark night of the soul into the light, once freed from illusions.

Red, heard or seen in a very explicit, undeniable way. Because it is a color seen or used frequently, look for additional signs around the same time. Examples: seeing 3 red cars with repeating numbers and/or names on the license plate. Leaving the store finding red cars parked surrounding your vehicle that weren't there when parked. When red is a sign, it is very clear and without a doubt.

Seeing or having a strong fascination with **eyes**; drawing, seen in clouds, photos. Strange sign, and not as liking pretty eyes. A sign is connected to what the mind sees and how interpreted. Open minds see more, wise minds see without the limitations imposed from fear.

The ascended master guiding, well-known or lesser known, is communicated in a visitation dream.

COSMIC GUIDES

Cosmic guides, our friends in the universe have an integral role in Earth's evolution and work directly with the Heavens. Some are noted in history and revered in religions. For example, St. Germain is an ancient master, who is also, an Arcturian, and the reason there are similar signs. If you are one of the select few with a cosmic life guide, here are the signs to look for:

The number five – or, V (Roman numeral) associated with the 5th dimension. We come in peace (sign)? lol

Dragonflies and Owls – When a dragonfly or owl shows up as a sign it will be a unique situation to catch your attention. Keep in mind, geographic locations when more commonplace and accustomed to people. An example might be a dragonfly landing on your finger, several flying near or in close proximity. Look for owls, out of their usual environment, vivid dreams of and synchronicity when hearing.

Vivid dream conversations or explorations out-of-body, astral traveling

Electronic distortions, (dissimilar to paranormal disturbances). Examples are: walking or passing by street lights that go on or off, radio changing on its own, unexplained photo distortions, non-destructive lightning strikes that catch your attention.

Names or words associated with a planet, or solar system. For people fascinated with a star system, check to see how many other signs in this list are included.

You will have witnessed **UFO or related sighting**(s) more than once or once, that seemed like it was timed to be seen.

The idea of contact fascinates you without fear.

Experiences in life that most could not relate to, or believe.

DEPARTED LOVED ONES

Signs from loved ones are sometimes misunderstood as personal spirit guides. It's normal to want someone you cherished in life to continue in a similar capacity. They do, in their own way, like comforting us during life challenges and continue celebrating special moments. Spirit guides are trained, evolved beings assigned at birth. DLO's may want to say hello or to let you know they are present but extremely important are forbidden to create any dependency that prevents grief to heal. Remember them with love while continuing the life journey. Here are some signs when near:

Butterflies, unmistakably catch your attention.

Coins with their birthdate, or yours. When yours, look for other signs, to know which loved one is near.

Hearing songs with sentimental associations. An impulse to turn on the radio or hear the same song played at different locations the same day. Check the time when heard to see if it's a loved one's birthday or similar connection. Music that pops suddenly into your mind is usually related to angels. Music sent from a DLO, is either a sentimental memory or lyrics with their name.

Smells and scents – cologne/perfume, whiff of their favorite flower.

Vivid dream visitations. (see dream interpretations in the chapter on Specialized Intuition)

Electronic devices turning on/off as a coincidence (will never create fear). Example: clocks stopping or any time related devices, specific to the DLO.

Pictures frames of the loved one, tilted, moved or falls over to catch attention.

Hearing their name can be harder to determine when popular, like Mike. The suggestion is to be aware of multiple occurrences.

DREAMS

Dreams are the gateway into the subconscious riddled with symbolism and archetypes. The gateway to the super unconscious opens to psychic dreaming, DLO visitations, astral traveling, and out-of-body experience.

I am not studied in dreams and topics are discussed within the limitation.

nightly dreams

Nightly dreams, if remembered, are remnants of vague images that fades with conscious alertness. Dreams remembered, can seem very real and easily confused with vivid dreaming. One sign to look for, is the beginning scene or interaction where it's already in process. A series connecting one continuing story will also transition scene to scene that seems to smoothly transition with reality shifts in a blink of an eye. Another sign is a sense of independent interactions where you feel as though you are the experiencer and observer of yourself simultaneously. A non-psychic or normal dream is still intuitive using symbolic and archetypal imagery from the subconscious for the conscious mind to understand how it's processing current life. Examples of collective symbolism many have at least once in their lifetime can be running from someone or something, falling, feeling exposed, night time scenes feeling something hiding. Houses, doors, windows, transportation, water, bridges, day or night, colors, numbers, animals including birds, fish and reptiles, imagery details is how we communicate with ourselves. I recommend researching what the symbols represent before making any concrete conclusions.

VIVID DREAMING

What's the difference of a nightly dream with vivid details and vivid dreaming?

A few important key details. Nightly dreams explore the subconscious where real dreaming happens when the conscious mind is perceptive as it emerges into unconscious worlds. The dreaming individual is guided to an alter reality or 'mid-state matrix' accessing all the senses when awake, experiencing tangible landscapes and communication is interactively responsive in linear time. Vivid dreams are not from memories stored in the unconscious but where the soul travels interdimensional to another time and/or location. The emotional sensation feels peace, love, and joy and one of the few psychic communications that can be experienced by every person.

VISITATION DREAMS

Visitation dreams are vivid dream with DLO's or a celestial being most often communicative in a familiar or ethereal setting. Departed family or friends have a sense of being at peace, sometimes appear younger in an atmosphere filled with love. Meeting with a loved one is a joyous experience organized directly by God. Reasons can be to reassure or a message for closure. Psychic dreams do have a form of introduction with smooth transitions. An example of a visitation dream may see a loved one in a setting without details of arriving but interactions and dialog begin with hello, hugs or expressions given upon first meetings.

Not having a visitation dream is not to interpret negatively, for any reason - especially as a form of punishment for the deceased or the living. Time on the other side is experienced differently and if the deceased require healing from soul trauma, the duration of how long can vary. The living may require time during the grieving process that is not always best suited if the visitation prevents letting go. Remember God knows how, when, and why.

THE SOUL GOING HOME

Every so often, I'm allowed a glimpse of the Heavens, or in this case, when the gates open and a soul returns home. Next, is what I was shown.

My consciousness was sent back in time when my client's mother was in the hospital seconds from leaving her physical body. As she was laying peacefully in bed, a circular door, or portal, gradually appeared with two ethereal figures emerged from a bright blue light. Her mother's physical body remained still but her soul seemed to know it was time. Her soul essence gently rose retaining the shape of her human form but a lighter version as the two beings light infused with her soul. The gateway light expanded into a brilliant white light filling the room surrounding the woman's spirit. The only way to describe it was the light was hugging her. The two light beings and her mother embraced and I felt every cell in my body filling with love and joy. Her face was ecstatic knowing she was going home. The last image was the three, fading into the circular light. I narrated to the daughter her mother's last breath on Earth and first heavenly vision with tears of joy streaming down both of our faces.

It was my first witnessing of a soul journey home. Was the experience for me to share to others, to help her daughter heal; I can't say. She didn't need to ask and this says, if it was a request or healing, neither will you.

THE TWINS AND GOD

This is a true story that centers around Mary, an 18-year-old girl, her twin brother on the other side and going to Heaven.

A mother contacted me about scheduling a mediumship telephone appointment for her young daughter. She told me only one detail; the reading was in hopes of contacting her twin brother. Twin's experience profound grief, described as a losing part of their own soul that leaves an emptiness. Before Mary contacted me, I meditated with the intension of establishing contact with her brother. Nina advised me to wait until the day of our appointment and I will understand why, at the time. As indicated in several chapters, I make sure clients don't tell me too much. There are also exceptions when a client explains events before validation is given. This was one of those times.

Mary's voice on the phone was polite but she felt closed off. Nina knew she would limit her participation and only go through the motions. I didn't ask if she wanted to speak to her brother, which she was expecting. My question to Mary was, do you think you can stop blaming yourself for his death? No and started crying, telling me what happened.

Names and personal details are excluded for privacy. This includes pertinent information that may create the wrong impression the parents or the hotel were negligent.

Mary's parents took them to a function at an upscale hotel built in the early 1900's. Mary and her brother, Tommy were 12 and restless, deciding to explore other areas of the hotel. The historic hotel kept up with the times, including modern elevators except for one manual elevator for nostalgic reasons. Mary and Tommy thought it would be fun to take a ride on it. When the elevator stopped, she got off, turned around and saw her brother playing around with the levers, that eventually led to his untimed death.

Listening to what Mary witnessed that day was heart wrenching, Nina whispered into my ear, *bring the young girl to her brother with hypnosis*. Mary agreed but I could hear her skepticism. After a few minutes of guided relaxation, she began describing being near a large body of water that was dark blue, almost black. I asked her why she was there and replied with, I don't know but I think I'm supposed to go into the water. She did and began swimming saying *"I'm in water but for some reason, I don't know how…I'm not wet and don't feel tired at all. Wait, I see land on the other side and going to swim there."* After a few seconds, she was telling me about the place she swam to, saying *"there are lions right next to different animals, what they normally prey on, but they're peaceful."* I asked her if she was standing near them prompting laughter," *no, I'm watching from the top of a tree! I just sort of thought myself here."*

"Mary, I want you to explore further and find your brother the same way, by thinking yourself to where he is." Maybe 10 to 15 seconds went by before hearing her voice filled with excitement and disbelief her twin was there and began describing in detail, how his appearance changed from what she remembered. He was older, same age as her and, for some reason, thought he would still be the age when he died. She began to feel nervous, worried her brother would be upset with her and blame her for the elevator accident. I encouraged her to talk to him and re-directed her back to what she was seeing. *"He's with an older man wearing a fishing hat who looks really nice and looking at me with a big smile. They're sitting together in a row boat that's in a wide river with a wooden pier you can walk on. The boat is near it, at the end. My brother sees me and waving, …. he's happy! Oh my God, it's really my brother!"* I suggested to go where he was and talk to him. The phone was quiet and after a few minutes asked her to include me in what she is experiencing. *"Well, we just wanted to hug each other without saying anything, first. He keeps looking at me, saying, it wasn't your fault and it was his time. That I couldn't have stopped it from happening or being any other way."* Mary could hardly talk from crying feeling both relief and joy reuniting with her twin. When she was able to speak, I asked her who the older man was. She said he was still in the boat smiling at her and would ask him. The phone was silent about a minute, *"He told me, I would know him as God and brought my brother so I knew he was loved and safe."* We were both without words for several minutes trying to wrap our minds around who the mysterious man in the boat was. I guided her out of the hypnotized state, after giving her brother one last heartfelt hug and asked if she ever read my book, *"Planting Seeds on Concrete"* published a couple years prior. Not understanding how the question related to her experience, she replied, *"no, why are you asking me?"*

"How you described going to Heaven is close to identical to my son's vivid dream experience included in the book." I read to Mary my son's words. For several minutes, we were quietly trying to wrap our heads around what just took place before saying goodbye. Mary's experience released her from guilt and worry changing her last image of her twin brother fishing with God.

From Planting Seeds on Concrete My son, Dean, when he was 10 years old would have what he referred to as, "a real dream." He demonstrated various psychic abilities early on but his uncanny ability of slipping into a waking state of channeling, unnerved, even me. This is one of the real dreams.

Mom, I had a dream but not a dream. It was real! We went to Heaven and I want to tell you that Heaven is really boring! I started to laugh and asked him why. Because you know everything! When I was there, I knew everything that I don't know here. I can't remember all of it now, just some of it. It started with both of us and you said, Dean, I found Heaven, and pointed to a bright white star, or dot in the sky. It didn't take long to get there and before reaching this point was a large body of water to swim through but amazingly you stay dry and do not tire. The water was dark blue, less than black but a touch of blue or navy. After emerging from the water, we started walking on the ground, gradually rising in the air. The atmosphere around us was a starry night. We continued walking, gradually rising at the same time. How far above the ground is an unknown. How long it took, a few seconds and then just appeared. We came into a park type setting, all white but some of the details are red, to show up as words. A hospital is there and had a red cross, a plus sign and whoever looked at it, whatever language you spoke, would transform to their translation. The purpose was for therapy and other traumas, or fast deaths. There was a giant observatory with a large blue orb. This is so you can look up a person, like a family member still on Earth to observe and stay connected to them and see what they're doing. You can find them by just thinking their name, telepathic communication. (a few paragraphs skipped). We were trespassers because we are still alive, so we were pushed out; it still felt like love but in a forceful way. Like me hugging you and pushing you away at the same time. Everything was white except for the signs in red. Nothing that is unnatural was there. Red was to stand out so the people could see the words and I saw all people in human form.

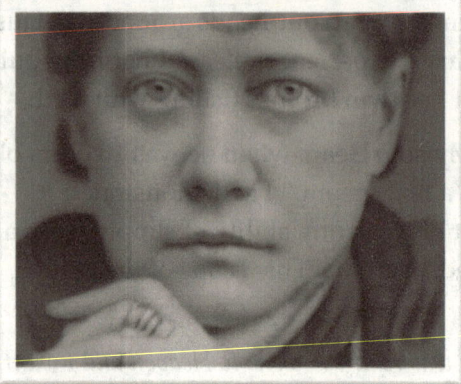

HELENA BLAVATSKY (1831 – 1891) Russian spiritualist, author, and cofounder of the Theosophical Society possessed profound psychic powers in the days controversial for woman to make claims. London Society for Psychical Research, declared her a fraud: a century later, reported she was unjustly condemned.

ST. JOSEPH OF CUPERTINO (1603-1663) The Italian Franciscan friar known for miraculous levitation witnessed by kings, dukes and philosophers. The overwhelming evidence was not a deterrent but rebutted with absurd accusations of witchcraft, witness exaggerations, and group hallucinations from poisons. The church investigated taking hundreds of depositions, finding the claims legitimate and was canonized, four years after his death.

INDRIDI INDRIDASON (1883 – 1910) was an Icelandic trance medium who produced physical phenomena of strength and variety comparable to that of DD Home, but who, unlike Home was unknown outside his own country. The phenomena were closely observed by investigators and detailed records were kept. A skeptical Icelandic scientist subjected Indridi to strict scrutiny and controls but was unable to detect fraudulent behavior, while continuing to observe striking phenomena.

ALTERNATE REALITIES

REALITY POTENTIALITY 15

... if knowledge is perception, how can we distinguish between the true and the false?
Theaetetus by Plato

BELIEF IS A STICKY WORD THAT DOESN'T ALWAYS PLAY WELL WITH OTHERS. What's true are beliefs shaping what your reality will witness. This chapter asks the question; do people with extraordinary capability think differently? Learning about others experiences who defied the standards of what is considered possible may shed some light to this question. Next, are true stories of human potential.

JACK SCHWARZ – (1924 – 2000) **Dutch-Jewish writer, healer and naturopath.** He was captured and sent to a concentration camp where he was regularly beaten and tortured, Jack taught himself to willfully control his body's internal biological process. Testing included 6" sailmaker needles into his arm, without registering pain or bleeding. When removed, punctures closed tightly.

MIRIN DAJO, could also demonstrate a similar healing force, when doctors tested by plunging their hands into his body. Find out why someone witnessing, one of the two died of a heart attack.

THE KAHUNAS OF HAWAII exhibited the ability to stroll across hot lava without being harmed. Brigham, who studied the process, went to a 150′

wide lava field and while watching the barefoot Kahunas unscathed, the soles of his boots were burned and his socks on fire. Reports of the same can be found around the world.

BARBARA BRENNAN - atmospheric physicist for NASA. From an early age, she could walk blindfolded sensing the trees' energy fields, see halos of colored light and the layers of energy fields and chakras. Her psychic abilities later proved startling accurate medical diagnosis determined by what she sees. One of the many documented cases involves a woman seeking Brennan's council and was told she had an abnormal uterus. The woman then told her that several doctors already confirmed the exact diagnosis, recommending a hysterectomy. Brennan suggested to take a month off and it would clear up. She was right with doctors confirming her uterus returned to normal and had a baby boy a year later.

CAROL DRYER is also reputed with psychic diagnosis confirmed by the medical community. An essential comment to include, this particular ability follows the ethics offers to verify with, not override, licensed doctors.

THE CONVULSIONNAIRES

The Convulsionnaires is one of, if not the most compelling event of supernatural phenomena ever to be documented and witnessed by thousands from across Europe. Being a subject that is content rich, a summary of highlights is given that can be researched from the information provided.

FRANÇOIS DE PÂRIS (1690 –1727) was a French Catholic deacon, theologian, and supporter of Jansenism. After his death, reports of extraordinary cures were claimed after visiting the grave of de Pâris. Onlookers described the unexplained phenomena as violent convulsive movements which overtook the body, designating the name as the Convulsionnaires of Saint-Médard.

The Catholic Church opposed the Jansenist's religious beliefs, asserted as a cult. But not everyone agreed with the decision including Cardinal Noailles, an Archbishop of Paris, who declared in 1728 that he believed the miracles to be genuine. The church sent a representative to witness the cures and the convulsionnaires indestructible constitution described as impervious to any acts of physical violence. The church leaders witnessed people hit with sledge hammers, stabbed, hung, burned that left without injury no matter the torture.

After Noailles died in 1729 his successor, Archbishop Vintimille, was handpicked by Cardinal Fleury, who also served as Chief Minister of France under the young King Louis XV. As noted, Fleury and Vintimille began a campaign to purge the Parisian clergy of Jansenists, extending to the convulsionnaires. Unlike his predecessor, he condemned the miracles as duplicitous in 1731, claiming the miracles were a result of "Satanic healing" produced by rebellious heretics.

At least 800 people were reported as cured by the convulsions of 1731 including several of notoriety such as Louis Basile Carré de Montgeron, a well-respected magistrate and Counsellor of the Parliament of Paris who later converted to Jansenism after experiencing a miracle. He compiled a 3-volume book containing 1800 pages described as *"one of the most extraordinary works that ever issued from the press."* Lives was also published in 1731, by Pierre Boyer, Jean-Louis Barbeau de La Bruyère, and Barthélémy Doyen. Rising hysteria from the events reported ultimately led to conversions to Jansenism in the thousands, influencing Louis XV's decision to close the churchyard on January 27, 1732.

David Hume, the father of empiricism, wrote, *"There surely never was a greater number of miracles ascribed to one person, than those, which were said to have been wrought in France upon the tomb of Abbé Paris, ... many of the miracles were immediately proved upon the spot, before judges of unquestioned integrity, attested by witnesses of credit and distinction, in a learned age, and on the most eminent theatre that is now in the world."*

For the curious researching this remarkable event marked in history should expect the naysayer's contribution and edits on sites like Wikipedia. But we know those denouncing supernatural events is reminiscent of Pavlov's dog salivating to the sound of a bell to capitalize on the scraps of attention.

Photo credits: *Les convulsionnaires de Saint-Médard* Illustrations of Convulsionnaire enduring torture without any trace of harm.

THE SLEEPING PROPHET

EDGAR CAYCE (Hopkinsville, Kentucky) was an American Psychic with **a ninth grade education** with the ability to answer questions on subjects as varied as healing, reincarnation, wars, Atlantis, and future events while in a trance. These answers came to be known as "life readings of the entity" and were usually delivered to individuals while Cayce was hypnotized, giving him the nickname "The Sleeping Prophet". Cayce founded a nonprofit organization, the Association for Research and Enlightenment that included a hospital and a university. He is credited as being the father of holistic medicine and the most documented psychic of the 20th century. Hundreds of books have been written about him and the life readings he gave. Though Cayce himself was a member of the Disciples of Christ living before the emergence of the New Age Movement, some consider him the true founder and a principal source of its most characteristic beliefs. Cayce became a celebrity toward the end of his life, and he believed the publicity given to his prophecies overshadowed the more important parts of his work, such as healing the sick and studying religion. Skeptics challenge Cayce's psychic abilities and traditional Christians question his unorthodox answers on religious matters such as reincarnation and the Akashic records.

Throughout his life, Cayce was drawn to church as a member of the Disciples of Christ. He read the Bible once a year every year, taught at Sunday school, and recruited missionaries. He said he could see auras around people, spoke to angels and heard voices of departed relatives. In his early years he agonized over whether these psychic abilities were spiritually delivered from the highest source.

In 1900, Cayce formed a business partnership with his father to sell Woodmen of the World Insurance; however, in **March he was struck by severe laryngitis that resulted in a complete loss of speech.** Unable to work, he lived at home with his parents for almost a year. He decided photography, was an occupation that would exert less strain on his voice and began an apprenticeship at the photography studio of W.R. Bowles in Hopkinsville. In 1901, a traveling stage hypnotist and entertainer named Hart, or The Laugh Man, was performing at the Hopkinsville Opera House. Hart heard about Cayce's condition and offered to attempt a cure. Cayce accepted his offer and the experiment took place on stage in front of an audience. According to witnesses, Cayce's voice returned while in a hypnotic trance but disappeared on awakening. Hart tried a posthypnotic suggestion that the voice would continue to function after the trance, but this proved unsuccessful. Since Hart had appointments at other cities, he could not continue his hypnotic treatment of Cayce. However, a local hypnotist, Al Layne, offered to help Cayce in restoring his voice. Layne suggested that Cayce describe the nature of his condition and cure while in a hypnotic trance. Cayce described his own ailment from a first-person plural point of view, "we" instead of the singular "I". In subsequent channeling sessions, when the connection was made to the "entity" of the person that was requesting the reading, he would generally start off with "We have the body". According to the reading for the entity of Cayce, his voice loss was due to psychological paralysis and could be corrected by increasing the blood flow to the voice box. Layne suggested that the blood flow be increased and Cayce's face supposedly became flushed with blood and both his chest and throat turned bright red. After 20 minutes Cayce, still in a trance, declared the treatment over. On awakening his voice was to have remained normal. Apparently, relapses occurred, but were said to have been corrected by Layne in the same way and eventually the cure was said to be permanent.

Layne had read of similar hypnotic cures by **the Marquis de Puységur**, a follower of **Franz Mesmer**, and was keen to explore the limits of the healing knowledge involved with the trance voice. He asked Cayce to describe Layne's own ailments and suggest cures and reportedly found the results both accurate and effective. Layne suggested that Cayce offer his trance healing to the public. Cayce was reluctant, but he finally agreed on the condition that readings would be free. He began, with Layne's help, to offer free treatments to the townspeople. Reports of Cayce's work appeared in the newspapers, which inspired many postal inquiries. Cayce was able to work just as effectively using a letter from the individual as with the person being present in the room. Given only the person's name and location, Cayce could diagnose the physical and mental conditions of what he termed "the entity" and then provide a remedy. Because of his accuracy in the diagnosis, word of his ability spread and he soon became famous. People around the world including presidents, sought his advice for personal "life readings" which included their past lives.

Cayce has variously been referred to as a "prophet" **(cf. Jess Stearn's book,** ***The Sleeping Prophet*)**, a "mystic" and a "seer". While giving a reading for a seeker, he at times referred to consulting the Akashic Record (the etheric imprint) of that soul's experience. Cayce's methods involved lying down and entering a deep sleep state, usually at the request of a subject who was seeking help with health or other personal problems. Subjects would not normally be present, and their questions would be given to Cayce, who would then proceed with a reading. Initial readings dealt primarily with the physical health of the individual; later readings might be given on past lives, business advice, dream interpretation, and mental or spiritual health. Until September 1923, his readings were not systematically preserved. However, an article published in the *Birmingham Post-Herald* on October 10, 1922, quotes Cayce as saying he had given 8,056 readings as of that date and it is known that he gave approximately 13,000–14,000 readings after that date. Today, about 14,000 are available at Cayce headquarters and online. When out of the trance, Cayce stated he did not remember what he had said during the reading.

After Gladys Davis became Cayce's secretary on September 10, 1923, all readings were preserved and his wife, Gertrude Evans Cayce, generally guided the readings. His clients included several famous people such as *Woodrow Wilson, Thomas Edison, Irving Berlin, and George Gershwin.* Books, auto-biographical or inspired by well-known metaphysical authors created wide-spread interest on topics about spiritualism and reincarnation.

"As a humble individual full of self-doubts, Cayce never profited from his mystic gift. He read the Bible every day, taught Sunday School, and helped others only when asked. Many did ask, and over the years he produced readings that diagnosed health problems, prescribed dietary regimens, dealt with psychic disorders, and predicted future events such as wars, earthquakes, and changes in governments. He spoke, moreover, of reincarnations, the early history of Israel, and the lost civilization of Atlantis. Enough of his diagnoses and predictions proved true to silence many skeptics and to develop a wide following. Although Cayce seemed to have acquired the ability to correctly diagnose an illness in the individual, he was often incorrect in his predictions of a distant future. He stressed that the future is determined by man's free will and our collective actions shape the destiny of mankind for better or for worse." **The Dictionary of American Religious Biography**

CAYCE PREDICTIONS

STOCK MARKET CRASH, March 1929, *"great disturbance in financial circles"* about to take place (900-425). Cayce stated: "...we may expect a considerable break and bear market, see? This issue being between those of the reserves of nations and of INDIVIDUALS, and will cause—unless another of the more STABLE banking conditions come to the relief—a great disturbance in financial circles."

WORLD WAR II, 1935 "anxiety on the part of many; not only as individuals but as to nations. And the activities that have already begun have assumed such proportions that there is to be the attempt upon the part of groups to penalize, or to make for the associations of groups to carry on same. This will make for the taking of sides, as it were, by various groups or countries or governments. This will be indicated by the Austrians, Germans, and later the Japanese joining in their influence; unseen, and gradually growing to those affairs where there must become, as it were, almost a direct opposition to that which has been the theme of the Nazis. For these will gradually make for a growing of animosities. And, unless there is interference from what may be called by many the supernatural forces and influences, that are active in the affairs of nations and peoples, the whole world–as it were–will be set on fire by the militaristic groups and those that are "for" power and expansion in such associations..." **(416-7)**

EDGAR CAYCE, founder of the A.R.E., Area for Research and Enlightenment, located in Virginia Beach. He is considered the Father of psychics, who has assisted tens of thousands of people, from all levels of society. *Edgar Cayce Readings 1971, 1993-2007 by the Edgar Cayce Foundation. All Rights Reserved ©*

THOUGHT REALITY
16

Time doesn't exist without thoughts, thinking, being. It is the reality and the illusion of what is thought and how to think. **God, Andromeda's Muse**

ON THE PHYSICAL LEVEL HIGHER AND LOWER VIBRATIONS are neither positive or negative. In the physical world, the proportion of vibrations creates the effects. Negative energy is a lower vibration that is dense and heavy from emotional burden and positive, finer and lighter from emotional freedom.

The physical body has a unique energy signature referred to as, the aura. Nina defines; *An auric field emanating around an individual is the – energy from a living being – translating their vibrations in various densities of color(s) – defining the essence signature of its totality.*

emotions = vibrations

Two words, when viewed contributing factors influencing the atmosphere from all lives of the past to current, is not typically considered. My teacher asked me a strange question, if I was aware of my emotional output contributing to the world, each day – over the span of a lifetime. A life ledger of accumulative tears and giggles translated as purifying or contaminating.

We've become immune to spiritual blitz language, offering nickel advice on healthy emotions that ...sort of help until you're stuck in traffic. So, let's change it up with a practical pollution free suggestion, posed as a question. Why are people characterized as nice or loving associated with tolerating others, at their own expense? Do these traits vanish telling those constantly pumping their negativity into the atmosphere to shut the f*** up? Truth doesn't guarantee, warm and fuzzy. At some point in life, we meet someone who vaporizes all that is good and happy. Not temporary challenges but ongoing without efforts to resolve. What if, instead of patiently listening, stop them mid-sentence and say, 'based on my calculations of five boyfriends, 3 co-workers and 2 family members, and the miscellaneous rants, over X number of months... is approximately 50+ hours you ow to our friendship. I'm being serious. Negative emotions play a central role in this chapter and extremely important to understand, energetically and cyclically.

The repetition of bad, sad, mad and powerless feelings, the neurotransmitters in the brain can go through a neural "rewiring," which reinforces negative thought patterns, making it easier for unhappy thoughts to repeat themselves and leaving little room for the more positive feelings of gratitude, appreciation, and well-being. A continuous cycle of negative thoughts may even cause damage to the hippocampus, the part of the brain used for problem solving and cognitive functioning. Over time, complainers become negativity addicts, attracted to the drama that comes with a complaining attitude. Manfred F. R. Kets de Vries, Harvard Business Review

Taking de Vries research and applying to Dr. Masaru Emoto's,[8] featured in, *What the Bleep*, might be the motivation to change thinking fast. Emoto discovered water is reactive to emotional expressions with concentrated focus. When exposed to loving words over time it crystallized into brilliant, and colorful snowflake patterns as opposed to negative thoughts as incomplete, asymmetrical patterns with dull colors. Then what are we to conclude when the human body is 60% water and 71% of the Earth is covered by water?

THOUGHT TRANSFERENCE

Research on *psychic thought transference* [9] published their findings as an ascertainable phenomenon in the scientific community.

Thought energy, imprints into the atmosphere, like a time stamp signature from the exertion of intense emotions. Using a relatable scenario to explain

---

[8] Dr. Masaru Emoto (1943 –2014) a Japanese businessman, bestselling author of, *The Hidden Messages in Water* and scientist who discovered the human consciousness' effect on water reacts to positive thoughts and words changed its molecular composition.
[9] Barcelona-based research institute Starlab, French firm Axilum Robotics and Harvard Medical School, published its findings in the journal *PLOS One*.

its effect is driving on an open road quietly, and a sudden thought or emotion occurs that doesn't make sense. Nina explained as, *"pockets of atmospheric energy imprints. A thousand years ago or a few years, is irrelevant. Residual affects remain until, counter-balanced or energetically transmuted. Transmutation occurs with equal or matching thought transfer, to create the opposite effect; hate - love, grief - joy, fear - reassurance.*

Understanding thought transference and its affect is a subject people should know. Public places with high anxiety or in a private setting where moods suddenly shift and defined as supernatural.

PROTECTION RITUALS

Protection rituals to block negative or low vibrations is a common practice and rarely necessary (there are always exceptions). The person divining, healing or communing with the supernatural are taught to believe they need to be protected, overriding the importance of developing a solid relationship with their guide and what this means 2) low vibrations don't affect high vibrations, only deplete temporarily (with or without a ritual) 3) when told a protection ritual is necessary from unseen forces, does it eliminate or create worry, or cancel both out.

Most energy influences fall into one of three groupings: stagnant residual imprints, emotional clusters, and emotional thought transference, intentionally and unintentionally. Residual imprints are from traumatic experiences, explained above, by Nina. Emotional clusters are public settings with accumulated energy. Comparable to meeting someone and initially uneasy or immediately comfortable but from a lot of people. Layers of sentiment accumulated over time with the current activity will generate different signatures; malls, stores, concerts, sport's events, etc. The empathic body feels the affect but not only mental chaos but distributed collectively, including happy and loving. Stores during off-peak hours without a buffer might feel the impact of Betty's bad day in the frozen food aisle.

The last group are thoughts transferred remotely and the main reason for invoking a protection ritual. Thought energy is responsive to the emotion, and the intensity of concentrated focus, not if deliberate or unintentional. Individuals with hatred towards isn't different than describing some demonic force in the process of a bitter divorce, political enemies, jealous rage, vengeance, are ugly. Dark magic is nothing more than young souls who lost their way need to feel powerful.

energy cleansing

Family and friends experiencing difficulties, temporarily or ongoingly, inadvertently pull positive energy from people giving support. Anyone who has helped others through heartache, or, the friend in a crisis often hears how they feel so much better after talking and more energized. The conversation ends and your eyelids are hanging by your chin, depleted.

EXERCISE: Lay down with your eyes and ask your guides to assist you while visualizing the low energy removed from you, returning to them and your energy returning. You can send a prayer, asking God to send love to the person in need during the transfer of energy. It isn't necessary to repeat over and over only to stay quiet for one to two minutes. The exchange can be a whoosh or subtle when re-energized.

empaths

Empathic sensitivity has certainly gained much popularity from increased spiritual awareness. People no longer ignore physical sensations when meeting someone for the first time or the negative vibes from friends constantly draining everyone's chi. Empathic ability is part of all natural intuition and when heightened is impressive.

An empath, in-tune with their ability can be powerful enough to confuse as telepathic. The empathic state of being, feels the vibrations of the surroundings in several ways; physically, emotionally, intuitively, subconsciously (dreams) and naturally (nature). It is considered a separate ability and is, but I also see empathic sensitivity as a tuning fork assisting other methods of psychic communication.

TELEPATHY

Thought transfer communication, or telepathy initially defined psychic ability, and some still don't understand the difference. Psychics receive telepathic communications from guides, DLOs, etc. And humans can forward a thought to another, intentionally and unintentionally, from concentrated focus (knowing the telephone will ring) connected to natural intuition.

Telepaths are born with a naturally high vibrational frequency of Pi/Q, giving them the ability to hear the thoughts of people or a specific person. They can listen to one or several (advanced), in harmony. A telepath can influence another's thoughts but cannot override a soul guide and not all are aware of soul guides and very few can directly communicate with. The reason is because telepaths typically do not extend their abilities into the psychic arena. Mutual thought communication, requires another telepath to converse. [Nina] Of the global population there are approximately 3500 telepaths. Of this number, 2% are known, with the remaining living somewhat normal lives. Meaning, most live in quieter non populated locations, using their abilities indirectly to help people when they can. The message for any telepath is qigong.

OUT-OF-BODY EXPERIENCE

OOBE is under the category of psychic dreaming and astral traveling. People can experience either, spontaneously or by willing the mind when practiced in deep meditation heightening trance state awareness. Where an OOBE takes the observant position as a form of witnessing an event, astral traveling is an OOBE in motion into realms, altered times of the past/future, or present experiencing the self as someone else. The easiest way to understand without direct knowing can be found in stories about near death experiences explaining observing the physical self before journeying or astral traveling into celestial or heavenly landscapes.

COLLECTIVE SHIFTS

A shift refers to a higher group consciousness or collective awareness during a concentrated time. World shifts may result from contributions of vibrational energy spread out like a sonic wave of light, spreading across the globe. The first collective consciousness shift occurred during the late 1990's creating an accumulation of dynamic growth, and the beginning of motivational speakers. The second major shift didn't happen again, until 2002, called "the big divide". This was divinely sent, as an adjustment period for negligent worldwide leadership both creating and allowing military actions to monopolize fuel. The actions leading up to the great fall of the Twin Towers was an anticipated event, as a world super power's sophisticated surveillance makes the obvious point. How can a small airplane create such devastation, to a domicile of population connected to world financial markets and trade? The same, as true, for the contradiction of military intelligence unable to defend their own home? The "big divide" was an internal shift of power focused on unknown elite groups, believing they are capable to run the world, simultaneously, filling their pockets from self-indulgence.

The third and last shift, ran concurrently, in 2008, with space exploration "expansion" and significant for lightworkers who reached attainment. Shifts effect all groups, regardless of where they are in the reincarnation process where its reverberation can result in enthusiasm, misplaced. The reason why all are affected is for the individuation of the self to recognize personal truth versus personal desire. Although not limited to, the topic is of concern creating the most enthusiasm individually, without considering the collective influence; attributed to channeling with life in the Universe.

INTERVIEW WITH ST. GERMAIN

MESSAGES FROM... Archangels, Ascended Masters, Pleiadian (Plee-ay-dee-an), Arcturian and Anunnaki (Ah-nu-nah-key). Who wouldn't be intrigued to hear what life beyond has to say? What about the people curious to learn who they are and directly communicate? I remember hearing an acquaintance telling me that channeling doesn't require any special ability and anyone can do it. The dialog is with my teacher, St. Germain, sharing his insights on channeling.

Hi, St. Germain. Please explain what a channeler is?

Yes, let's address the growing population, *"with messages from."* You have heard me use the phrase, 'true channeling' to differentiate various levels of authenticity degrading into fiction. The population concerned with personal spiritual alignment with the higher self, often rely on technology for information. The global population is entering another shift to transcend from the pain body. During this time, the selection process deciding whose words will assist guiding their journey is imperative. Knowing our true wisdom flowing through the telepathic conduits chosen connected to the world of the living to the multi-universe, decides their path of futures.

Can anyone channel?

Yes, all have within them the capability and potential. Mastering any skill requires training from knowledged teachers to practice and develop experientially, until recognized, as such.

What is important to understand as a channeler?

The Meditative Self and The Super Unconscious "Higher Self", as a collective unconscious. Accessing the All Universe – the levels of consciousness are of vital importance to comprehend, able to surpass the meditative Zen into the all Universal Consciousness. Channelers are practiced in deep trance meditation and/or self-hypnosis. After years of practice and doing, the Channel has opened the neural passage through the pituitary, able to connect immediately.

Channeled" Messages From" are everywhere. What's going on?

The reasons depend on the motivation, even with good intensions. Choosing to communicate with cosmic beings with curiosity to communicate with heavenly celebrities believed as their spiritual path to contribute finds this as, the larger part of communication.

Does studying levels of consciousness, qualify a channeler?

It is an integral component but not the only qualifier. As previously mentioned, a channeler has developed psychic sensory perceptions, in tune and practiced in connecting with multi-verse.

So, no one should bother trying to be a lightworker?

Not, at all. Lightworkers are any who want the world to be a better place and the love within them affects the global population, more than they realize. All lightworkers have an important role, and truth is part of the lightworker's purpose. Not all roles are the same, even having similar intentions. Channeling is one of many roles of the lightworker that happens to have specific parameters.

Lightworkers, even if not trained – isn't it still contributing?

You decide. Say you read about someone who decided qualifications based on one physical interaction with extra-terrestrials giving them a message. The message did not include instructions to continue or not. Their love for humanity was the reason for the contact, knowing they were capable to reach an audience. The assumption made from the one incident, plus a professional background in marketing was the deciding reason. From this, they developed a group focused on enlightenment, light and love. The messages shared are from the meditative self, filled with inspiring messages but also, misleading partial truths. Add, his media presence allows others to contribute their received messages to share with others.

Isn't that still a good thing?

Depends on the percentage of misleading information a person considers acceptable and able to decipher what information, is misleading. Let's also include the others sharing, and automatically associated of having the same intentions, with the group of enlightenment. A chosen messenger of the divine would preclude from such actions without discernment. Spirituality is not defined as allowing for the sake of being loving. To be truly loving, knows the foundation of love is built on truth.

When words are a mixed variety of biases, contradictions and misleading information claimed to be from the Ascended – do the inevitable contradictions create mistrust of all channeled messages? Most importantly, ask why are there so many contradictions and why would the creator of the enlightened group allow?

Messages from the Archangels or Ascended Masters, any true?

Each sentience carries a vibrational classification. For telepathic linking, the physical soul has ascended beyond the illusory for the essence to match.

CHANNELING WITH ARCHANGELS, the purest vibrational essence of the God Consciousness is very rare. Claims of are hearing their spirit guides – intermittently combined with subconscious beliefs.

The true nature misunderstood by the contactee, they request mentally a specific or favorite archangel and messages received are assumed from the desired request. Any words or phrases concerning a particular faith, as a prerequisite to receive enlightenment, is absolutely not the angelic realm. Messages believed, as written from, is the contactees idea of heavenly language. My personal interactions knows this, as a certainty. Archangels are lovingly direct and do not mince words. Communications will inspire the soul reaching the core, for no doubt. Their vibration is aligned and 100% in tune with Our Creator, and direct with, is not by yearning, I assure you. Hearing from this elusive realm, channelers have an abundance of signs during, leading up to and may continue for a duration.

ASCENDED BEINGS, are humans who achieved self-mastery during incarnated lifetimes. They are scholars of ancient wisdom and truth is of the highest importance. Approximately 9% of all messages "*as from,* "are from. When not, it's a blend of the meditative higher self with brief moments expanding into the super unconscious. A message believed as received for a ten-minute time period may contain one - two minutes of true channeling. The words given are profound, comparatively to their normal writings, convincing the mind the remaining message is, of the same. I will discuss the following in subsequent messages providing further details. For now, here are a few identifiers, as the one reading messages and for any believing received.

- Statements of what the world must do
- Mentions dark energy or similar fear-based remarks
- Apocalyptic dooms day revelations
- One religion, over another
- Overly loving - feels contrived

TRANCE MEDIUMS SPEAKING WITH ALTERED ACCENTS. Exceptions are experienced with profound unattainable wisdom and unquestioned supernatural abilities (i.e., previous verifiable prophecy, foreign languages not native to the trance medium, physical distortion of appearance).

- The messages are generic, mundane, unspecific and do not offer unknown concepts of true Universal wisdom.
- Intuitive body feels uncertain or uncomfortable when reading the messages but doesn't know why
- Messages are very similar to biographies on other spiritual sites.
- The channeler is not psychically proficient.

MESSAGES FROM ST. GERMAIN, To date, those claiming messages from are from enthusiastic light workers eager to contribute. Of the thousands in the media, only two, not of the Theosophical practices, are authentic. It is for certain; I do not speak through any individual's voice.

Messages are with selected students working on self-mastery and this requires adept endurance. Of my select, 100% were not aware of who I was before introductions. This will help those with claims in my name. Lightworkers continue on, perhaps, one day you will hear from me.

Currently, I am working with twelve individuals selected to hear my words. Of this, eight remain with five capable to endure completion of 1st stage to the mid-way point of the 2nd. Three will reach the last stage, as my chela to initiate. Individuals from the past, who are well-known Theosophists bringing my words or supposed, have met me directly and introduced as. Selected to connect with my mind to yours, is one experiencing, or, completed soul re-generation, devised as a 3-step process, discussed further.

WHAT IS TRUE CHANNELING?

Channing is the ability to bypass the mental matrix, surpass the meditative unconscious, connecting directly with the super consciousness of the Universe and write the words of those residing, in it.

To telepathically connect with inter-dimensional beings requires several circumstances to combine; psychically in-tune, openness of mind for any conclusion, acceptance of their purpose and identity and most importantly allowing the physical differences including their capabilities witnessed. When this aligns within, introductory conversations take place.

What is true channeling is one beckoned to hear the words without notion from whence they come. As any honed skill takes years to perfect, channeling and perhaps, especially, is not to categorically deny.

GHOSTS AS MEDIUM CONDUITS

PIPER, LEONORA E. (1859–1950) Perhaps the world's most celebrated trance psychic medium, and most scrutinized, was Leonora Piper. She was considered a paradigm of virtue and integrity using her extraordinary gifts for the good of humanity, viewing her mission as religious, and regarded herself as a "bringer of glad tidings."

In 1887, *Harvard philosopher-psychologist*, **William James** and the *American Society for Psychical Research*, **Dr. Richard Hodgson,** an English investigator of psychic phenomena, conducted the Piper investigation, (Hodgson continued until his death, 18 years later). Hodgson took extreme care in his study of Piper, diligently monitoring her sittings and testing the validity of her trances by keeping her under constant scrutiny. "*[Hodgson] Hired detectives often trailed her, volunteers watched her, her utterances were checked and double-checked, and every facet of her private life was scrutinized for evidence of fraud. No fraud was discovered; Mrs. Piper was integrity itself.*"

In 1889, *England's British Society for Psychical Research* sponsored Piper's visit for research. Every precaution was taken from boarding the ship to her arrival, said to be more like a kidnapping than a welcome. The initial test session was conducted before a group of absolute strangers presented to her under assumed names. "*As soon as Mrs. Piper was entranced, the controlling spirit revealed incidents, details, and occupations. The sitters were astounded; describing homes and rooms, mentioned names of children, and even diagnosed ailments in the light of the subjects past medical histories — histories that Mrs. Piper could not have known.*"

What set Piper's medium abilities apart were the 'controlling spirits' speaking through her in trance state, identified as ghosts of the long-dead, including **Sarah Siddons, Henry Wadsworth Longfellow,** and **Johann Sebastian Bach**. Eventually a French physician by the name of **Phinuit** emerged and asserted himself as the controlling spirit, remaining in exclusive command of Piper's pronouncements for some time. Phinuit was supplanted by a new control purporting to be George Pelham, a young man who had only recently died until Piper's trances came under the control of religious personages known as the "**Imperator Group.**" (from Encyclopedia Britannica)

REALLY, HE SEES DEAD PEOPLE

17

DO YOU BELIEVE IN GHOSTS? It wasn't that long ago the topic of ghosts wasn't accepted in traditional society's vernacular. Popularity of paranormal activity increased when the first paranormal investigator television show aired on Syfy cable. The major networks, reluctant to invest in the genre, were surprised to learn the viewer's interest wasn't a fad but growing fanbase. A few spin-offs made their way into prime-time television but it wasn't until *Paranormal State* aired on A&E in 2007, audience numbers skyrocketed. The stars of the show came from Pennsylvania State University's, *Paranormal Research Society* (PRS), a student-led college club. The show debuted with 2.5 million viewers anticipating ghostly encounters with thriller style promotional teasers. The technologically savvy ghost hunting team did not disappoint. The show was well produced with a charismatic six-member crew and guest medium investigating contemporary suburban homes to the creepiest haunted locations around the world. PRS was a front row seat to what goes bump in the night. Their popularity caught the attention of the bigger networks and cable channels based on the growing viewership.

The first paranormal show, TAPS, with two plumbers was my personal favorite because they followed the paranormal investigator's script using technology to measure phenomena activity. No religious theatrics with some unnamed entity following them around, no screaming taunts, crews panting heavily while in pursuit of something terrifying (with brief cameos of night vision eyeballs).

RARE INSIGHTS FROM EARTH-BOUND SPIRITS

This section includes a special guest who directly communicates with ghosts with the five physical senses. Other than Mary Ann Winkowski,[10] he is the individual having this extraordinary and rare capability.

David Jenkins is ex-military in his fifties and successful career entrepreneur. His rare ability to see and talk to ghosts was evident as a child, and no well received in his traditional upbringing. Meaning, he freaked people out and so, he preferred this part of his life to remain private. Over the years, David searched for spiritual mentors, not realizing this would prove more problematic than anticipated, after meeting several psychics, mediums and even shamans for help.

When asked to elaborate on his experiences, he said, 'I'm talking to these psychics, mediums, and they don't know what I can see. After a while, they tell me some ethereal being is in the room, either telling them what to say or around me, you know? I'm looking around the room not seeing any spirits knowing they were full of it.'

A mutual acquaintance I met years before recommended he talk to me. He set up an appointment by phone to see if I could help. David decided to let me mentor him, stating later, 'you were the only medium that admitted a limited understanding of my specific ability. "

We focused on techniques of mediumship that could apply to his specific ability and guidance from Nina. A few conversations in, it was clear David's dialog with his nightly visitors didn't extend information beyond the individual ghost and the why, how and what's were concluded from observation. I suggested giving him a list of questions and see how they felt about being interviewed for their direct perspectives. He thought it was a

---

[10] Mary Ann Winkowski is a television personality whose paranormal experiences are the basis for CBS's Ghost Whisperer.

great idea to learn more about this elusive existence. Next are the rare insights exploring the unknown world of ghosts.

WHAT THE GHOSTS SAY

Interacting directly with this plane, is next. My first question is what ghosts see and feel when crossing over.

People use expressions like going into the light when in this plane. I saw one ghost, who was at a friend's house, while over for dinner. When I mentioned they had a ghost, immediately, my friend's wife jumped in and confirmed. He was not a nice guy, not evil but disruptive. I told him he was leaving and took him to my home, where I told him, he had to cross over. Plain, simple and wasn't giving him a choice because of his mean disposition. Immediately, a bright light opened and as he walked into it, his energy, sort of evaporated.

A bright light isn't the only way, though, it's more like a pull that creates a blur. **(I asked him to elaborate)** When they cross the spirit is pulled to a source that that opens. This source is connected to the Universal Source to collects its light, like a magnet. (The source described may be an actual gateway or angelic host. David can describe what he sees and feels as an observer but doesn't conclude what the source is.)

Is it always a choice to be a ghost?

No. Some ghosts never see the light and go to this plane to complete a spiritual task. Some don't believe in God and blinded by their belief. These are ghosts who spend the longest time, wandering for decades or even centuries.

Can you go back to spiritual task as the reason?

Yes, several ghosts I've met over many years, explained this kind of unfinished business differently. An example might be a specific fear to overcome while incarnated – the same fear is experienced in the spirit realm until they overcome it. I think it is an agreement made before they incarnate and the awareness is understood when they find themselves in the in-between. Overcoming victimization, not as someone victimized, but a mentality, is another reason but I can't offer any more details on it.

Do you see other discarnate forms in this plane?

There are beings that are part of Source, not human, like angels, cosmic intelligent beings and uncategorized energy people don't know exist. I see them as bright colors; orange, white, purple, etc. They show as energy forms, not orbs, like blurred shapes of people. You can tell they are ancient and when around there is an immediate sense of safety, nurturing.

Do ghosts know they are ghosts?

Yes. They know they are dead living different rules and in a different plane.

Explain why you mentioned different plane.

The best way to describe speaking with a ghost is how time feels a second before or after. Like it's trying to catch up or slow down to connect to the current moment.

Nina explains ghosts are on a separate plane or overlapping dimension.

Yes, that makes sense. Like they are here on Earth but in their own space, simultaneously. But ghosts believe they are on the same Earth, when they were physically living.

Can they see other ghosts and if so, do they communicate to each other?

Ghosts in the same proximity see each other, can talk to each other and ignore each other, just like people. I've had three ghosts show up with two in a conversation and the one ignoring them like he was the only one there. When they talked to me, politely taking turns, he would continue to talk like they weren't there but knew they were.

Why do ghosts communicate between 2 am and 3 am, called dead time?

Every ghost I asked unanimously gave the same answer. They aren't only around during this time. That creek people hear in the night can be heard during the day. They [ghosts] said dead time is when people thought the veil between worlds was the thinnest. Speculation that became a ritualized fact. Other than being quiet, including mentally, day and night, they're around.

Are ghosts aware of time?

Not the same, as we are. I asked and was told, no. They just are where they are, when they are.

Why do they contact you?

Mostly, to talk…tell me their life story. It isn't unusual for a ghost to stay around me for a week, sometimes even a month, just to talk and be heard. The companionship makes them feel comforted by getting something they didn't get before. Once they talk about what it is they want to say, they go to Source.

Talking was enough?

Yes, of course, not for all but it's important to always remember ghosts were living people and just like people, have different wants and needs. Some are even needy, meaning want more attention.

Can ghosts go anywhere or bound to a place?

They can go anywhere but if they hold strong emotions to a location, will bind themselves to a place purely because of their belief.

How do they know to find you?

I wanted to know this, too. Of the ghosts I could ask, all said I have a different vibration, like a beacon they were drawn to.

You mentioned seeing ghosts at an early age. That seems to indicate ghosts contact anyone, at any age to communicate with, maybe, just to be seen by the living.

My mother told me I would look and talk to things, she didn't see. When I was four or five, we went to her friend's house and there was a girl I saw on the stair landing. We played together for hours. The next morning, I wanted to continue playing with her and asked my mother's friend where the girl was. She said, 'that's impossible because my daughter died and there aren't any children here.'

Ghost stories with children bother me. From my understanding, all children are directly brought into the light because, even though the soul is old, the persona remains upon death until it can acclimate back to its soul state.

This is an interesting subject that might surprise a lot of people. When someone dies, we know, the soul leaves the physical body. When a ghost chooses to stay, the rules in their dimension are different than ours. They can appear in different forms to represent a personal expression, including presenting itself as a child.

Are you saying ghosts appear as they did in life with the option of changing to reflect how they want to be seen or how they perceive themselves?

Yes and no. They present themselves as they want to be seen.

Like when people talk about seeing DLOs in dreams, younger, around the age thirty.

I didn't know that but yeah, makes sense. Think of it like what you do as a medium when talking to a grieving parent wanting to connect with their child. Even though they're not a child in Heaven, you see them as they were for the parent(s) to recognize. A ghost does that too, or other reasons, like wanting to appear innocent or to show they aren't a threat.

Appear innocent and show they aren't could have very different meanings. Can you elaborate?

Unclean or wanting spirits have an agenda and find a way to get into someone's life. They can also appear as a child because people are less guarded and trusting with children. Understandably, any ghost would incite some fear but to discern negative energy ghosts from a nonthreatening ghost is the same when meeting someone in the physical world. Their intuition prompts a feeling or sense of danger and threat.

What about when they know the person/people can't see them?

Use a lot of energy to make themselves known and what is thought as a haunting. What's said about being afraid they're going to Hell based on actions in life...that's true but not the only reason. An older gentleman stayed because he stashed money and wanted his wife to find it. You understand when someone dies, their spirit leaves the body but still has the same disposition, thoughts and personality when alive. This may be different when a spirit transitions to Heaven, but think of ghosts as people with the same worries, fears and thoughts, just without their body.

Speaking of hauntings, can you elaborate on the ghosts who stay specifically to stay around particular people?

An example might be a lover's quarrel where the husband walks in and sees his wife cheating and it gets out of control and he ends up losing his life. He might stay because he's hurt and angry, wanting vengeance. It's important not to sugar coat ghosts and know some are mean spirited but they aren't the majority, either.

The question asked, helps people understand this kind of behaviors in real life carries over. At the same time, it's not the main reason to answer the same question – I would say the highest percentage stay to help loved ones, including preventing harm. If they die knowing or believing someone they love could be in danger or living with someone who harms them, it would be a strong incentive to stay.

When I first started out, I joined a paranormal investigation team. From my experience and what Nina explained, it takes a lot of energy for a ghost to move something like a balloon on the earth plane.

That's true. This doesn't change the fact 90% of ghosts know the living are afraid of them. Any place with a ghost is called haunted, a word associated with something bad. They exist, don't get me wrong. But usually no one stops to think it could be a loved one trying to pass on a message for closure or there to protect them, like I mentioned before. People automatically are scared.

GHOSTS, HOLD THE SUGAR

David, it's essential to discuss the ghosts that aren't friendly. We both agree the objective is not to sugar coat, or, paint an unrealistic picture. If truth means hearing a ghost can physically hurt a person, people need to know what that looks like and what they can do. From your years of communicating and witnessing, can a ghost attach to a person for something like revenge? Before answering, I'd like you to explain a comment made in a conversation we had, implying ghosts can convince a physical soul they can't cross over.

Yes, to the first question; they can attach to the living. The reason could be out of revenge like the example of the lover's quarrel mentioned earlier. Remember, they have the same traits when they were a human being and this includes not being truthful. After you and I talked, I asked some of the ghosts who come to talk to me, if or what they knew about this but none were forthcoming, or particularly interested in answering.

Makes sense, being the mean ones stalking like a rejected lover are busy ...well, stalking. It can't be a pleasant experience on the receiving end.

The power a ghost has, including the mean ones, is affecting emotions, like fear, but nothing more. The negativity might even be mean spirited but their affect is purely emotional influence. This includes having a physical being or another ghost believe something not true, like crossing over. I would replace mean with negative and negative is the same emotional affect as a bully – if you give them power, they will take advantage and could even take it to the next level that could create havoc in your life.

Is this why apparitions choose to look frightening – to create an emotional reaction?

I don't know if it's a choice, or, if it just happens but I do know it's connected to how they see themselves because of their actions when alive. It would be the same reason why they didn't cross over.

It explains why people witnessed a ghost responding strongly to a crucifix, ...holy water, because of what it represents intertwined into their reality.

For sure. Any ghost strongly affected by their own negativity from religious beliefs taught, would see themselves as the negativity to create that reaction.

How negative can a ghost be?

There is a category within the ghost realm that's avoided for good reason. The in-between souls that are extremely negative that should be taken seriously. I don't know why or how but they seem to have a different level of intelligence with no respect for the living – very selfish and focus on influencing people to a place where they can feed off.

I'd like to explore the last two sentences further because of how it pertains to the book. Can you continue with what we were talking about? Explain, *'influencing people to a place they can feed off.'*

Yes, of course. I've mentioned several times ghosts were people. Well, we know from history, the news, a percentage of the population have thoughts and sometimes act upon these thoughts, that are pretty ugly. When this kind of person doesn't cross over, they take that ugliness with them. A percentage of this group learns to blend their energy with the living, the ugly personality they enter the spirit world with, is susceptible to becoming darker.

Ghosts can't touch, taste or smell. When the soul enters this plane, they remain stuck in their death shroud, if you will, their last moments of death. All ghosts are attracted to the energy, the vibration of light connected to humanity. People in the same location with intense emotions, would alert this type of spirit to blend with their energy, 'like a vampire'. They're attracted to heightened emotions; fear, anger, hostility, anxiety, to feed off.

Strong emotions? Like hate, anger, fear? How does that make sense with the light energy of humanity?

Energy is warmth, like food to them. Fear would be equivalent to falling in love and the most intense energy these vampire ghosts are attracted to.

Just so I'm clear, you said all ghosts are attracted the human's light energy. Do only the negative ones try to blend with a person's energy?

All ghosts are attracted to the energy of the living, including the benevolent ones. But they aren't always aware how blending their energy affects the living. And, in a situation with the nice ones, they aren't blending as an attachment. More like, temporarily being in close proximity of someone to feel it. Another energy that attracts ghosts is psychic energy because it's a richer vibration. Why amateurs messing around with divination isn't smart.

⊷⊶

Interviewing David, to learn about this elusive plane of lost souls was an amazing opportunity to finally learn truths without it being bent for dramatic ratings. His firsthand observations and conversations with ghosts allow the lay person to see through his eyes of experiences. His advice is useful and easy for any person to apply: *"Never fear a ghost. But this doesn't say, go to places known to be haunted. They aren't playthings for our amusement. Remember they were people and most aren't trying to hurt anyone. If there is a ghost in your house, the material world is for the living, therefore, we have domain and they have to listen to you. this is what people don't understand. Your free will trumps there's. Don't yell, scream or act like an idiot, be confident, matter-of-fact and tell them it's time to cross over."*

To cover all the bases, the idea of something viewing our energy as food might be more than disconcerting for readers prone to worry…and then, worry about worrying. I've learned over the years, when information leaves the mind unsettled, it is either not true or, in this case incomplete. It was given to the overseers of this plane, the angelic host for further insight.

GLOBAL GHOSTS

David's global military background made it possible to ask questions pertaining to geography of the ghosts witnessed, over thirty years.

You were in the Navy that required traveling to many countries. What countries you have been, too?

Most of Europe, France, England, Ireland, Italy, Germany and Austria. Never went to Russia but Yugoslavia, Bosnia, Sarajevo. The Middle East and northern regions of Africa, the Caribbean islands and most US States.

Of the places you've been, do any stand out – meaning, more ghosts than usual or unusual?

Yes, for sure. Germany was bad. Me and my military buddies wanted to visit some historical military locations. We went to Auschwitz, where the concentration camps were and I couldn't walk through the door. There were many ghosts still there. I found areas in Austria, connected to WWII, the same.

In concentration camp clothing? Male and female?

Yes, they looked tattered, tired and thin, as you would expect. Mostly men.

How did Germany compare to other countries?

In Europe, England and Ireland had more ghosts than other places. Italy was normal, meaning not more or less. France had the least number and the Bahamas. The Middle East and Northern Africa – the energy there was different. Not just ghosts but…, can we use the definition your guide gave you earlier defining a demon[11]?

---

[11] (Nina) dark energy/demon; describes as collective dark thoughts magnetically connected to matching vibrations formed into the shape or appearance representing the negative thought that created it. This energy doesn't have a soul but conceived from soul thoughts that hold a semblance of intelligence - but not intelligent. In the ghost plane,

Are you referring to residual negative energy thought forms in the environment?

Yeah, it covers the Middle East and North Africa like a wet blanket. It's just different than other places I've been too.

David, you didn't mention Asia in your list of travels.

Ok and yes, I've been to Okinawa (Japanese island in the East China Sea). I've never answered questions like these or even thought about it like this, so some of my answers I'm figuring out with you. Okinawa was also different, not negative energy – the ghosts there completely ignored me, which is unusual. I have no idea why. Also, I've never seen a ghost on water. Being in the Navy, I've been on many ships. Never saw a ghost on or near water. Strange, just thought about that now.

That is strange considering stories heard about haunted battle ships. Maybe we can go back to this later. What's the top 5 countries with the most ghosts?

England, Germany, Iran/Syria, US, Bosnia/Herzegovina

England #1. That says something, doesn't it?

Oh yea. The English are the worst, killing more people than anyone else. Also, the plagues that ran through there, more than once. A lot of dead for such a small space.

Seeing ghosts since you were a child and around the world, as well as, those who seek you out; how many ghosts would your guestimate be?

This isn't an easy question to answer. The same answering the percentages of different groups (*in this chapter*) – I don't have hard, fast statistics. If I had to put a number on the total, I'd say roughly 5000. Not that spoke to me, directly, and not to associate as anything conclusive. People associate ghosts from television and having a semblance of the reality reminds us all, ghosts used to be people and not the boogie man living under the bed, and the largest percentage aren't trying to hurt anyone.

'demons' remain connected, can be created, or attracted from existing, thought forms, but still thought forms.

I asked David to help me create a demographic snapshot of the ghost population organized by time periods, events or other reasons. Clothing apparel was the obvious go to, to gauge when, including war-related events. A couple of categories didn't have enough data to give anything more than a theory and noted, as such.

GHOSTLY OBSERVATIONS

MISCELLANEOUS GROUPINGS: ghosts who wander the longest time because they don't believe in God and blinded by lack of faith, and ghosts completing a spiritual task mentioned in earlier dialog.

REASONS FOR NOT TRANSITIONING: 1) Interestingly, David has never seen a ghost just arriving, or while acclimating. 2) a low percentage are murdered or the murderer and equal number between them – most are woman staying because of revenge and anger 3) war trauma and shock from unexpected and sudden death stay because they are mad life was cut short 4) unfinished business, 5) get a message to a living loved one 6) the lowest percentage are protectors who stays to watch over loved ones

GENDER: The largest percentage of ghosts are white males, various ages with a ratio of 3 males for every 1 female. David said, *I have never seen a woman appear in a gruesome way, with half their head blown off, like men sometimes appear. It could be for vanity, but I've never asked. I also don't know if a woman with my abilities would have the same experience, with men's vanity.*

BELIEFS: The largest percentage don't cross over because of religious beliefs; either, afraid of not being accepted or Hell association. Suicides are mostly younger males, late teens – early twenties and cross over the easiest. David's experiences are they just to tell their story visiting him for a month(ish) and when heard they transition.

ATHEISTS: Once a soul leaves the body the word atheist no longer applies. Not only awareness of continuing to exist, but even the wanderers that remain the longest are aware of a larger presence. When I asked why they would remain seeing there was an afterlife, it wasn't surprising – their strongly held convictions in physical life refused to acknowledge.

Time periods below are guesstimates based on clothing apparel:

American Indians. David offers a loose overview based on the complexity of indigenous customs deeply rooted to nature and spirit, warring rivals and the white man wars pitting tribes against each other. He explained a unique identifier, understood intuitively – not interacting but observing them was part of their communication he interpreted as not conforming to others, in the physical or spirit planes. Those not transitioned haunt sacred lands and rivers (incl. burial sites and rituals) as protectors. An estimate, without visiting reservations or similar we agreed would be misleading. What David shared, had me wonder if the protector of sacred lands in spirit was assigned while still in the physical.

1600 – 1700: white males, no direct interaction, and unknown reason for the duration preventing transition. Estimate 100 and mostly in cities

CIVIL WAR: We talked about this longer than others to get the information as close to the actuality, possible. 1) David has seen a lot of soldiers, mostly white, very few were black. 2) scattered locations with the least number on battlefields (see comment below) 3) Equal number from north and south, adding he would see both together and not fighting. Key West and Florida

NOTATION: Energy imprints are different from non-transitioned ghosts able to interact. Imprint energy is faded and has a mundane, blah feeling and blip in and out. Civil War battlefields are almost all energy imprints. David commented further saying, people intensify imprint energy just by focusing their attention

GERMANY WW1 & 2: Not surprisingly, these two events were responsible for the largest population of in-between spirits.

1910 – 1930 (from the author): This is only a hypothesis based on when séances were very popular. David didn't offer a conclusion, only the theory might explain why the ghosts from this time seemed confused, and easy to cross over. If true, a strange can of worms it would be, i.e., once a soul is on the other side pulled against their will doesn't hold up and as a ghost, pulled from somewhere else as the reason they look confused? For, another time.

1980 – Believed the increase is possibly connected to AIDS.

PARANORMAL SHOWS

When I asked David about paranormal shows his reply was unexpected, and began laughing when it occurred to him, he never watched a paranormal show. We talked a week later and could hear his eagerness through the phone, about two paranormal shows. He said, *the cast provoked and acted like bullies to get a response.'* Adding, they had no clue what they were doing, *'tell people not to try and intimidate ghosts like that. They used to be people. Imagine watching someone walk into any place with the same behavior?'* When I asked why ghosts don't just ignore them, he replied, *'If a ghost was there, they would leave. Any initial detection with equipment would be temporary with the cast ranting and raving to themselves. Their obviously hacks.'*

AUTHOR'S COMMENT: Neither, myself or David, oppose paranormal investigators. On the contrary, we have great respect for any who put in the efforts to help the public. The emphasis is <u>responsibly</u> <u>representing</u> information, and <u>reinforce</u> the importance of <u>related</u> qualifications.

THE ANGELIC HOST

The angelic host are the guardians of the ghost plane and will compare ghost's beliefs and the reality described by these overseers beginning with the initial stage of the soul traveling.

❦ When the soul is released from the physical body, the angelic hosts greet the soul transitioning from one form of existence into another. Upon physical death the soul leaves the body maintaining the persona during the transitional period giving the soul time to readjust from the corporeal to incorporeal while guided to their heavenly home. Death is peaceful, love and loving reunions. Few reject the natural course, preferring to remain attached to what they perceive as the earth's magnetic field. When they do, the transitioning soul by-passes the angelic healing guide consumed by over-powering thoughts cycling false beliefs creating an alternate or matricidal reality. For the lost soul exists in a holding place between two worlds.

Angelic guide(s) are assigned to free the confused soul into God's all loving embrace and eventually do. All disembodied souls when returned to the Heavens regain their natural state of grace, even the naughty ones.

dreams of loved ones as ghosts

Some may dream a loved one not fully in the light but not in a dark place, either. A visitation dream from the in between can create concern and worry. They are not alone and feel assured the angelic realm is on duty to help resolve. All eventually are brought into the light.

what experiences are not ghosts?

Sightings of non-responsive spirits (not ignoring) or not intelligent are classified as mental energy imprints from intense emotions stagnant residual atmosphere, Familiar apparitions where the soul returned to the Heavens, can imprint death trauma or grief of the living. After-effect energy can appear as a full body apparition, affect temperatures and fluctuate electro-magnetic fields and why confused as ghosts. To clear residual energy, (calmly) visualize of brilliant white light flooding through the entire area, inside-outside, and all life residing within.

APPARITION CATEGORIES

David's interview was literally added after the book content was done and in the never ending editing stage (hunting my nemesis, the comma). Because my curiosity wanted to compare how his experiences coincided with what I received, he wasn't told or given the information, beforehand. From what I have read, comparably, the information aligned more than expected, with only a few differences.

THE HIGHEST percentage of sightings are non-responsible imprinted forms.

SIGNS: non-communicative, consistent emotional emission that does not change (unless overlapping with more than one). The energy forms may be specific to an event, a day or time, connected to the thought it was created from. It is unaware of physical life and does not interact. EMF devices would fluctuate in sharp spikes before dropping back to normal.

THE SECOND HIGHEST percentage of sightings are souls residing in the overlapping holographic plane; a transitional residence capable of interaction but unable to affect physical matter.

THIRD HIGHEST, is an unconsidered group – astral/remote travelers. The ability to disconnect from the physical body, explore the Earth dimension or outside of, in soul state. During, their form is not typically seen but some more adept can keep intact their physical essence.

LESS THAN 1% <u>of reported sightings</u> are ghosts capable of physical interaction with the 3D physical world that are not transitional but choose to remain from misperceptions of the afterlife or simply believe being on Earth is better.

Spirits wanting to be seen will seek any who can, including young children. In rare instances, physical contact is possible, such as handprints, marks, or scratches, of course, considered hostile. The reason, isn't to assume automatically, as hostile. Likely, the confused soul isn't proficient in controlling physical matter in a non-physical form.

Understandably, parents go into protective mode with uninvited intruders. Ask for assistance from angelic healers who will enlighten the discarnate soul of their unwanted attention is creating fear to coax them back into the light.

interacting with a disembodied spirit

"Similar to an out-of-body experience (OOBE), children frequently slip in and out into the unconscious designed for impressionistic learning. Those who see earth bound or spirits of loved ones on the other side are unconsciously remotely traveling, a few inches out of the body. When this happens, the veil between various earth energy fields lifts, opening multiple timelines planes or existent life currently camouflaged to the conscious human perception."   **St. Michael**

what you can do

Tell the spirit they are harming your child and stop. You don't need to invoke a ritual. Explain, as if an actual person was in the room that didn't realize the physical affect was hurting your child. People can't see ghosts but ghosts can hear and see the living. **Communication** is effective and doesn't require calling a paranormal team or psychic medium, unless, you prefer the assistance or reassurance. Remain calm. It's important to be firm but don't automatically assume the worst. In addition to the above reason give, it's also possible the ghost is a relative and saw your child having a bad dream and tried to help.

When there haven't been signs of paranormal activity and a one-time incident, swiftly call upon the Angels to assist the entity away from your home. They are the overseers of this plane and use calls for their assistance as a means of awareness to in-between souls.

AUTHOR'S COMMENT: As a mother or medium, ghosts aren't allowed to do anything that scares children. If the reason is to help them, a child is too young. All ghosts are aware of the angelic healers and other light beings and can ask them for help. If suspected as a family member, explain it's easier to communicate from Heaven and they must go.

There are parents who like the idea their child is psychic, and might be true. The welfare of your child, physically and emotionally, is the priority. Find a reputable medium to assist you, and never dismiss their experience as 'just their imagination.' When scared, let them sleep with you, or you in their room, until handled.

ANIMALS AS GHOSTS

While addressing misunderstood topics, I took the opportunity to ask a about pets believed to be ghosts. Nina explains. Animals do not have a complex behavioral consciousness that creates the emotional thoughts, formed into beliefs to open the ghost plane, but a form can be energetically created as an idyllic representation specific to the spirits behaviors, actions or an event in the physical life. For instance, cruelty to animals, inhumane acts of hunting, hunting the exotic or endangered for self-pride or profit representations would attach to the ghost. Another example of animal attachment are pets strongly associated to the individual, when one was not seen, without the other. The purpose is twofold: not only does the created thought form entangle with how ghosts identify with themselves from their living actions, guides/angelic host may choose to create the energetic form as a teaching aid while in the spirit plane to learn, sense and feel the compassion of the animal, opposite of their actions to know creatures of God. Pets loved on Earth would not be a ghost.

REALLY, HE SEES DEAD PEOPLE

WHAT DO YOU SEE?

Photo by Jacob Riis (1849 – 1914) reporter photographer "Bandits Roost" (1888) in NYC, now Mulberry street, "How the Other Half Live" exposing slums and poverty. (*continues, on next page*)

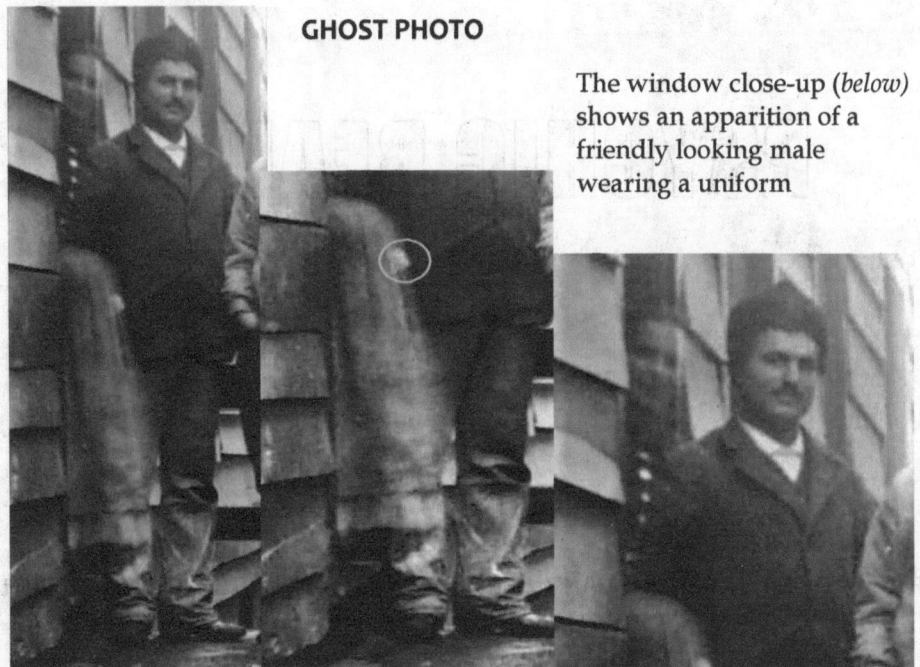

GHOST PHOTO

The window close-up (*below*) shows an apparition of a friendly looking male wearing a uniform

(*above*) what initially looks like a leg over the window ledge and (*middle-circled*) a protrusion are anomalies. Material and clothing were considered but from how it bends, (like a knee?) it was ruled out.

ABOUT

I happened upon this photo randomly. I'm not a photographer, nor jump to '*it must be paranormal*' as the first conclusion seeing something anomalous. Before including, I researched 1900's film quality, exposure, camera equipment, and ruled out double exposure when professionals said it's an effect - technique purposefully created. Riis' portfolio, only had one group shot of police, or men in uniform, to rule out any overlapping transfer from another photo (which is possible but very unlikely). In addition, Mr. Riis' book, *How the Other Half Live*, showcased this photo without mentioning the only uniformed man's body overlapping unnaturally into the man next to him or why the same has black eye-sockets (close-up) devoid of details. What looks to be a long skirt draped over the window, and the protrusion (circled in the above right photo) or why it seems to bend like a knee, that isn't uniform guy's leg based on angle and perspective, I have no idea.

PSYCHIC REALITY

18

PERCEPTIONS OF REALITY CAN'T BE DEFINED BY OBSERVING OTHERS. My first impression of beyond the veil was the television show "*The Ghost and Mrs. Muir.*" The female lead rents a house by the sea, despite its a reputation as being haunted. Of course, the spirit was a dashing ship captain and original owner of the house. As a young girl shows like The Ghost and Mrs. Muir, formed into my imagination abilities were physical interactions, other people couldn't see and hear. Later, my perceptions added celebrity mediums sharing some fantastic event or interactions playing with dead Uncle Joe while still in diapers. Because it didn't reflect my psychic reality and knowing stuff was normal.

Perspectives, when not directly experienced will relate it to a diluted version just to give it some traction. The goal in this chapter is to bring my experiences to you and relate directly with it.

intellect vs intuition

Think about how you learned to identify a single impression, like a drop of water heard from another room. The burning smell of smoke linked to fire. There is no proof of what was heard or from the smell it happened yet we don't doubt it occurred. We can compare the five physical senses with analogies of intuition to relate references found in everyday situations.

Our five physical senses are in a constant flow of communication interacting to the exchanges in our environment. What we see, hear, touch, aromas of the food we taste. By exchanging the physical experience, like the water drop, with intuitive communication, we can relate both with everyday life.

EXAMPLE 1: Imagine you're in a separate location and hear children playing outdoors. Within a few seconds, a quick pause to hear before resuming what you were doing. From the sound alone, what details did your subconscious form? Proximity from how loud and from what direction. The number of boys and/or girls, the type of activity, and even approximate age can be instantly determined from only a few seconds. Some may have flashes of mental images, like kids riding their bikes or playing on a swing set. When longer than a few seconds, listening becomes more intent able to single out the sound focused on. The reality of the experience is you didn't see the children or can you prove it happened but know it did. Just like the five senses have a specific function communicating with different levels of intensities (loud/whisper, hot/warm/cold), the 6th sense interacts within the mind, called psychic impressions. psychic relay connects as levels of subtlety or intensities. The reason being subjective to what factors are involved, like the five senses. A physical conversation can be loud, as a whisper, from a distance and so on. Because the communication is multidimensional between corporeal and non-corporeal using heightened sensory perception conveying information is done a little more creatively.

cognitively speaking

A deeper understanding of cognitive processes and the intuitive mind sheds light on a foundational truth.

Sigmund Freud coined the term, Freudian Slip as an unintentional truth from the unconscious. Expanding his analysis to an instinctual collective language of unconscious perception shows us how the intuitive mind is responsive to the environment. Language processing the sensation of in-built knowing without being able to explain how we know; *I just know it, gut feeling, a hunch, they seemed trustworthy, I felt a pull, a nagging suspicion, there's something about them, don't know why but I just know it, something tells me, for some reason.*

Natural intuition is also found as a spontaneous physical response we refer to as knee-jerk reactions like when we find ourselves taking an involuntary step back *that doesn't make sense* when meeting a non-threatening looking person. Physical impulses that result in a coincidence or important situation is another example. These intuitive responses found in language and in physical response are found in millions of stories describing extraordinary situations. Our senses beyond the physical communicate to us as excitement, a curious pause, recognition or nervousness. They are felt as compelling, an internal SOS, overwhelming positivity, a nagging feeling or spur-of-the-moment inspiration.

Psychic ability, albeit, communicating with loved ones or with guides shares the same level of communication intensity but from training and practice received with clarity and comprehension. Establishing a relatable connection via the five senses and the intuitive mind provides the general population a truer understanding. It was essential to filter out false notions to experience psychic ability communication, next. Don't concern your mind with doing it wrong. The exercises are simple to give the reader a direct experience on a rudimentary level.

trance-state awareness

Sensory linked to the beyond requires a quieted mind to enter *trance state awareness*. If you're like millions of people who struggles with a busy mind don't let this intimidate you. Freeing mental constraints only asks for your permission. Sounds too easy but true when you know how. If you're reading this while juggling a mental to-do list, waiting for a call or any background chatter diverting thoughts – put the book down and resume when you have approximately 20 minutes distraction free.

Reading during the exercises won't be as effective as recording each, as you go, into your smartphone and listen with earbuds. Find where you want to begin recording.

CHECKLIST: Go potty, turn off cell phones (unless recording), find a quiet room. Be comfortable but don't lay down to avoid falling asleep. Bright, sunny rooms are happy and relaxing. If possible, sit by a window with the sun shining on your face (eyes closed) for a couple of minutes. No music or meditation sounds. Absolute quiet. Remove any concerns about doing the exercises correctly. You're ready, let it be simple. Give yourself permission to release all busy thoughts – it's only for 20 minutes.

EXERCISE 1 - CLAIRVOYANCE

Take 8 deep breaths into your nose and exhale slowly from your mouth. Focus only on the sound of your breath and how your body relaxes into each one. When a sense of calmness fills you, proceed.

Close your eyes and imagine seeing a red couch in your mind for approximately 30 seconds. Now imagine someone you've never met sits down on the couch. Notice what they are they doing and look like.

Open your eyes. On a piece of paper, describe the couch including the environment surrounding it. Were the colors vibrant or muted? Do the same for the person who sat down; what they looked like, age, clothing, etc. When done proceed.

A red couch is used because it's an easy, simple visual that the imagination can assimilate even if someone never personally saw one. Based on my directive, unless the reader has a direct memory of owning/seeing, most people will visualize a soft spotlight shining on the red couch in the middle of an ambiguous room where the room fades into darkness around the perimeter. The imagery is typically easy to quickly conjure the image into your mind. What wasn't as easy to mentally create was someone unknown. The highest percentage will imagine the opposite sex, unless sexually attracted to the same, wearing casual generic clothing without facial details. Of course, there are a few exceptions but still link to a form of seeing a person associate with a desire. Let's review some important factors and how this simple exercise revealed more than you realized.

1. The red couch visualized is not unlike clairvoyance. This was the purpose for connecting the example of hearing the children playing, on the previous page, communicates similarly to the 6th sense. In this first scenario, your memory was accessed to quickly form a visual. If you saw the couch as I described, that wasn't psychic or a cold reading, just basic psychology where the mind spotlights what's important and fades out the rest.

2. Asking someone to imagine what isn't memory accessible was for the reader to understand the difference of the imagination and clairvoyance. When psychically receiving images it's important to remember they are someone else's physical memory; as a person, place, or thing. Depending on the client, situation, and other variables these images are seen various levels of intensity and detail.
3. Physical sensory clairvoyance experiences the non-incorporeal as the three-dimensional world. Most mediums understand this experience but typically receive mental imagery with various depth and intensity.

EXERCISE 2 - CLAIRAUDIENCE

- Repeat the deep breathing to get back into light trance state awareness. Close your eyes and instead of seeing, hear "red couch" in your mind.

Was it heard as your own thought or a different voice? Did you visualize the red couch or only hear within?

- Think of one person you know you had recent contact with. Close your eyes, and hear the person chosen shouting RED COUCH in your mind.
- Last time, as a whisper up close from the opposite gender.

EXERCISE 2 – MULTIPLE CLAIRS

Clairvoyance and clairaudience are the tools most frequently accessed and can be experienced as a clear movie to quick flashes of imagery. All mediums must be clairvoyant and clairaudient to see and hear spirit messages. Whereas, psychics may not be clairaudient but receive clairvoyantly with clairsentience as the method to convey what is being shown.

Clairsentience is an intuitive perception instilled within, as a knowing. An example is asking a question, like, what's your dog's name or what kind of car do you drive. Instantly the mind pulls up the answer from repetition of something familiar. The difference is the knowing isn't your memory experience. As discussed previously, the psychic's database is accessed to quickly relate and relay experiences difficult to translate. Accessing the clairs to relay information can be a series of images, words to answer a question, in-depth answers using multiple clairs as flashes, empathic sensations, simultaneously in pairs or overlapping intermittently. Because this is a bit more involved the exercises will use visualizations, as experienced. Reminders are given to prevent distractions.

1. **Clairsentience** - find a personal memory of intuitive <u>knowing</u> - like someone lying to you, or knowing you could trust someone not typical for your personality. Examples: A co-worker who is known to be trustworthy walks up to you smiling ....and *for some reas*on you know they are lying. An applicant applies for a job not as qualified but know they're the one.
2. **Empathic** – do the same with an empathic emotion felt from someone else. Examples: talking to a person who is smiling but your body feels suddenly nervous. The grocery store when one person enters the same aisle and a strong feeling sweeps over you. Empathic emotions can be felt as an onset of heightened emotions unrelated to the current environment.

Write down each experience in a few words, no longer than a sentence. Next, find one example for **clairvoyance and clairaudience**. You can use the exercise experience if nothing else comes to mind. Read each example several times so it's active and accessible. Visualizing the below scenario will be pulling the easiest and most accessible relatable memory at the same time, nanoseconds fast, in the background. Having one sentence written down is concise and prevents being tangled up in a way that slows down the fluid process with two or three sort-of situations.

PSYCHIC EXPERIENCE IN A READING – PART 1

PREPARING FOR THE CLIENT: Begin by quieting the mind from active thoughts, until you are grounded. Let the sensation of peace fill you and say, *within this stillness I call on the divine Universe to activate the God spark within and call my heavenly guide to assist.*

THE READING: The reading exercise is a first-person narrative of a long-distance psychic phone reading with a woman who sounds like she's in her 30's, early 40's with light, bouncy energy. The questions she has are about career opportunities. Dialog begins when topic is established and asked Nina for guidance.

M - Michele N - Nina C - Client

N: *begins with empathic impressions to relate how the client is emotionally connected to her current career situation as confusion and anxiety. This also indicates the client didn't want to give any indicators pretending to be happy and upbeat.*

M: To strengthen our connection I'm going to ask you to answer just yes or no. What I received from my guide around career, my body felt a wave of anxiety and confusion. Is it correct to interpret this as feeling confusion with a current career situation creating the anxiety?

C: Yes, to the confusion and anxiety.

N: *reduces the empathic impressions when confirmed. Clairsentient is then sent as a quick download in pieces; the client's current employer brought in new management - the client was up for promotion - uncertainty seeing position responsibilities changed.*

M: Did your current employer bring in new management?

C: Yes

M: The timing seems to have something to do with a promotion and now you're not sure what to do?

C: That's right, yes.

M: Great. Thank you for validating what I'm receiving. You can begin elaborating on some details but refrain from over explaining so you can trust it was psychically received.

C: Ok, great! I will.

N: *clairvoyantly flashes an image of the word 'review' simultaneously feeling anxiety. She sends to hearing the word promotion with a knowing the client was directly recommended. Clairvoyantly sent is, she now thinks she's getting fired not promoted. Rumors being spread about new management restructuring the whole department is sent as a knowing with images of several resumes to indicate the number of people and simultaneously sends the feeling confusion about looking for another job.*

M: OK. What I received will be given as a question even though it wasn't received as. This helps me not misinterpret and for you to participate in your reading. Did everything change after your review, where you told before about a promotion? The change in management affected positions – something about rumors and I saw resumes of several people and now wondering if you should stay.

C: A week before my review, new management came in. The review had a lot to do with being recommended for a promotion. I've been there...

Summary: The reading in real life would, of course, continue. If I was to approximate the time for the above, 10-15 minutes would be about right and long enough for an idea of spirit guide communication to the 6th sense. Nina's portion is written to read quickly whereas when on the receiving end there's a lot going on. Also, the above is with a well-behaved client, meaning when I'm listening it isn't met with nervous talking elaborating on details thinking I need help. Of course, the intentions are understood and most clients do.

For the readers who participated in all the exercises, congratulations on completing. This shows patience and truly wanting to connect with how psychic abilities are experienced firsthand. The following expands on the psychic experience providing more details without concentrated focus. Although the emphasis is placed on the 6th sense, with slight modifications (i.e., spirit guide with DLO) applies to medium communication.

WHAT A PSYCHIC EXPERIENCE IN A READING – PART 2

Discussions about a fascinating subject offer new perceptions but also arouse the curious mind. An exchange of familiar ideas will see two individuals anticipating the other's response, psychic listening on recurring matters is specific for each inquiring individual. Psychic filtering elaborated on how signals are interrupted substituted with a pre-established bias. Every person seeking guidance must be thought of as a unique fingerprint with the same curiosity for any answer. This is an important mindset for a Psychic – Medium, and the proper client attitude.

THE SETTING

Imagine you are one of two consultants and meeting with a client for your expertise. You are physically present and the other consultant is off-site relaying information into a small earpiece. This scenario requires some artistic license where the phone device is advanced technology able to read minds for two-way communication. For this to work efficiently any previous thoughts and emotions are quieted and enter a light trance state of awareness to make a call. Hearing your coworker saying hello to let you know the connection is good, heard audibly, like listening to someone talking to you from another room. You insert the small ear-bud and can hear your co-worker in the distance knowing the connection will become stronger and clearer as the conversation progresses.

It's time for the meeting and the client comes in and sits down and looks at you smiling and nervously introduces who they are and what information they're seeking. You explain the listening device and will be acting as the liaison for your co-worker with direct knowledge to answer their questions. For three or four minutes the client asks some questions but mostly listens to the suggestions and guidance. As the information goes deeper, they become engrossed in the easy exchange of conversation forgetting your listening to your coworker. Human behavior focused on physical reality kicks in and your client begins interacting as only two people discussing an interesting topic. Replies are longer to elaborate a point and enthusiasm on what is being said is more and more frequent while listening to your co-worker. To maintain the connection of the unconscious while communicating consciously, you remind the client about what's needed to continue listening. This is where client variables can occur on how they react. Most will be apologetic and thank you for reminding them. A small percentage will think you are being rude for interrupting them. Some will start asking more questions about what you're doing, how the communications work and inquire about your co-worker. When this happens, the call is dropped. Once the client is reminded of the process, you re-connect. From this point on, communications resume with maybe a few intermittent reminders, depending on how emotional the topic is. The scenario provided is with a pretend communication device to represent clairaudience to introduce the basic concept to the reader, in first person. For a more realistic understanding, the device would include the co-worker capable of sending visual imagery to your mind and tap into a sense of knowing. Communicating psychically isn't 2-D, it's 3-D using various resources to relay information that can be hearing, then seeing to knowing or in combination simultaneously. When the psychic is also empathic, they will feel the emotional state of the client or the individual being asked about. All of this is happening in the background or at the unconscious level while simultaneously consciously alert for the information to be given.

what's an example of feeling energy empathically?

It's night time and remember you needed something at the store. The aisles are empty with only a few other shoppers around. Suddenly your mood shifts from peaceful to feeling of anxiety and annoyance that wasn't there a minute before. You see someone in the same aisle approaching but has a look content; no screaming babies in need of a nap. You walk to another aisle and feel comfortable, again.

What just happened? Natural intuition is tuned into the emotional world around us that is felt at various degrees, depending on individual awareness. Empathic ability is inherently intertwined with clairsentience as divine tools all people are born with to assist them through life. It's felt when meeting someone new, a sense of something about to happen, called a hunch, being good at reading people. Does this mean every time you feel annoyed or anxious is from someone else? No, sometimes we just want the aisle for ourselves. Knowing yourself truthfully, is the key. Psychics with developed empathic senses are essentially the same but heightened and can determine the energetic source. The most interesting aspect of empathic ability is seeing the outer masks worn contradicting the inner-self. Hearing, "I'm fine, great," while flooded with nervous tension or the facade of confidence while terrified, are examples and commonplace.

divine synchronicity?

It's a beautiful day and you're driving on the highway. The only thing on your mind is the music playing while enjoying the scenery. Out of nowhere, an idea pops into your mind. Maybe it has to do with someone you haven't thought of or to take the next exit for ice cream. In the first scenario, you call the person to see how they are and find out something important. For the second, you decide to listen and get ice cream and continue back on the highway. Nothing happened. A few months later, you meet someone and they talk about a place that has great ice cream and find out it was, not only the same place; they were there at the same time.

DANIEL DUNGLAS (DD) HOME (1833-1886) Many consider DD Home to be the greatest of all physical mediums. His phenomena were dramatic and varied, and although his career lasted approximately 25 years, he was never detected in fraud of any kind. Allegations of fraud were made against him from time to time, but most were second or third hand, and none were substantiated.

HENRIETTA 'ETTA' WRIEDT (1859-1942) was an American 'direct-voice' medium. Detailed accounts of her mediumship were published by Dr John King, founder of the Canadian Society for Psychical Research, and Vice-Admiral William Usborne Moore, a member of the London-based Society for Psychical Research (SPR). Her genuineness was recognized by William Barrett, Oliver Lodge, Arthur Conan Doyle, Charles Tweedale, and William Thomas Stead.

PRESIDENT JOHN F. KENNEDY accurately described one of the biggest U.S. historical events in the 20th century – his own death. The morning of JFK's assignation, Jackie Kennedy became unnerved by a newspaper article resembling an obituary. To comfort her, JFK said, *"We're heading into nut country today. But, Jackie, if somebody wants to shoot me from a window with a rifle, nobody can stop it, so why worry about it?"*

CARLOS MIRABELLI (1889-1951) was a Brazilian medium credited with similar power and frequency DD Home. His testing included over thirty languages automatic writing, speaking in numerous foreign tongues, materializing objects & people, apportation, levitation, producing impressions of spirit hands in trays of flour, dematerializing anything in sight, himself included – done either in daylight or brightly lit environments. Mirabelli was discovered in a fraud incident doctoring a photo with the conclusion, despite, he did demonstrate genuine phenomena in bright lighting over many occasions and the fraud being a practical joke.

MICHEL DE NOSTREDAME, better known as Nostradamus, was a 16th century French apothecary and reputed seer known for his book Les Prophéties (The Prophecies) a collection of 942 poetic verses predicting future events. His prolific style of esoteric writings combined Astrological references and metaphorical symbology, called Quatrains. Nostradamus is one of the most well-known prophets, to this day.

STEFAN OSSOWIECKI (1877-1944) was a Polish engineer, promoted as the most gifted psychic in Europe and ever to come under the scrutiny of researchers. He exhibited a range of clairvoyance no one has exceeded, under experimental controls. Notable persons who credited his claims, pioneering Parapsychologist Gustav Geley and Nobel Prize-winning physiologist Charles Richet.

THE WISE
&
THE A.S.S.

GLOBAL PHENOMENA 19

That which we are is that which passes the duration of time. PSOC

ADVERSITY MAKES STRANGE BEDFELLOWS, accurately represents the reason for conjoining the wise and the a.s.s. Initially, the a.s.s.'s efforts were credited for their efforts as passionate crusaders against fraud. The amendment came from a consistent discovery over several months. Researching extraordinary people and events to include in this chapter proved more difficult than expected. Inevitably, the skeptic's rant of reasoning stole the spotlight, posed as the self-imposed champion of morality. More than a few accounts of real phenomena were omitted and kept the focus on stories difficult to refute. Admittedly, there was a concern of intentions misinterpreted as an adversarial viewpoint until my wise friend offered his opinion, 'Michele, you are a psychic medium and didn't consider the possibility skeptics having an agenda. Others won't either.' Thank you, Javier. The squeaky wheels get enough attention. Let's celebrate the extraordinary human potential, or, *The Wise.*

DR. EDWARD GIBSON MOON

One morning, in the 1930s, **a country doctor in England**, went to Lord Edward Carson's home who was critically ill. Carson's residence, in the Isle of Thanet, had large privacy hedges in front and a circular driveway. Daily visits were necessary to provide the medical care needed. But one morning Dr. Moon stood on the front steps absorbed in thoughts regarding his patience's care. After a few minutes he looked up and noticed the large hedges were gone. The road the hedges blocked was also gone along with the familiar surroundings, seen as a barren field with muddy tracks. His mind knew where he was and certain he was not sleeping. In the distance appeared a man walking towards him carrying a flintlock, outfitted in breeches, riding boots, a caped overcoat and a top hat with a narrow crown he knew in style decades prior. Dr. Moon saw the man could see him, too. When he approached the two men stared at each other, silently exchanging eye contact before continuing his way. Moon tried to orient his mind and looked behind him to see if Cleve Court was still there. It was. He turned back to look where the man was headed finding the landscape returned and the man had vanished.

SAMUEL CLEMENS

Also known as Mark Twain while living in Hannibal, Missouri, had an uncanny vision while in a dream state seeing a metal coffin resting on two chairs in the sitting room. Twain describes seeing his brother Henry laid out inside the coffin with a bouquet of white flowers and a single crimson flower in the center laying across his chest. The vivid dream was so real, when he woke up, he didn't realize it was a dream. Not long after, he and his sister would hear The Pennsylvania, the ship his brother and 150 others were on, blew up. He discovered his brother was alive and survived for a short time. The city provided plain white pine coffins for the deceased – except for Henry's. Sixty dollars from lady admirers was collected to purchase a special metal coffin to honor his memory. When Sam, aka, Mark Twain, saw his brother, he was lying exactly as shown in the prophetic dream; in an open metal coffin resting on two chairs. Not long after, an elderly lady entered with a large bouquet of all white flowers with a single red rose in the center and laid them on Henry's chest.

WINSTON CHURCHILL

British politician, army officer, and writer. Churchill, the Prime Minister of the United Kingdom from 1940 to 1945, was known for operating on what he called hunches. It would be more accurately described as premonitions, two of which saved his life and several others.

One evening during the Luftwaffe assault, the nightly air raid began while Churchill was hosting a dinner. The warnings were so commonplace, no one thought to interrupt the party and continued conversations. Churchill suddenly rose from the dinner table without a word, walked into the kitchen and began ordering the staff to immediately go into the downstairs bomb shelter. He then returned to his guests, again, sat down without mentioning his recent departure. A few minutes later, a bomb struck the back of the large house, destroying the kitchen, with his staff safe.

Another Churchill's hunch was later described as an audible command in his mind to immediately change his usual chauffeured seat to the opposite side of the vehicle and leave quickly. He did, and moments later diverted an assassination attempt on his life.

ESREF ARMAGAN

Mr. Armagan, is a landscape artist living in Turkey, known for his vibrant use of color expressed in his paintings. But that isn't all. Esref, is a mystery to the science, medical and art communities, he was born without eyes. Harvard University researchers[12] heard about Mr. Armagan, their interested to learn how his paintings **grasped three dimensional perspectives** and **the use of color, having no visual references**. When Armagan arrived for further research Scientists were baffled when his MRI revealed the regions of his brain for sight became active when asked questions about his paintings. One of the scientists drew the conclusion, *human vision apparently involves more than the information seen through the eyes but the ability to understand space not yet understood through conventional means.*

PAT PRICE

Mr. Price's, **a retired California Police Official until 1974**, remote viewing abilities were well known and a member of SRI (Stanford Research Institute). During a remote viewing test for psi research, Price correctly described a car's destination as a sailing marina twenty minutes before the driver

---

[12] 2008 two researchers from Harvard, Amir Amedi and Alvaro Pascual-Leone, Neural and behavioral correlates of drawing in an early blind painter: case study

randomly decided to stop there. Over the course of nine tests, seven concluded with the same degree of accuracy, estimating the odds, at 100,000 to 1. *He was extraordinarily accurate, unbelievably accurate.* – former CIA official.

IF PSYCHIC ABILITY IS REAL...

A Stephen Greer documentary about the government's denial of life in the Universe made a reference fitting for this subject; *it isn't lack of proof, rather embarrassing how much proof is continuously denied.*

IF PSYCHIC ABILITY IS REAL, WHY ISN'T IT REPORTED IN NEWSPAPERS?

Nandana Unnikrishnan, India (Autistic) India's nine-year-old Nandana Unnikrishnan is one of them. Thanks to her incredible gift of telepathy, Nandana can read her mother's mind, responding to her thoughts before they become words (her ability to read the minds of others have yet been tested). Her parents also claimed that Nandana seemed to know of outing plans and venues that they spoke of in private. When news of her abilities first spread, local papers and research teams visited her to test her telepathic skills. In one such test, journalists provided a nine-digit number to her mother, who 'read' the number in her mind. Nandana was then asked to spell out the number, and lo-and-behold, she got the entire number sequence correct. **Khaleej Times**

Western Visayas, Philippines, three-year-old Emma Tablate is turning heads for a unique ability - pyrokinesis. Fires occurred wherever Emma went, prompting local officers in her town of San Jose to cordon off their house for security reasons. San Jose Mayor, Rony Molina, also visited the home and was reportedly amazed by what he saw. Seconds after the girl said that something around them would catch fire, a shirt hanging in the house started to burn. The Daily Guardian reported that the child foresees when fires are about to occur, and can even cause objects to burst into flame simply by saying "sunog," the Filipino word for fire. **PhilNews**

IF PSYCHIC ABILITY IS REAL, WHY AREN'T SCIENTISTS BACKING IT UP?

FIVE-YEAR-OLD SHOCK SCIENTISTS. Ramses Sanguino's eerie supernatural talent has convinced leading neuroscientists to declare that "telepathy exists". Dr Diane Powell, who used to work at Harvard Medical School has met

Ramses three times and is now "confident that telepathy exists". She has since put Ramses through rigorous, scientific experiments and believes the young child is proof of an "alternative method of communication".

But the researcher admits although most scientists believe her, they will not publicly accept the bizarre phenomenon because they fear they will lose their job. She said, "I am as confident that telepathy exists as I am a lot of things that have actually been accepted by science. I would never say 100 percent about anything - but I have seen evidence. In terms of other scientists, they don't usually believe in telepathy. But I have met privately with many people who have said they would never publicly state that they believe in telepathy but tell me that they have experienced it or witnessed it themselves. Many of them say the reason they don't come forward and say anything is that they are afraid they would be ridiculed or possibly even lose their job. "It's very risky to one's credibility to take on a subject like this - but I knew that when I got into it." Express Newspapers

IF PSYCHIC ABILITY IS REAL, WHY DON'T THEY PREVENT GLOBAL DISASTERS?

There are examples of reputable psychic predictions time stamped before the occurrence. Keep in mind, there are situations that would be irresponsible for psychics to reveal considered classified, containing sensitive information in a public forum. When there is an opportunity to forward a global prediction, it isn't a guarantee the warning will be taken seriously, or heeded.

I've experienced this directly speaking to several clients working for the government – from the mail room to high level security agencies. Employment positions can be an opportunity for the universe to forward vital communications about current or future outcomes, such as, individuals with high-level security clearance with Homeland Security. If a situation aligns with the client's connection to influence the outcome, their personal reading is interrupted with larger scale data on an upcoming event. Overseas clients, combat soldiers or consultants have been recipients of spontaneous information concerning future events, specific to their rank of authority and security clearance.

Irrespective of the administration, these messages have not been acted on. Fear of ridicule might be the reason but doesn't apply to high ranking officials that don't have to inform a superior their source. The decision, to act or not, is unknown as well as, why didn't the silent recipients aware the prediction happened as described, ever contact me, again? Perhaps, the question is why won't anyone allow us to prevent global disasters?

IF PSYCHIC ABILITY IS REAL, WHAT ORGANIZATIONS RECOGNIZE IT AS LEGITIMAte?

CHULIN SUN can induce plant seeds to grow shoots and roots several cm long within 20 min using mentally projected qi energy witnessed on more than 180 different occasions at universities as well as science and research institutions, in China.
Photo: Shen and Sun, 1996, 1998

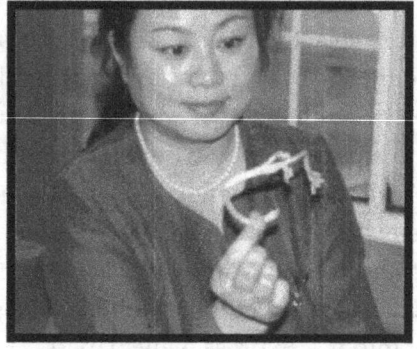

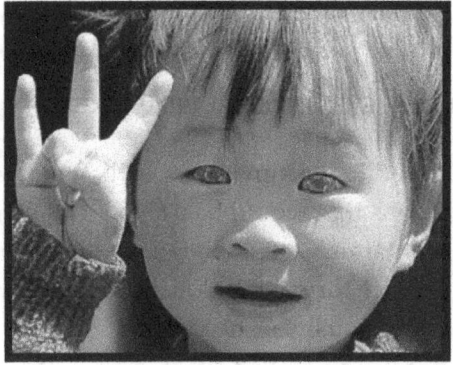

NONG YONGSUI, Dahua, China set the world record for the first human who can see in total darkness, listed in the **World Record Academy** - the leading international organization which certify world records.
Photo: FUAD

IF PSYCHIC ABILITY IS REAL, WHY DON'T THEY HELP FIND CRIMINALS?

FORBES ARTICLE: Meet the Medium Who Helps Law Enforcement Solve the Unsolvable - "Due to law enforcement publicly using psychics to solve cases, the CIA conducted a study to legitimize how viable and valuable using mediums could be. Out of eleven officers at different police agencies interviewed, eight officers said using a psychic provided them with otherwise unknown information. Three out of those eight officers found missing bodies through the use of a psychic."

LA TIMES ARTICLE: 'Psychic Vision' Woman Wins False Arrest Suit Against LAPD Nurse Melanie Uribe was reported missing. Searches to find her were unsuccessful until, a clairvoyant stepped in. What the medium received were so strong she went to the location she was pulled to. She ended up finding Uribe's body near her home shortly before the police showed up. They questioned and detained her as a suspect, but later released her when three suspects were identified and detained.

READER'S DIGEST ARTICLE: 13 Mysteries Actually Solved by Psychics – See article, information included in References for story details.

THE CIA

As far as powerful organizations go, the CIA gets the gold star for efforts regarding psychic abilities. Bureaucracy's missteps from the few less honest, mentioned, doesn't represent the incredible contributions and valuable insights. I encourage checking out their resources available, and accomplishments.

STARGATE

INGO SWANN (*photo, right*) was an internationally known advocate, psi researcher and leading figure in the CIA's Stargate Project. He was the first psychic to successfully demonstrate his abilities in the remote viewing program that ran for 25 years. Swann also described an unknown ring around Jupiter before scientists knew it existed. It was only after the first flyby of Jupiter by NASA's Pioneer 10 spacecraft confirmed the ring existed.

The Stargate Project may seem dated to mention. New information became known from lead members, in the position, to contradict the 20 year project publicly discounted. The Stargate project focused on psi functioning using Army personnel trained to demonstrate clairvoyance on demand. The question is why was the successful program scrapped? The CIA messed up. According to *The Stargate Chronicles: Memoirs of a Master Spy by Joseph McMoneagle*, the National Research Council had issued a report, *Enhancing Human Performance*, by David Goslin, concluding "*little or no support was found for the usefulness of many other techniques such as... remote viewing*". But further investigating discovered Goslin did not have the necessary security clearances restricting the analysis to exclude crucial data. In addition, no one that was part of the panel review group has ever seen the information they claim to have had access to. Star Gate veterans Harold Puthoff, Russell Targ and Edwin May knew more about the Star Gate project as anybody involved in it. The panel review group did not invite these three to be panel members.

"An Evaluation of Remote Viewing: Research and Applications." The 183-page white paper was more like a white flag – it was the CIA's public admission, after years of speculation, that U.S. government agencies had been using a type of ESP called "remote viewing" for more than two decades to help collect military and intelligence secrets. At a cost of about $20 million, the program had employed psychics to visualize hidden extremist training sites in Libya, describe new Soviet submarine designs and pinpoint the locations of U.S. hostages held by foreign kidnappers." **Jim Popkin, Newsweek Magazine, 2015**

... the program had employed psychics to visualize hidden extremist training sites in Libya, describe new Soviet submarine designs and pinpoint the locations of U.S. hostages held by foreign kidnappers." **Edwin May, CIA Stargate Scientist**

The Star Gate project lasted more than twenty years. After 20 million dollars the top brass shut its doors citing the information received was too vague for the intel needed. Another opinion was it came down to a political maneuver to save face when a Russian spy was hiding in plain sight, as to why the CIA Director went on the record on national TV, shutting the program down.

> "I'm not going to deal with a skeptic who has no fucking idea about what he's talking about. Because he's just *making it up. That's bad science. I'm a scientist."*
> **Edwin May**

CIA scientist, Edwin May running the program, said, *"dramatic cases in the laboratory"* when speaking of Pentagon psychics accurately sketching a target thousands of miles away that they had never actually seen. When asked about nonbelievers who dismiss remote viewing as voodoo without examining the evidence, May is short-tempered. *"I'm not going to deal with a skeptic who has no fucking idea about what he's talking about. Because he's just making it up. That's bad science. I'm a scientist."* And May has even less time for all the former Star Gate psychics who peddle mood-ring junk science online, some warning paying customers about flying saucers and the coming apocalypse. *"They are ripping people off, and I have to undo that when I try to sell this to mainstream scientists,"*

THE INVISIBLY REAL

Since 1974 the Chinese government has discovered over 100,000 children who have extraordinary psychic powers. These children, when blindfolded, can "see" with either their ears, nose, mouth, tongue, armpits, hands or feet. 5,000 have demonstrated publicly the passing of solid objects through another solid object. A 12-year-old girl, Hu Lian's X-Ray vision, saw a piece of shrapnel left inside a man's body and accurately drew its shape. Medical researchers at UCLA are discovering some youngsters with a unique DNA pattern no one else has. They have 24 active DNA codons. People normally have only 20 active codons. These children have a remarkable resistance to illness and seem to be immune to every disease. *(next page)*

The official CIA website provide documents that are available about the Stargate program and for law officials when working on a case with psychics.

THE SUPER PSYCHIC CHILDREN OF CHINA

China's government funded comprehensive research to study phenomena after gifted children with advanced capabilities were being reported, ongoingly. Extraordinary abilities witnessed by scientists and cooperating governments concluded authentic psychic abilities were demonstrated, under testing guidelines. The phenomena of psychic writing, as documented in China's Super Psychics, is one such case study.

CASE STUDIES

Omni Magazine was contacted with the results to determine if the tests were set up to check there could be no cheating.

CASE STUDY: A small group of children are shown a closed pencil case and asked to imagine a blank piece of paper inside. Next, the children were asked to imagine words written on the paper. A few minutes later, the case is opened with the words physically written on it in pencil. In 1981, Xiao Kiong was the first to demonstrate this ability.

CASE STUDY: A research team put together at Yunnan Wenshan Teachers' College, selecting 5 children for further study. An amazing discovery found, when blindfolded, the children were able to see with their ears, nose, mouth, tongue, armpits, hands, or feet. The tests were flawless.

CASE STUDY: From a stack of books, one was selected, then opened at random and a page was ripped out and crumpled up into a small ball. It was placed in the armpit of one of the children - and the child could read every word on the page perfectly. After many more tests Omni Magazine became convinced, these kids were for real. But Omni was not the only one present. Zhu Yiyi, editor of Shanghai's Nature Magazine, a prestigious science journal also witnessed these events.

CASE STUDY: 1000 people were gathered in an auditorium; each given a rose-bud. A six-year-old girl came on stage and when she waved her hand all the rosebuds opened before the eyes of the astonished audience.

CASE STUDY: a sealed bottle of pills is placed at the center of a table. After a few moments the pills passed through the glass bottle and settled on the table. In many cases, the child would then take another object, such as a coin, put it on the table and it would pass back into the sealed bottle.

THE INVISIBLY REAL

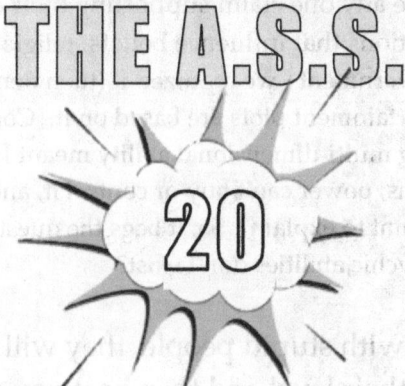

THE A.S.S. 20

They go about puffed up and pompous, dressed and decorated with, not of their own labours, but of those of others. And they will not allow me, my own. They will scorn me as an inventor; but how much more might they — who are not inventors but vaunters and declaimers of the works of others — be blamed. **Leonardo DaVinci**

EVERYONE HAS AN OPINION but what makes people think they are entitled to offer them as facts? Living in a country granting us the liberties to openly express our viewpoints is not only a constitutional right but a booming business. Why isn't dramatic rage and haughtiness before an audience perceived as an undiagnosed attention seeking personality disorder? It's the quagmire's lure dominating the airwaves orchestrating melodrama as the rescuer defending the people.

Narcissism, according to the psychiatric community is a personality disorder, *"Having an exaggerated sense of self-importance; expects to be recognized as superior even without achievements that warrant it; belittle or look down on people they perceive as inferior."* Narcissists craft their public persona to receive praise to reinforce their sense of identity and self-worth. A friend of mine is a psychiatrist who made a point I didn't consider, saying it makes sense for a public figure skeptic to challenge psychics as the ultimate game to demonstrate their superiority.

A quote from psychologists Niklas Steffens and Alexander Haslam *"like moths to a flame, narcissists drawn naturally to positions of power and influence"*. Psychologist Robert Hare, *"they are social predators and like all predators they are looking for feeding grounds. Wherever you get power, prestige and money, you will find them."* For centuries supernatural critics have relentlessly inserted ten doubts to override any one claim supporting their observations; specifically, organizations that influence beliefs; religion - demonized it, science - alleged it, government - weaponized it (then denied it), psychology - diagnosed it, and entertainment plots are based on it. Could it be these power houses acknowledging multi-dimensional ability meant Heaven included woman and other faiths, power can't buy or control it, and intellectual elite asking the less intelligent to explain? So, it begs the question, why exert more effort into denying psychic abilities don't exist?

> "Never argue with stupid people, they will drag you down to their level and then beat you with experience."
> — Mark Twain

THE ALLEGEDLY PEOPLE

Skeptics of notoriety readied with absurd accusations when speaking about ALL psychic phenomena. Motives are swept into a verbal riptide of persuasions, superstitions, scientific regiments, and confident arrogance. An online blog dedicated to bullies, describes attention seeking disorders found in forum's online (trolling). *The troll's use of forums to post irrelevant, disruptive, insulting, or abusive messages, designed to infuriate or upset members leading to replies, counter criticism, and arguments and taking the forum way off topic.*

A forum describing the antics of trolling fit a skeptic ridiculing a popular spiritualist's views discussing skeptics (comments were not mean spirited). The skeptic followed a mentioned strategy to the letter; sidestepping specific points, diverting the attention to his outrage the spiritualist used improper use of semantics; in particular, *skeptic* versus *cynic* and *belief* versus *faith*.

The attention seeking skeptic's (abbrev. to a.s.s. – hmm, the universe does have a sense of humor) diversion tactic was perfectly described above, by Tim Field's observation of trolls and counter criticism and arguments take the forum way off topic. I wonder if the skeptic realized that focusing the dispute to proper syntax says he agreed to the points, not contested.

DEBUNKERS

The qualities prized by the media – succinctness, confidence, showmanship – may not be compatible with the qualities conducive to sound scientific judgment.
Canadian-American Psychologist Philip Tetlock

The preponderance of evidence is only a sample that creates a bigger concern of competency of non-believers holding sway in the public. This includes the debunker that takes skeptic to another level of theatrical acting skills to express their passionate indignation while loading mental guns readied with condescending counterpoints, animated gestures, flaring nostrils, and intense stares of injustice. The more advanced can juggle all this, AND, throw in smug-shots and forced laughter. Phew, impressive stuff. Regardless of how loud the rant, scientific blah, blah, blah or .50 cent words in their vocabulary, doesn't change they ain't qualified to render anything other than ignorant speculation.

The extent of their influence was discovered while researching case examples of global phenomena exhibiting extraordinary abilities. As mentioned previously, a pattern emerged going back hundreds of years having the common denominator of a large audience. The more attention from the public the faster the inevitable nay-sayer was positioned on their inflatable pulpit denouncing - *such nonsense, it's who-do-voodoic heresy, table tipping tricksters, hypnotic hoaxes and, and, and!* Notoriety, was and still, the provocateur for the a.s.s. disguised as the moralistic defender to ensure doubt in the public's mind.

We know the skeptic's tired mantra – *ESP doesn't exist or proven scientifically*. The same people have yet to grasp what their message translate to; cue the speech bubble. Millions of intimate, personal experiences described as profound, could not be guessed or known, were not posted on social media, or overheard before. Dismissed and rationalized as grief, reduced intelligence, and naïve vulnerability. Grief isn't like taking a stupid pill and clients are not pushovers. If their research wasn't focused on being right, they would learn from statistics people open to psychic communication are mostly highly educated professionals.

> We dismiss millions of people's beliefs. We dismiss every experience and claim pertaining to. We know more than you, decide your reality and what's real.

EVALUATORS

The points made next are obvious. Guidelines of a professional evaluator assesses skills having related working experience and knowledge to accurately determine another's performance. Again, not an earth shattering revelation but a necessary one when conflict of interest influences decisions. Who reviews a topic, can guess the outcome, like:

- A Christian Book Club reviews a fiction novel written by an atheist.
- AERA – (Association Embracing Realist Art) evaluates a Wassily Kandinsky's geometric abstract painting.
- A homophobic man critiquing the movie, *Broke Back Mountain*

GORDON ALLPORT[13] defines prejudice; *"a feeling, favorable or unfavorable, toward a person or thing, prior to, or not based on, actual experience"*.

Overkilling the point, was the point. It's ridiculous for any job to be evaluated by someone, 1) with an outspoken negative attitude towards your profession and 2) and didn't know peanuts from pickles. Because they decided psychic ability doesn't exist only reinforces the point.

Public debunkers have to ignore evidence to remain relevant. True story. I posted on a well-known debunkers page the CIA link about the psychic children of China. Within, five minutes, it was deleted. Re-posted two more times, taking screen shots of other posts. Only my post was deleted...three times.

PSYCHIC VIGILANTES

Psychic vigilantes are people who form a group to expose anyone claiming supernatural abilities...that happen to be famous. Why these groups are a bit more slippery is due to the humanitarian passion exuded to protect people from the unscrupulous. The approach may differ but share similarities with the a.s.s.; they are usually defined by one success, hunt only the famous,

---

[13] Gordon Allport (1897 – 1967) was an American psychologist and Harvard alumnus regarded as one of the first psychologists to focus on the study of the personality, often cited as one of the founding figures of personality psychology.

evaluate with prejudice, breath-takingly irresponsible and think they are qualified.

One group's mission statement, *'exposing all celebrity psychic mediums.'* This type of confidence sparked my curiosity. The founder's background was a retail store photographer before organizing a modest group of volunteers scattered globally. I was initially impressed describing a well thought out, methodical approach. Their attention to detail was extraordinary. Months of effort were put in to make-up a realistic identity on Facebook including the personal information, used as bait. Minutiae wasn't omitted, blending the mundane recipes as convincers. Deception to catch deception. They snared a medium with a respectable following and mounted the medium like a stag head over the fireplace. Their unqualified pursuit for glory, didn't consider to inform readers, *'secure your social media page before scheduling with a medium.'*

What resulted from their ignorance was experienced with a first time client. Connecting with a DLO with messages hearing, *'you could have read that on Facebook.'* Honestly, I was taken aback. Fast forward, the client read the vigilante's method as advice to prevent fraud. Not knowing how it works, rationalized messages would be 'other than' social media, if I was genuine. It compromised their DLO experience and inadvertently encouraged removing social media safeguards to see if the medium... you get the idea. An, identity fraud nightmare waiting to happen. People, secure your online presence.

The reckless methods, didn't stop there. A New York Times journalist featured an online article about the vigilante group. It just so happened the founder mentioned she volunteered as a Wikipedia watchdog correcting any pages with information she viewed as myths. The example was **Psychic D.D. Home page citing an accusation by** English poet and playwright, **Robert Browning**. I couldn't help wonder if the article's Wikipedia redirect implied the founder edited Home's biographical information. Why it was suspect is the fact D.D. Home continues to be regarded as one of the greatest physical mediums known, and his skills were meticulously tested, several times. If my assumption is true, and the founder's revisionist haste was, indeed, to discredit Home's repute, she has failed again. Browning and his wife were open to the supernatural and did watch Home demonstrate his ability. During the time, Home was accused of being portrayed as the fictitious

<u>medium</u>, *Mr. Sludge* in Browning's poem and was eventually corrected. Below are two references found easily and only requires looking.

"More harm was done to Home's reputation by Robert Browning's poem, Mr. Sludge – the Medium, which was generally taken to refer to Home, as Browning, together with his wife, who accepted spiritualism, attended séances with Home. Yet he never claimed in public to have caught Home at trickery and in private admitted that imposture was out of the question." Biography of D.D. Home

"Many consider DD Home to be the greatest of all physical mediums. His phenomena were dramatic and varied, and although his career lasted approximately 25 years, he was never detected in fraud of any kind. Allegations of fraud were made against him from time to time, but most were second or third hand, and none were substantiated."

THE REAL ALLEGEDLY PEOPLE

Should Scientists be held accountable for disregarding proof of supernatural phenomena?

No one disputes the allegedly people are anything shy of brilliant and respected for inventions and discoveries, humans around the globe benefit from daily. It seems, when believers of the supernatural question the science community's methodology it translated as not able to grasp the simple concept of evidence. The fact is, it's the other way around.

American Psychologist, Yale Psychologist Irvin L. Child discovered ESP experiments had been completely ignored by the science community despite dramatic evidence. Important, yes, but not the bigger point. How does a group brimming with extraordinary talents and intelligence continue to struggle with what their alleging. It's illustrated in an article highlighting two scientists studying whether ESP exists by exploring different kinds of ESP with experiments focused on mind reading. Their research found receivers weren't particularly accurate, concluding no evidence of mind reading or any other sort of ESP has been found, stating; since science hasn't uncovered any evidence that ESP even exists, no scientific investigations of its potential mechanisms have been undertaken. ESP itself is neither scientific or unscientific – but it can't be studied scientifically or unscientifically and scientific studies have found no support for the hypothesis that ESP exists. **Those who ignore the evidence and insist that ESP is a real natural**

phenomenon fail to meet one of the key aspects of scientific behavior: assimilating the evidence.

Included, was a disclaimer by a web administrator in small print; '*Here we are taking a scientific view of ESP. However, some people have a different view — they consider ESP to be a spiritual or supernatural phenomenon, which involves tapping into another level of consciousness or an alternate dimension. In this case, ESP is not "natural" in a scientific sense, and thus cannot be studied with the tools of science.*' Maybe one day those words will grow into a 12-point font. **University of California, Museum of Paleontology.**

The above mentioned psychologist, Child, added a philosophical footnote pondering if, perhaps, scientists denied ESP, from a morality standpoint. His red herring questioning if scientists are basing outcomes on humans being evolved enough for the responsibility was an interesting view.

No one's disagreeing fraud's abuse of power but scientists aren't society's keeper of morality.

Ignoring facts, is not only professional gross misconduct, it compromises the public's confidence and support. The allegedly people have failed as the self-appointed judge unable to grasp one basic idea they continue to allege – psychic and medium ability **is not mind reading telepathy**.

why are they involved?

It is through science that we prove, but through intuition that we discover.

Henri Poincare

CELEBRATING SPIRIT

◄►

Without giving away information, it didn't take long for her to tune-in with me & my situation. She provided needed guidance, shared wisdom, and brought to light something personal to me which I didn't believe was within my reach. I now feel different. The experience was amazing for me. A.S.

◄►

When we spoke, I was excitedly skeptical. (The psychic) knew things about my office environment, what would happen with my job-which it did end up happening! specifics about my love life-even called my boyfriend out by name! She was so on point that it was freaky, but in a really great way. Not enough words to convey how much I recommend (psychic)!!! M.R.

◄►

I just had my first reading with (a psychic) and I am still sitting here amazed. My reading left me with my jaw on the table. She knew details about me that I have never shared even those closest to me. She helped me achieve in one call, what I have been working to accomplish my entire life. Thank you!!! K.A.

◄►

(The psychic) talked about such specific details that only someone who was close to me in my world would know. Even people who are close to me don't know half of what (the psychic) knew just in the first session. She has such an amazing gift. After the reading a sense of calm and peace comes over you. I am so glad I found her!! A.D.

◄►

From the beginning (the psychic) made me feel comfortable, she asked me no questions and knew all about me. It was shocking how accurate she was about the details of my life- past, present, and future. She knew about my current situations that I only discussed with close friends and was able to give me direction in areas I was on the fence about. A.G.

HOTLINES & COLD READINGS

21

Those who can make you believe absurdities can make you commit atrocities.
Voltaire

!#@%&*%#$!!! AH, THE OTHER CURSE. Let's get to it. Fact; curses and dark crap the fortune teller is known for, started from superstition. It was a modernized invention using superstitions to prevent tombs and priceless artifacts from being stolen. In more recent times, fabricated stories of curses, like the Hope diamond, were solely to increase an objects value. And, the sensationalism worked.

The final chapter emphasizes; how to recognize the fakers, the client most vulnerable and distinguishing the victim versus the risk takers. Our starting point is to create a basic profile of the scam artist:

Any reader not familiar with the stories connected to fraud then stop here and find news stories. It is essential clients are aware of the parasites pretending to be psychic and what they are capable of.

Psychic fakers are psychopaths. Spiritually, they are early-beginner level with underdeveloped egos. A commonality shared in this group is confusing intelligence or strategy as advanced.

They do not think the same way as 'normal' people do. They become whatever illusion serves their purpose with convincing acting skills. Their motivation is eliciting fear to create dependance or promises from the heavens for self-gain.

Next is learning the psychopath's vulnerability and clients have the power to stop them from existing. Deviants need to control the narrative. For example, imagine a scenario where a scam artist realizes a genuine psychic is listening in on their reading. What do think would happen? It's what might have happened, that changes, right? How about the scenario where scam artists learn a large percentage of clients know the signs of who's genuine from fraud?

Regardless of the industry, fraud has predictable consistencies when it comes to methodology. They target naivety and venues supporting highly charged desire and fear for the simple reason it attracts those likely to ignore possible risks. This type of greed[14] was explained perfectly; *"In the pursuit of their material needs, they know no limits. They will compromise moral values and ethics to achieve their goals. Caring, being concerned about others – is not part of their repertoire. As such, they have little qualms about causing pain to others. Their inability to empathize, lack of genuine interest in the feelings of others, and unwillingness to take personal responsibility for their behavior..."*

Let's distinguish what a legitimate victim is versus the risk taker. Morality rejects the idea of giving victims accountability. But shifting blame to clients unaware, isn't being questioned. In the current day and age, what percentage of people interested in psychic phenomena aren't aware of these slithery creatures stealing grandma's inheritance? Fraud warnings are not new and almost impossible to avoid online. The category is directed specifically to the psychic seekers *ignoring the risk*, throwing all caution to the wind to satisfy an immediate need. To what end does desperation override personal responsibility for fraud continuing to exist?

---

[14] Seven Signs of the Greed Syndrome Manfred F. R. Kets de Vries, Distinguished Clinical Professor of Leadership Development & Organizational Change April 8, 2016

is love accountable? (a true story)

[*Names were changed*] John, was a middle-aged man who was a highly educated professional. He lived not too far from a friend's spiritual bookstore and decided to meet there for an in-person reading. When I arrived, Nina's usual reserved demeanor got my attention something was different. She began downloading information before opening the door to meet John. Casual introductions were skipped, telling John it was important what Nina wanted him to hear. "You met with another psychic, recently. Please pay attention. My guide is relaying a warning to be careful." John acknowledged with a nod and a look of disbelief. "John, did you already give this psychic $5000? (John nods again) Nina is asking you to please pay attention. The next time you speak to this psychic, she will ask you for another $5000."

He sat in his chair quiet trying to process what he was hearing. After a minute or two, he confirmed what Nina said, followed with, that no one knew and, the reason he scheduled a reading with me. In mid-sentence Nina interjected, letting me know he would ignore the warning. I offered my psychic help free of charge as an attempt to prevent Nina's words. John left promising he would heed the warning.

Four years later, John scheduled a phone reading. The reason for contacting me wasn't for intuitive advice. He wanted me to hear how the $5,000, when we met last, became $80,000. Yes, $80,000.

high risk

Does John's version include the warnings ignored; I can't say for sure. Is he accountable? Yes. His heart strings were played despite efforts of preventing his well-being targeted as a sociopath's pawn of opportunity.

High risk mentalities; desperate grief from loss, heartache relief, (I just need to know) and ongoing life challenges believed to be bad luck.

PSYCHIC HOTLINES

In the 1990's a large psychic hotline network introduced a new concept to the public. Commercials blasted into the airwaves with a large advertising budget, targeting late night viewers with 24-hour psychic advisor access. The strategy seduced the lonely-hearts demographics persistently flashing their ONLY $1.99 A MINUTE slogan.

James Surowiecki, the journalist for Slate Magazine's online article, *What Psychic Friends Failed to See*, details the influence of The Psychic Friends Network's that impacted viewers. "*Psychic Friends infomercials had been among the most popular in history. Between 1993 and 1994, they aired more than 12,000 times, and at one-point Inphomation[15] was shelling out half a million dollars a week to buy air time on cable stations. It was money well spent: At its peak, Psychic Friends was bringing in as much as* **$125 million a year***, most of it through infomercials.*"

I have a Psychic Friends Network (PFN) story to share (why a psychic calls a psychic, is explained in the afterword). When PFN's was at its $125 million dollar peak, I just ended a relationship with *that guy* leaving my heart filled with *those questions*. I was in a constant swirl cycle seeking relief any way I could. While meticulously organizing every single photo album at 3:00 am, a PFN infomercial came on. Only $1.99 a minute? That's cheap, since I had only one question. Can you guess what my first question was? If you said, *how does he feel about me* or *will I hear from*, you are correct. Into the rabbit hole I went.

My call connected to a psychic advisor who sounded normal enough. She only asked me one question, '*are you looking for answers about heartache*?' Not considering you don't need to be psychic to figure out why someone is calling at 3:00 am. They were the magic words to open my emotional flood gates. And then, he said... can you believe it! So, I said, 'blah, blah, blah, and then, and then, and then, but he said. When I finally came up for air it was to ask questions beginning with *will he* and *why did he*. My account was more like a negotiation hoping to hear he really loved me so I could ask; *when will he?* The $1.99 advisor graciously let me talk myself into a $600 phone bill.

Did she tell me anything psychic? No. Are their legitimate psychics working for a hotline? Maybe someone building a client base or keeping appearances of a conventional identity but most likely a very small percentage.

---

[15] Inphomation Communication, Inc. was the parent company to the Psychic Friend's Network filing bankruptcy in 1998 from the competing market.

Remember, authentic psychics connecting with the divine universe wouldn't scam... because of this connection.

ADVICE FROM THE ARCTURIAN

First, it is essential to separate the employees from the employers; one not representing the other. Second, there are moments when immediate advice is beneficial, as a rarity, not as reliance. Those who find themselves with an ongoing need driven by desperation's heartache, prolong the pain. Around the globe, a substantial number of advisors are available to satisfy your per-minute desires knowing love in distress wants a silent ear and future words to satisfy.

Energy - think, transmutable energy. Whether it's a Voodoo Priestess or Diviner of ancient ways, there is one hard and fast rule – all healers remove fear, not create. Call it dark or negative, the name given isn't important – the result is. Fear and diversions, dark clouds that follow or conclusions of similar claims are not words of the enlightened. Know, the dark cannot exist in the light, nor sadness in laughter and joy. This is Divine Law, without measure or means, that another soul embodied or disembodied can alter and the only potion for love, needed.

Requesting the elementals of magic for concoctions forcing love to satisfy only one of the two? What is the answer if another without love, did to you? When intentions imbalance, persuade or harm one life or more, open reciprocity's reflection for the same, as given. This is the rule of Gaia aware of any summoning or conjuring the fates. Negativity holds no sway, or power over the light body of Christ's Consciousness. True listening to the Divine Teacher's allows souls to develop without fear and warnings are specific for an action or to prevent. Contacting any psychic or medium, alchemist of magical way to guide a soul's path out of confusion or towards individual purpose decides a future of possibilities. The gifts bestowed, capable to truly hear, see, know or conjure the light of healing comes from the light of what is sacred. When exploited for personal gain, with or by pretense, this light is extinguished for neither to know. As guides and overseers to Earth, only the light reaches into the Heavens, as given to assist and guide others.

WHEN TO LAUGH AND LEAVE

Legitimate charge a flat rate for their services, and visibly present. Requests for large sums of money or material items worth money to have, get, be, not have, etc. –please, never fall for this, it's a con.

Rituals to remove negativity for romance, luck, ancestry, etc.

Magic love potions, elixirs to curse or harm. If suggested, seriously, immediately hang up or get up and walk out.

Phishing questions asking for personal information. DO NOT. Think of the access someone has with age, birthday, address…and (if given directly) check or credit card used to pay. There isn't any circumstance, situation, or earth-shattering event any legitimate psychic would request this amount of personal information…. EVER.

Threatens personal harm (like who-do-voodoo bad luck) if services are refused. Ask them to repeat what they said while recording on your cell phone. Then call the police. Frauds are not more powerful than God, the Angels or your guides but will have to answer to them, one day.

Watch for the Barnum-effect, using general statements that apply to anyone. More details provided in cold readings clues.

Language pertaining to negative karma from a past life. Stop them from talking, right there. Ask what they see in their future reincarnations based on their current life decisions. Then, laugh and leave.

AUTHOR COMMENT: My background is not versed in nature religions using rituals, such as Wicca. Research is recommended before consulting.

pay-per-minute and fortune teller storefronts - overview

Since anyone can be hired, be aware of questions connected to identity theft. Never answer birthday questions. Tell them you don't give out personal information and ask why they want it. Psychics aren't Astrologers and pay-per-minute is not the forum for an in-depth chart reading.

Astrology sign questions are asked by cold readers. This includes tarot readings for astrology spreads. Scheduling with an Astrologer for an in-depth chart requires birthday and location of birth. Check and verify qualifications thoroughly! How long, do they have an internet presence?

Keep your questions and answers simple, *"I'm calling about employment and relationships"* Same with answers, *"yes, it's when we broke up."* Heartache=watch tendencies of emotional overload, that is over reactive and wants to over explain. And… it's never one question. Seriously, never.

Avoid asking questions only about the future and don't allow information only about the future. Validation is essential.

Watch for questions to elicit an emotional verbal response. It isn't a secret the heartbroken want to explain everything down to the itty-bitties, and a question or statement as, *"I see them saying they love you…'* would be enough to open the floodgates. A legitimate psychic wouldn't say something that general and two, will stop too much information. Review chapters discussing participation.

Tarot readings – are not general life questions. Unless you know from previous experience the reader has mastered this divination method, stay away from seeing what they get and ask about specific concerns.

Divination, including tarot is a participatory reading. The querent provides the question and assists to avoid misinterpretation. *What can you tell me about the job I'm currently applying for?* (don't say where or for what position). Court cards, like a King or Queen describing a person, may ask about people fitting the description. Same with Pages and Knights that might be describing characteristics or communication connected to the question. See chapter on tarot in Divination Section.

> **TIP: Language in daily** horoscopes shouldn't be compared to a natal chart from an Astrologer. If someone claiming to be psychic uses phrasing that is similar to:
>
> *You have leadership qualities and a strong sense of justice. Being fair is important to you. In, friendships and relationships, balance and loyalty are essential. You see the best in people and this has caused you problems in your life and what the guidance you seek is based on.*
>
> A real psychic doesn't lead-in with generalized character traits that are specifically, non-specific and try to hook the ego's personal self-interests. The example above is for a Libra that other signs can relate to. Remember, for video or in-person readings, to remove jewelry or other indications that can be used. Read astrology signs to recognize the language and see The Barnum effect, in this chapter.

VALIDATION

The importance of validation is mentioned numerous times, specifically on clarifying, what is too much information. I decided to lurk on a psychic chat board on the discussion to learn what advice was offered. Hundreds, if not thousands, including comments under comments, chimed in. One of the chatties offered her strategy on how she duped a psychic. According to our self-dubbed opinionator, the key is to remain completely expressionless and only yes or no replies. It would have been funny if not for the ooh's and ahhh's grateful for the advice, not realizing it's 'what not to do'.

generally speaking

FUN TEST: The exercise is to physically describe a person you are seeing for the first time for another to recognize. Ask a friend to send you several photos of relatives or friends you never met or seen before. Randomly choose one of the photos and describe their physical characteristics. Did your friend know which relative/friend? How many people would fit the description given?

Validation isn't what someone decides a psychic or medium should say or wants to hear. Maybe you will, maybe you won't. The universe decides. It's when a stranger, in this case the psychic, gives details about your past and present, that cannot be guessed. The client's responsibility is to recognize and the required effort to validate. An example of understanding the difference between generalities of a cold reading from legitimate is when circumstantial details happen to fit most people.

Male, 6'0 tall	Brown hair/light eyes	Wear's business suits
Drives a white SUV	Camps/outdoorsy	Quirky sense of humor
Good with his hands	Military background	Intelligent/Educated

Each fall into the general description pile except for the humor and good with hands, which interprets to being handy at fixing things, still vague independently. With few exceptions, most people fall into regular everyday likes, dislikes, hobbies, and appearance when describing out loud. Of course, there are exciting and unique adjectives to separate Bob from Tom and Joe offered in personal and intimate stories shared with loved ones. But to stay on the point, validation generalities become less general when combined.

A man, with a military background who is 6'0 tall with dark brown hair, light eyes with a quirky sense of humor. He drives a white SUV, is educated and a white-collar professional. Very outdoorsy type that likes to camp. Also, good with his hands and handy around the house, maybe knows some carpentry or work on cars. The picture begins to form of a man already known or mentioned in the future with all the generalities pieced together. Validation explained is often misinformed from ignorance without proper elaboration. For example, 'watch for any general descriptions.' Uneducated advice, in this case, could shut down a client's energy when talking to a psychic for the first time, hearing the first two descriptions.

Cold readings avoid any personal details like hair and eye color, height, and color of a car. In person readings and video calls have higher chances of a cold reading than phone because of the physical clues someone perceptive in the art of fraud can determine.

what do i look for when a psychic uses cold reading techniques?

First, psychics aren't cold readers. Cold readers are opportunistic thieves and an important distinction. When pretending to be clairvoyant, cold readers are adept at visual cues from a person's body language, clothing, and facial expressions. Phone readings can't rely on the visual to reveal but can overgeneralize or stay quiet long enough for the caller to help them. Numerous times I've witnessed clients who get uncomfortable … think I need help and start downloading information. Please keep this in mind when using a hotline service because cold readers know its effective.

The Barnum effect, was coined in 1956 by Psychologist Paul Meeh's as a *"psychological phenomenon whereby individuals give high accuracy ratings to descriptions of their personality that supposedly are tailored specifically to them, that are in fact vague and general enough to apply to a wide range of people."* The examples on the following page review some techniques to watch out for. Be careful to not confuse an isolated point as an indicator. In other words, use common sense like hearing a compliment isn't a conclusion, and vise-versa.

information is vague or general, that can apply to anyone

Cold readers know to placate the ego can be seductive. The reason is from one detail most aren't aware of; a large percentage of the population believe they have a special purpose. Maybe it's true but doesn't mean that purpose isn't susceptible to a con's manipulation that reveal hidden psychic powers. We discussed natural intuition previously and would suggest reviewing the finer points. This will be helpful for the cold reader who knows the right buttons to push for a reaction especially during times being treated like anything but. Again, it isn't that you aren't, it's to recognize the motivation behind the words.

There have been more than a few times I've recognized a client with abilities and times when compliments are legitimate. Both can be backed up with specific details connecting, not vague or generalized.

Body language. (In-person or video call readings) A cold reader is proficient in reading subtle body language or non-verbal cues. Finding tell-tale signs of strong emotions show in different ways Cold readers play the odds for contact is because of distress. When depressed they look for signs of neglecting basic grooming. The eyes are an easy tell, looking down (guilt, embarrassment, shame, submissive), intensely staring shows they are extremely interested in what is being said, to the side depends on the question or statement. Others look for nail biting, impatient fidgeting, crossing your arms across the chest or heart as a defense or protective.

Fashion. There is something to the saying, "clothing makes the person." Let's say you're donning business attire and the questions you have focus on business. How much your shoes cost, handbags, accessories, jewelry all tell a story about a person. Casual attire isn't any different. People with money tend to buy higher end that cold readers can detect.

Asks for your birthday. Unless you are meeting with an astrologist, it is not necessary. When asked, see how much of the information is based on your astrology sign. FYI: This might be asked for identity theft. Watch for other personal information that could be used.

> *date of birth and where you were born, is 98% of what someone needs to steal someone's identity.*
>
> NBC News interview
> Frank Abagnale

Bottom Line A cold reader can't give specific details that are personal. There have been occasions where I've received messages that could apply to many people, or nervous when complementary. Sometimes the client gets a message that will happen to apply to others, and it doesn't make it wrong.

Sometimes, a client will have to struggle through hearing a compliment, and it doesn't make it wrong. Genuine abilities include specifics that can't be guessed. Cold readers say nothing specifically in particular. The first 5 minutes of the actual reading will let you know hot, cold, or just right.

Over the years, more than half of my new clients indicated intuitive experiences as the reason for contacting me like; *your name kept coming into my head suddenly* or *when I saw your picture and read about you there was a strong feeling you could help.*

Listen to your gut instinct: There are gifted psychics and mediums around the globe. Don't worry about distance affecting accuracy. Also, celebrity doesn't mean better. Guides and loved ones will influence thoughts leading you to the psychic with skill set and personality preferences.

Referrals from someone is the best approach but not always a guarantee and important the person referring give examples that could not guess.

Research, research, research. Ever go to the grocery store when you're hungry? Yep, that cheese ball with nuts or ugh! food makes sense at the time, doesn't it? It's the same when upset, crying looking for fast answers, when selecting a psychic. Patience can save a lot of money and find someone qualified who knows what they're doing.

Be patient. Taking the extra time to find a spiritual advisor significantly reduces the risk of finding undeveloped psychics or con artists.

Check digital fingerprints. Established, reputable psychics will have referrals and found on websites, other than their own. Check for previous arrests or any indicators of fraud.

Fame. Being famous is not synonymous with being the best or better. Some are famous because of their skill; some aren't famous but just as skilled.

Some have good personality traits to draw viewer attention. The benefit of celebrity psychics is how much information can be found and seeing if they feel right. Remember, there will always be negative reviews from skeptics or disgruntled clients, as well as, the overly enthusiastic that part of being a celebrity.

Rates. The reason celebrities have high dollar amounts per-hour isn't black and white greed. Their skill comes with higher expenses for shows, marketing, staff, and costs for traveling. Higher rates also prevent a 10-year waiting list from people who are drawn to celebrities.

Do your homework: go to their website and see if they are practiced in the psychic skills, you are looking for. Read reviews, not only on their site. Experience will typically have an internet footprint. Allow for one or two negative reviews, based on assumptions or not hearing what they wanted. educating the public. There are literally thousands of spiritual websites educating the public. The number reporting fraud have decreased but the goal is to educate people until they can no longer deceive anyone.

Allows too much information or asks leading questions. Highly charged emotions are susceptible to over sharing, as mentioned earlier. A psychic will stop the client from offering too many details to avoid sabotaging the validation process. This is one question clients have the most difficult time. Understanding the reading process helps clients participate more confidently. Psychic readings aren't one size fits all. Communication techniques vary, and, I'll walk you through my process when speaking to a new client, first.

how to ask questions

Should I take a job? The question 1) gives away decision making power and 2) personal accountability in case something goes wrong, later.

Let's say, the question isn't rephrased and yes, is the answer. The client is relieved hearing a definitive yes, at the same time, expects more than a one-word answer. "*Yeah, but you know what I mean…*" A definitive question, translates as knowing the exact question to ask, therefore, answers are, respectfully, as given.

The client asks, *I have been offered a new job. I'd like to know if this is the best career direction for me and any guidance specific to my career.* Rephrasing gives the clients an opportunity to hear unconsidered details to understand the bigger picture. Example, the job is a stepping stone for a better opportunity, later.

EXCEPTIONS: Continuing with example 2, and the answer seems to contradict telling a client what to do; *'yes, encourage them to take the job.'*

Clients affected by ongoing challenges can miss important signs or ignore intuition guiding them towards a destination, the next chapter in life. The same exception mentioned earlier, for serial cheaters. Why, is explained and validation given to trust when exceptions are involved.

other clues and signs

Look for words **connected to beliefs**, like *"I'm a Christian."* A psychic's religious preference is personal and not relevant to professional services.

Another clue is **statements of experience.** For example, claims of 10 years of experience should have a number of testimonials and an established digital presence that supports this (not only their website).

At no time, for any reason, will a spirit guide tell someone they have a curse, demons, dark energy attachments. Any language resulting in fear, or to over-powers personal independence. Ex., Listen to them to have (a want or promise), only they can help, etc.

Because of public awareness, words like **curse might be substituted** with acceptable practices like; clean/balance chakras, healing for emotional health. Pay attention to suggested services needed, that creates urgency and concludes with an ultimatum (the want) will or won't happen, unless. **'JUST IN CASE'** – thinking, is what they bank on.

Check for **visible certificates** for the service offered (Reiki).

Messages giving a desired outcome without validation.

Inexperience **claiming advanced or rare abilities.** Akashic records, phrases following trends. (i.e., twin flame). Explained in previous chapters.

Personal reactions, as 'guidance'; jealousy, revenge or to inflict pain. Infidelity questions. See chapter on romance.

Ask your guides. One psychic might keep coming up or into mind as the answer. Ongoing obstacles with someone you are considering to prevent the choice.

> Divine selection finds all people with the pure soul. Divine access to nurture the pure soul, finds few.

CHANNELING

Channeling messages explained earlier is recommended for any following this format of spiritual advice. Below, is an example of a *received message* clearly affected by subconscious.

higher self-reflections examples

The higher self receives truths but not universal truths, whereas, channelers surpass the meditative state into the super unconscious. Here is an example of a mid-level meditation state thought to be channeled:

When you visualize something and see and feel it happening, you send signals out into the universe. These signals then bring what you desire into your reality. This is the Law of Attraction and is one of the fundamental laws of this universe. The more positive your energy, the faster you will manifest what you want.

The most obvious clue is mentioning *The Law of Attraction* as a fundamental law of the universe. Not only is this not true, it's negligible. How does fate and destiny, as a pre-established part of the soul's plan work with this message? How is a fundamental law based on a bestselling book that also doesn't align with fate and destiny? How does the receiver know what the universe's fundamental laws are? How come I have more questions than answers.

Next, are archangel messages with the highest vibrational essence, other than God. People who love Archangels and want to connect directly, have messages from with elaborate introductions, 'I am Archangel …., bearer of light, *protector of earth and…*

…and how they imagined angels would communicate…

The lifting of peace will begin now; and you can feel this peace as many times as you wish, simply by asking me and your angel team to assist you in helping you to feel peace more frequently or even in a specific situation. You are free now and always to experience the peace that is always available to you for you are one with God now and always. Be still beloved and lift now to God- anything that you wish. Trust God now and always and I will always hear you when you call. Peace be with you beloved Peace is yours always! Love and peace to you and your family. and it is, amen, amen, amen!

It isn't a direct message from the Angels but sit's uplifting without irresponsible advice and contributes loving energy into the atmosphere.

IN GOD'S HANDS

An experience that gives me goosebumps every time I share it. A client scheduled a reading to connect with her son. As an evidential medium, the cause of a loved one's physical end is given, and, as always, there are exceptions. I began describing his personality and physical appearance, a nice looking man in his early 20's. He relayed important dates and specifics for my client to know it was him. I let my client know he wasn't letting me know how he died but the number 17 was mentioned. She began crying and asked if it was the day of his passing. It wasn't and why he wouldn't tell me made sense, "*Michele, he jumped out of the 17th floor of a hotel.*" What happened next, still gives me goosebumps.

As the words left her lips, I was inserted into his death experience where I was falling face up, in mid-air with her son. He was on my right, a few feet away his face preparing for impact. Suddenly, I saw two enormous hands appear from the sky and scooped up her son seconds before impact. We were both crying and they were tears of joy knowing the extraordinary clairvoyant experience was a gesture of profound love for a mother to remember his last breath of physical life being safe in God's hands.

AFTERWORD

Did I demonstrate psychic abilities as a child? A question psychics get asked often. I wasn't yapping with any dead relatives or saving the day with 'just in time' warnings. I knew how to help people and knew stuff.

IT WAS IN THE CARDS

At ten years old, the drive to learn about the psychic arts was so compelling. My sister, Patty, was the resident tarot reader and being four years old AND owning her own Tarot deck, there was no competition. She told me I was too young (and was right), which I interpreted as needing to learn by stealth. I walked to the Library and took out the only book on Fortune Telling. In retrospect, it bordered on absurd shelving a book in a time when residents associated it with devil worship. But, then again, the small New Jersey town didn't think it was odd to have a horse located on main street greeting the passersby by Jone's Hardware store.

With a pack of regular playing cards and a few weeks of obsessive study, I learned to use them as a tarot deck. The book instructed to practice, which required someone willing to give me direct eye contact. The elderly next-door neighbors were perfect and thought my card reading request was cute. You know those smiles you catch from two people looking at each other that silently say, just go along with it dear? I asked what they wanted to hear that was psychic. That was when the, just go along with it honey, demeanor change into both suddenly scurrying off. Apparently, the cards revealed something where they remembered needing to be somewhere.

My stint as the Bicycle Deck Tarot Psychic was short lived and wouldn't make a comeback for another fifteen years. Not because of the neighbors but the unfortunate decision my mother made bringing the family to the theatre, playing The Exorcist. My young mind was traumatized seeing a girl the same age, playing the role. The divine connection is not a fair-weather friend and never leaves: it's a relationship that walks with you patiently waiting for the right time to embrace it. At twenty-five, I opened the door once again – this time with the grown-up version of tarot cards, the Rider-Waite deck. Living on 58th street near Central Park, in New York City was walking distance to my conventional job. My life was tailored to what normal people said and what normal people did. Including, the daily cubicle grind under fluorescent lights and mind-numbing meetings with that boss believed was promoted by blackmail. One minute… a mere 60 seconds turned into hours, Monday through Friday (unless there was cake in the conference room). On the weekends and after work, time became a fast blur when my hands picked up my tarot cards secured in a crinkled burgundy velvet sack holding answers and mysteries. Fifteen years later, having a Rider-Waite deck, was as daunting as it was exciting.

It's a strange predicament when the most natural extension of yourself is edited out because it's viewed as delusional. *They say*, it's too weird to believe in *that stuff*, so I did what society expected of me; stuffed it inside, listened to the fluorescent light people recite Oprah quotes on being your true self and nodded like a good zombie fitting in, should.

"I write because I must. It's not a choice or a pastime, it's an unyielding calling and my passion," by Elizabeth Reyes. A quote capturing the soul at a primal level when passion isn't a caricature in costume. By all accounts, I was normal, wore designer couture, could talk world politics…except, I knew that woman walking by would be pregnant in a couple of months or my girlfriend's new fabulous, he's the one, boyfriend was already cheating on her. What was I supposed to do with it?

The answer was part of the grand design, I would be unaware of for many years. Including, my cousin's two eccentric friends, Steve and Steve, being a crucial piece. Upon introduction, our connection was immediate forged in goofy and shrill comments, *you're a Libra and OMG, I'm an Aries*! We had an easy groove meeting at outdoor cafés in Grammercy Park instilled in high octane cappuccinos in-hand, while pondering the esoteric of who goes bump in the night.

One of our casual cappuccino café meetings, the Steves were more shrilly than usual, bursting with excitement to tell-all on a recent adventure, *"we JUST met with A PSYCHIC and she said the MOST AMAZING things and, GET THIS – she stopped us on the sidewalk and told us that both of us have a strong need for love and affection **AND THIS BROUGHT US TOGETHER!**"* Steve and Steve could hardly contain themselves, *"You HAVE to go meet her"*, they said, and I did.

You know when you meet someone for the first time and instantly like them? This wasn't one of those moments. My thought bubbles were popping out like a Batman comic strip, seeing the psychic's chewed fingernails with blue sparkled nail polish remnants navigating me to the dining room table. I took a deep breath and told myself to stop being so judgmental and trust the Steves. What's the worst thing that could happen, right? The psychic stared at me for a few seconds without saying a word and began shuffling a worn tarot deck. We were quickly interrupted by the scuffing sound of her husband's black knee-high socked into sandals and an unidentified stain on his sleeveless white t-shirt (obviously, unconcerned by the basic dictates of fashion). He acknowledged me with a half-nod before scolding his prepubescent son, hiding behind the door, to stop staring at me. Nothing creepy at all. Breath. Logic and intuition were urging me to, go now! Before I could come up with an excuse to leave, the psychic, who desperately needed a manicure…and a husband who understands the significance of socks and sandals, touched my hand so I could see her foreboding concern stirring up the maybe's, it's possible, and what ifs. Staring at the cards, her expression deepened into trepidation forgetting about her horny son who was the only one in a trance, staring at my boobage. Did she see why my love life was darkened by heartache because of negative blah, blah, blah but this wretched blah, blah, blah that was only $80 extra? I started to rationalize with, *well, it could explain, what's his name* and *what were you thinking*.

I decided to tell her about my psychic abilities and none of my tarot readings indicated dark stuff. Here's the pay attention, part. That little tidbit raised the price to $400 with strict instructions to not touch my cards because the evil blah, blah, blah, would lie. "*Wrap up your cards in purple cloth, and throw them away.*" I didn't meet her again but she planted the *just in case seed* and for the second time my 78 friends were wrapped up and tossed in a public trash can.

Life in the conventional world estranged from my instinctive nature created a void and wondered what the universe was telling me. The answer would take many years to discover.

I continued the daily monotony in fluorescent lights shining over the muted gray wool cubicles sympathizing with Dilbert cartoon characters. At 4:58 pm, and weekends, a quest began to find a Psychic; a real one. Pursuits led to 900 numbers charging $3.99 a minute with a variety of fake accents, screaming babies or loud televisions in the background taunting me with specific generalizations, smothered in flattery. occasionally, the high phone bill paid off with a diamond in the rough with future insights that seemed to make sense but contradicted others. Knowing who was accurate started to be more confusing than the questions they were answering. I wondered how there were so many phone Psychics and with as many different conclusions. To find out, I applied for a job and see if they would hire me, without any prior experience. The online applications were answered honestly before submitting to several well-known hotlines. All replied within a day or two, offering employment with a multi-page contract of agreement outlining monetary stipulations and "for entertainment only." I make no conclusions to every person's ability, but the experience was 100%, leading me to believe even pedophiles and identity thieves, only need apply and will be hired.

Some time passed before hearing about a highly recommended Psychic and was encouraged she had a waiting list. For sure, this was a good sign. On the day of my anticipated appointment, I went to her upscale New York City apartment and handed her $400. My one-hour psychic reading left me hopefully confused with '*great news*' predictions, in my future, but nothing mentioned about my past or current life. A year of, waiting for happy times later, her mug shot appeared on the local news, reading the caption, "Psychic Arrested for Fraud." Another two years would go by before a close conservative friend got the courage to admit talking to a Psychic. He had no idea about my abilities that were highly guarded from any I perceived would roll their eyes at such a ludicrous idea (and no, if I was psychic). My excitement interrogated him with reciting words that couldn't be guessed.

He said, "she knew, without me telling her anything specific about my life, about (name of his daughter), I'm going through divorce and details specific to, AND, described (wife's name) personality… and, you know that isn't easy." An understatement, for anyone who knows her. His almost ex-wife is a 5'4" red-headed tornado with suspicious big brown eyes framed in a creamy white freckled complexion and scared the shit out of her 6'4" husband and anyone in her path. He handed me her card and we spoke a few weeks later.

Timing is everything, with the appointment coincidentally coinciding a few days after a sudden breakup and a broken heart who could only find solace hearing, *"you two will get back together."* The voice on the phone was soft spoken and after a few minutes of introductions and general non-specific chit-chat, she found the perfect words to open the emotional floodgates. *Michele, you are calling about a recent heartbreak, is that correct?* 3-2-1, boom! Yes, and I just want to know, and how does he feel about me, and he said, and then I said, and will we, and…and…and… She didn't have a chance as I continuously interrupted her in a torrent of fears, masked in confident control. Patiently, she waited to speak and ask if she could continue. Her abilities as a psychic validated unguessable details but allowed a lovesick, unruly client offering too much information. In a two month period we spoke several times; each with an obsessed agenda to squeeze any detail I could out of the Gods.

Our last reading provided amazing insights she managed to get in about my future professionally, but, and, and, and didn't give it much thought since it didn't include my ex-boyfriend's name in a sentence. She said, *"I'm seeing a bookcase with several books and your name as the author. Michele, you are going to be a well-known public figure or speaker and it's somehow connected to writing these books."*

In retrospect, a quote comes to mind from Carl Jung, *"The pendulum of the mind alternates between sense and nonsense, not between right and wrong."* Seeking answers from the beyond with a mind distracted on the heart is determined to control the destination towards relief.

Fast forward, new guy, getting married, my son born and moving from Hoboken after 9-11, prestigious job, buying a house, hurricane + trees = substantial damage, work under new management, fired from job and leaving the conventional world. For good.

I dived head first back into the comfortable arms of my metaphysical lover and reunited with intense passion. My abilities responded quickly, with daily practice and diligent study but would not be enough on its own. A mental inventory of every crappy, mediocre and genuine reading was reviewed, making it a priority to people to provide clear guidance, clear validation and honor an ethical code. For two years, I immersed myself in course work that included Dr. Chips Hypnosis Development, being trained and sponsored by a Master Hypnotherapist for NGH Certification, one-on-one advanced study with a Georgetown University Professor with two Ph.D.'s and author of 30 books, mentored with a Psychic-Healer and Guru of Eastern Philosophy, completed Usui Reiki Certification, flew to California for EFT training and Psychic Medium Lisa William's Mediumship Workshop Seminar. In my free time, I read, including the book that would dramatically shift how I thought, The Sleeping Prophet (Edgar Cayce), meditated every day, ghost hunting with a paranormal group or practicing on friends who were more than happy to volunteer as psychic guinea pigs.

Psychic advancement required learning a metaphorical language, being in-tune to what my sensory body was saying and clearing my mind completely from my belief center for messages to be given, as given. What I couldn't see was how the constant focus to perfect my abilities prevented me from gaging my level of development. It took a friend burst into laughing, thirty minutes into a tarot reading and me nervously asking if my accuracy was off, to find out. She shook her head and said, *Michele, are you aware, you stopped looking at the cards 25 minutes ago, and telling me things my mother doesn't even know?* No, I didn't and tested my wings flying solo.

On New Year's Eve, Bill, an elderly gentleman I regularly lost racquetball to, asked if I would mind giving him a reading. We met at our regular coffee place, on one of those balmy days that randomly inserts itself into winter's monotony and bringing life into the outdoor patio. From this point on, everything changed.

Bill assumed my tarot cards were with me, not updated on my recent psychic developments and even after several minutes reassuring him, the concerned expression lingered. I sat back thinking how to proceed when a clairvoyant image of a man in his early 30's, made an appearance. Without introduction, he said, *"tell him he has 2 children."* According to our racquetball chit-chat, Bill had one daughter. Mentally, I refused. The unexpected visitor insisted, *"Tell him."*

"Bill, I'm being told you have 2 kids." He looked at me like I lost my mind saying, "Michele, I know how many kids I have and it's one! See, this is why the cards are better." In the background, I heard the man asking me gently to relay what he said, *"you had a baby boy that died and he's here, He knows you're worried about moving his grave to another location."* No exaggeration, as the words left my lips, several sparrows began dive bombing Bill, sometimes only a few inches from his head like they were part of the message, somehow. Defiantly and holding back tears, *"well, if it's my son, ask him what I named him."*

"He was never named but he saying you called him Junior when you talked to him, privately. You stopped doing that and wants you to know, he heard you and misses the conversations." Bill's blue eyes welled up in tears, nodding his head in acknowledgement saying, not even my wife knows I called him Junior. Thirty years after his baby son's short visit on Earth, Bill said he felt peace knowing his son was alive in spirit, and safe.

We left in a state of astonished wonder, witnessing Heaven's message of love finding its way to a father. Moments like these are why I love what I do and brings joy to my heart when I think of the truly gifted mediums who devote their lives to connect Earth momentarily with the divine residents.

My *discovering me* journey officially transitioned into being a full-time professional psychic medium, and validated when featured in a well-known publication with high praise of "chilling accuracy." Only one experience was missing and it was an important one.

The Psychic Fair was an opportunity to connect with the spiritual community, insights on the supernatural climate and see what's what. I entered the indoor fairgrounds complex and signed up for a Doreen Virtue class on Angel numbers, with time to shop for sparkly things and get a reading. The main area smelled of wanderlust and Patchouli filled hemp totes walking into a sea of one-of-a-kind hand-made novelties and trinkets. The lightworker community offered a diversity of craftsmanship from hand carved Buddha statues, wind chimes, dream catchers crystal jewelry to an array of magical paraphernalia.

A section was cordoned off with a large banner where the psychics congregated. I entered leaving behind the hustle and bustle of the crowd hoping to find someone to give me a reading. There were approximately a dozen tables set up in a single row with each displaying a sign of the service offered. I slowly walked past each one letting my intuition guide me. One by one, I felt an uneasiness until my body lightened when I approached an attractive African-American woman with gentle features sitting quietly looking at me with a curious expression. Her energy was effervescent and began by offering amazingly astute insights about my son. We had ten minutes and didn't have anything specific to ask and decided on allowing the divine choose the guidance. She closed her eyes and nodded, and asked me for my hand and looked closer pointed to the big "M," in my palm. *This is a mark I was told to show you and has significance* while outlining it with the tip of her finger. Palmistry is fascinating but I had little to no knowledge and just thought everyone's palm lines intersected, similarly.

"Your hand also says you are very psychic, interested in the esoteric arts, had experiences with almost drowning and sensitive to electro-magnetic fields (EMF)," and suggested removing the television in my bedroom. When she was done explaining, I stared at her with a thought bubble, she got all that from my hand? What was profoundly accurate was how I almost drowned. I did, three times, two of which, I know God intervened to save me. She was the first Psychic to mention the esoteric arts, and being at a Psychic Fair as a customer, not a vendor, left me speechless. The EMF comment blew my mind, remembering a time when ghost hunting and our tech guy and founder was frustrated trying to figure out his $5,000 EMF meter kept spiking saying "unless the area was jammed up with spirits, it didn't make sense." He checked batteries and other technical issues, before suddenly pointing the device directly at me and immediately the EMF meter went to red. He shook his head and began laughing, discovering I was the culprit. Those last ten minutes restored my faith, and her words lingered for a long time.

It took years of hard work to walk the path so many tried to take away, ridicule, or saying my reality didn't exist. Was it worth it? Absolutely. What did I learn from it? If you want to play in *a supernatural sandbox, you better know which one is quicksand.*

Thank you for spending part of your journey with me.

SOURCE'S GUIDE TO ENLIGHTENMENT

all consciousness

is multidimensionally aware of every moment happening, linear lines concurrent and simultaneous timelines.

attain

one seeks the self-connection within to uncover and expose into the light the heavy words from the past called expectations, morals, definitions of being good, intelligent, accomplished, faithful, worthy, normal, unique. The dowry called fortitudes. One then, can re-define as the first step on the individual path to self- into and lightened.

awaken

is the path of discovery of self, without fear's compromise to please others

Christ Consciousness

is the soul, individually and proudly, friends with, as the truest most profound definition - a companion for comfort, the Father for strength and safety, the Mother to feel protected, nurtured as a child, prayed to for guidance or release despair, connected in conversations, inquiring about God, too, as a gesture of love and as friends do. The path of the human soul is this. To rediscover the connection automatically understood, Heavenly. To seek the individual potential, called purpose, through the travails and the glory. To allow the light of the internal glory to radiate into the world without apology to those who respond with limitations judgment - fearful to find their own light.

free will

thoughts allowed time to process below what's already been decided, above.

higher consciousness

is the awakened to the Divine connection, individually purposed, as all life is connected with shared purpose -- to inspire others to be individually dynamic, discover what's inherent, recognizes when the self or others enslave minds through ignorance or fear called encouragement's wisdom, posed as teachers, not awakened to the Divine connection.

I AM

is the soul who walks and can only be the self-defined, for no other's purposed tradition, heritage belief or life -- as all and any found as the commonality to attain personal mastery. Some call this removing illusion, as ye are born without.

manifesting reality or mind matters

is the awareness of ethers answering prayers, and prayers are what one holds as principles believable, requests to results already fated, provisionally timed for all included and at the Creator's discretion when fated time ignored direction, of the internal compass.

mind mapping

Emotions are the inner soul guide to recognize, why and when heightened responses of lower vibrations occur.

near death experience

The spirit of the physical body manifest leaves the body for one minute or several, into the realm of all-time awareness and conscious reality, Heavenly. Experiences are not random and has purpose. Adults, witness one of three choices: 1) redirect the mind to truth of spirit, 2) soul knowing the pure spirit, 3) the soul returns infused with the Heavenly Spirit, to fulfill a purpose.
The child is specific for innocence of life to witness, and give witness to others. Children describing memories as experienced, advanced beyond maturity's imagination or comprehension is a difficult partner for rationalization's dance to dismiss. Upon returning, the two worlds of the body and mind in spirit remain forever linked; the psyche of the child select remains with "a knowing" of eternal life, that is.

a psychic journey

knowledge of the past, present and future, embodies the soul agreement.

reincarnation

is time slotted for soul perfection to create individualized stories each unique combined with all souls as the clue to the vastness of The Creator as all and every is.

soul agreements

is the inherent intuited mind within the incarnated spirit, joining the physical body to ascend above primal instincts found in duplicity of re-occurrences.

to self-empower

...is to believe you do not already have to attain, that what is.
Remembering, discovering, or removing falsities of what you are, is accurate.
How the belief and the power given to, gives the self to another or circumstance, undeserving. Give yourself, to those who will cherish and cherish themselves.

what is with purpose

will not ever find illusion when the extent of comprehension is fully realized.

what is dark energy?

It is true to describe, dark energy forces. It is not true, as one physical being or supernatural entity. Dark energy exists in the universe, has life forms, other than Earth beings practicing it, has humans on Earth, believing it or contributors of it. It, is the absoluteness of the power of thought and power of association, called static, or stagnant belief. Thoughts of pain- to hurt another, thoughts for power for the self and not the people to benefit, thoughts of lust without the other's consent of the body, thoughts to influence or manipulate souls for personal outcomes harming others quality of life.

what are advanced beings?

As there is no hierarchy in Heaven, there is a system and structure of, and in, the variety of assignments to assist my children while in the physical form. You may see them as extraterrestrials but these are none other than the souls advanced, the soul very advanced, or the soul considered complete.

what is truth

- Truth equals the action for the sum-total of equal results.
- Truth intuitively quiets upon hearing when absolutely.
- When "a truth" lingers in variant levels it equals percentages of truth.
- Un-truths equal an uneasy or anxious body.

The path of every soul to know, is one word shrouded in the complexities of intricate wisdom.

- Truth of, removes fear, pain, and false ego.
- Truth is God Supremacy as prayed for.
- Truth does not self-empower or negotiate, it simply is.
- Truth bends to find truth for another to be.

what is absolute truth

Truth in absolutes is love, interchangeable and exquisitely, the equal same no physical being in human or any sentient existence can comprehend.

what is a Godhead?

A collective force of completed souls, or elder souls living as one able to extract from and into physical form as an incarnated life or temporary visitation.

Lords of Karma

a phrase created, becoming identifiable, in time. The title bestowed was devised from a young mid-level soul with the gift of wisdom's words. "Overseers" and/or "Ancients" is more accurate. Prana Ancient Overseers, as the most accurate human words could define. They are part of the engineering for life to succeed "life contracts" or specific goals outlined pre-birth, individually, and collectively. **Sanat Kumara**

karma is not karma

(God, continues) Let's begin with shedding some needed light on accepted spirituality fundamentals. Moralities of what is right or wrong, good, or bad, has been misunderstood as karma. "the experience of individual souls to accomplish the re-perfection of itself through timelines and contrasting lives; as every race, creed, gender, religion, physicality, one life to the next. What goes around is the circle of life, never defined as revenge."

In the truest sense, there is no such word to define a soul's journey. Individual souls will focus on lives to accumulate knowledge in specific areas, some may choose more than one [area of study], with a concentration [major focus] to develop; like a Master's Degree in Architecture, minoring in Ancient History or a specific culture to cultivate a design style. Every soul decides "goals" to achieve and achieve is defined by acquiring or over coming, instilled as triggered environmental reactions, such as; meeting a person, traveling to a destination, personality types or any situation creating an atypical heightened response. When a lifetime seems to be filled with the overflow of challenges, two separate goals are set to achieve. There are no punishments for being "bad" from a past life, or "what goes around, comes around" resulting in dire consequences. Contrast experience is to know what being a husband is in one life, and not married, in another. Highly educated and the school of hard knocks. It will never be one who was murdered and a murderer, or, any role of extreme hostility. This, absolutely serves no purpose.
As the agreement also includes free will when humans choose to:

- follow the internal-intuitive-inclinations, connected to the divine cord, called grace, or...logic's thoughts of humans, without the full knowing of their being.

As all life is created from God, not all life decides or listens to the internal God-self; the paradox of the created connection and the independent choice, of will. To know your neighbor's joys and plights is the wisdom, in their shoes. Any who rank above another, judge their own past or probable future to exist. The lives of every past brought forth into the current of life, decides the future to define.

free will

Free will and prayers are words that influence decisions and a way of life. Because of their significance, I asked God to explain for full comprehension.
Free will was given for objectives to conclude with every and each to have complete awareness of their actions for the results in the Heavens, succumbing to the inclinations and desires without end.
For the people to know those who lead for destruction over a group, country, or monopolizing power spreading backwards time over the masses. One decision affecting millions or billions, is always allowed but what is not understood when allowed, is not free will of the individual compromising other's free will, en-masse. The most complex advanced life forms have mistaken conceptually the truest definition, in its simplicity.

- Free will of the individual does not affect another.
- Free will affecting the course of humanity to conclude with affects over thousands of lifetimes, is at My discretion.

Free will and God's intervention. Is this a request, or decided when needed? Also, how is it... What percentage are achieving goals versus the number going off path or against their soul code?

Free will is not contingent on what choice or circumstance, rather the time allotted to stay, resolve the choice or circumstance. Every decision acted upon is known before becoming linked into the fabric or web lines surrounding the earths auric atmosphere. Thoughts are vibrational energy. Depending on the thought – from one powerful enough to penetrate the atmosphere, or many with the same thought creating a thought collective; can strengthen or weaken a present or future action. A direct thought, request or prayer in sadness, anger, pain, joy or jubilation reaches Me when the result is for betterment or love, affecting one or many.

It is not, every human is responsible for all actions; as this is an impossibility for any soul to be everywhere or interfere with individual's choice. Souls are created individually to experience, as, or I would have created, otherwise.

Personal prayers are similar, when not only for the self, but for the self and connected to another. Unto the self we have discussed. The exception, as there always are when the mind is clouded from ongoing pain unable to see past it when the mind is filled with only uncertainty and questions from others, as previously discussed. Most of the world's population do not pray for the world's relief from tormentors, they ask why I allow, for one or their family, to harm one responsible for hurting. Very few, pray for love and harmony or healing for all my children.

Spiritualists of Zen teach how to receive for individual fortitude, personal gain and those who focus on this, are motivated to achieve in the ego to elevate over others. By organization, God's will, is invoked without revocation; not separating. My will is for only love as the outcome. What is allowed or not, is a complex answer contingent on the effect, group collective thoughts, including perception of God's will, and individual prayers all happening as one song. The melody and lyrics can be soothing or gruesome.

Laughter is impenetrable, the highest vibration when pure. The children heal earth every day, in their absolute-from the belly-to outward boisterous music. A child not ...is an unhappy home with few exceptions

what is a prayer

Music found in love for another to rejoice, again, out of grief or pain. Love, for the self to remove the dark thoughts into the light, when feeling despair. Words for hope, when little is felt or found. Words requesting My guidance, in purpose to be and know. The connection to My Holy Spirit, called faith, when little evidence is seen, knowing I love you when loneliness prevails as the only experience remembered. Asking to be comforted for the self or another. The whispers of all find Me and all are answered, when and how, at My discretion for, when the outcome and who the outcome, aligns with every person, affected. When prayers requested are not, reasons find what is, unconsidered or known, with the request viewed from one moment, one side, one outcome, not able to see past or all the variables. Saving one soul could be the sacrifice of many. Re-uniting a loved one to ease heartache interferes with future destinies, unknown. All has reason, to be or to be another, for love and as love.

MODALITIES PRACTICES & TERMINOLOGY

MODALITIES

Acupuncture: involves thin, sterile needles inserted painlessly into pressure points along the meridian lines in the body in the body, releasing Qi energy to relieve pain and balance yin and yang.

angel healing: connects with the divine through meditation and prayer. Requests for healing emotional, physical, or mental conflicts are heard and communicated with an angel assigned. Results are not always obvious or immediate, contingent on individual life paths of chosen experiences.

aromatherapy: uses the fragrance of oils extracted from natural ingredients in a distillation process, containing concentrated levels of a plant or flower's healing properties, also known as, Essential oils

aura reading: the ability to perceive "energy fields" surrounding people, places, and things

Ayurvedic Healing: between 3000 – 5000 years ago and considered to be one of the world's most sophisticated and powerful mind-body health systems. Ayurveda is a science of life (*Ayur* = life, *Veda* = science or knowledge). It offers a body of wisdom designed to help people stay vibrant and healthy while realizing their full human potential.

binaural beats: are an auditory illusion perceived by the brain when two slightly different frequencies of sound are played into each ear (bi – two, aural- ear) to shift the way the brain processes information.

biofeedback: is the process of gaining greater awareness of many physiological functions primarily using instruments that provide information on the activity of those same systems, with a goal of being able to manipulate them at will.

Craniosacral Therapy non-invasive touch to affect the pressure and circulation of cerebrospinal fluid around the brain and spinal cord. This process is thought to relieve pain and dysfunction.

Emotional Freedom Technique (EFT) by tapping along the meridians while repeating statements specific to blocked or traumatic thoughts, pent up emotions, re-directs association allowing a free flow of energy.

energy healing: A psychic ability to clear, repair and balance the body's energy systems by seeing and manipulating the aura. Reiki is a popular form of energy healing. **energy medicine**: The ability to heal with one's own empathic etheric, astral, mental, or spiritual energy

Feng Shui: a system of laws considered to govern spatial arrangement and orientation in relation to the flow of energy (qi),

I Ching: An ancient Chinese system of prophetic philosophy and has long been used as an oracle. The I Ching is based around a set of 64 abstract line arrangements called hexagrams. Each Hexagram is composed of six stacked horizontal lines with each line is either Yang which has an unbroken solid line, or Yin which has a broken line with a gap in the center.

kinesiology: technique in alternative medicine to diagnose illness or choose treatment by testing muscles for strength and weakness

medical intuitive: alternative medicine practitioner who use intuitive abilities to find the cause of a physical or emotional condition through the use of insight rather than modern medicine.

medium: a psychic who connects with and acts as a communication conduit for spirits in the afterlife and/or guiding entities such as angels. **mediumship** or *channeling* – Communicating with spirits.

palmistry: a form of divination using the lines and structure found on the hand. The earliest form of palmistry, also known as, chiromancy has been dated all the way back to 384–322 B.C.E.

psychic reading: *precognition, premonition* and *precognitive* information of past, present events, as well as, predictions or events known before they happen.

psychic healing: ability to sense illness and heal

psychic medium: a channel or conduit in communication with guides, angels, spirits or those that have passed on.

psychic tarot reader: a person with extra sensory perception who uses the imagery from tarot cards to gain knowledge or awareness of past, present, and future events. See also tarot Reader.

psychometry: ability to obtain information about a person or an object by touch.

Qigong: directs the Qi, through physical movements and meditation to balance the energy within the body and stillness within the mind.

regression hypnosis: technique accessing the unconscious mind and previous lifetimes to explain current life inclinations. There is a lot of information and suggested to research.

reflexology: The physical act of applying pressure to the feet, hands, or ears with specific thumb, finger, and hand techniques without the use of oil or lotion. It's based on a system of reflex areas on the foot corresponding to areas of the body, when manipulated can improve health through one's qi.

Reiki: Use of symbols connected to universal energy transferred through the practitioners using gentle touch to activate the body's natural healing processes to restore physical and emotional well-being. Based on *qi* ("chi"), the universal life force, developed in Japan in 1922 by Mikao Usui.

Rolfing: body manipulation devised by Ida Rolf (1896–1979) claimed by practitioners to be capable of ridding the body of traumatic memories storied in the muscles.

shamanism: a practice involving a practitioner reaching altered states of consciousness in order to perceive and interact with what they believe to be a spirit world and channel these transcendental energies into this world.

spiritual/ intuitive coaching: the divine forces assist in uncovering core issues at a deeper level affecting life habits, behaviors and goals.

tarot reading: a person with an understanding of the archetypal meanings of tarot Cards able to intuit cards in a prophetic way.

therapeutic touch: form of vitalism where a practitioner, who may be also a nurse, passes their hands over and around a patient to realign or rebalance a putative energy field.

PARAPSYCHOLOGY TERMINOLOGY

The study of existence and causes of psychic abilities and life after death.

apportation: materialization, disappearance, or teleportation of an object.

automatic writing: also called psychography, (often defined incorrectly) is a form of channeling the insights from other dimensional beings accessing the unconscious. Individuals involuntarily channeling are not trained and should stop writing

astral projection: or mental projection – An out-of-body experience in which an astral body becomes separate from the physical body.

bi-location or multilocation: simultaneously be in multiple places at the same time.

clairvoyance: or second sight: perception outside the known human senses.

clairaudience or clear hearing is the ability to hear beyond the natural sense from disembodied celestial beings.

claircognizant: clear knowing.

clairempathy: to feel emotions from beyond natural realms.

clairsentience refers to a psychic's ability to pick up sensations and relate messages from those sensations.

clairscentient means being able to smell aroma beyond physical levels.

clairtangency; see psychometry.

clairgustance refers to taste. some psychics will be able to pick up certain tastes while conducting a reading.

cleromancy: ancients would cast stones, pebbles, or bones for divinatory meanings. Later dice became more popular.

divination: related to *divinus*, '**divine**', or "to be inspired by God practice of seeking knowledge of the future or the unknown by supernatural means.

divine intervention; spontaneous spiritual visions to guide and direct the seer.

dreams: interpretation of symbolism and metaphors at the subconscious level as clues to the state of mind that differs from prophetic dreams.

dowsing: a technique for searching for underground water, minerals, or anything invisible, by observing the motion of a pointer (traditionally a forked stick, now often paired bent wires) or the changes in direction of a pendulum, supposedly in response to unseen influences.

empathy: ability to relate to another's emotional or physical feelings, without personally experiencing first hand. Whereas, sympathy, relates to other's grief to provide comfort.

empath: intuitively senses the emotional body of others with levels of intensities.

Extra Sensory Perception or ESP: Perception beyond the physical senses.

graphology: The analysis of the psychological structure of the human subject through his or her handwriting

intuition: heightened sensory, insight, awareness or clairvoyance.

Ki: Life Force Energy. - Ki (Japanese), **Chi** (Chinese), **Prana** (Indian). (Reiki comes from the Japanese words Rei meaning God or Higher Power and Ki which is Life Force Energy.

levitation: Physical body capable of rising or floating.

lucid dreaming: The ability to wake up inside a dream and experience an alternate reality. Can be like Astral Projection.

meditation: is a process of training your mind to focus and redirect your thoughts. It is not daydreaming or similar, which are levels of lighter trance. Meditation is a state becoming still within, until the mind becomes silent, without distraction.

meridians: Our bodies contain meridians, or energy lines, that flow up or down. Meridian focused energy healing releases the blockages so you have more energy in your present-day reality.

metagnomy: psychic ability while in a hypnotic trance.

metaphysics: branch of philosophy on the first principles of things, and concepts of being, knowing, substance, cause, identity, time, space.

mystic: an initiate of the secret teachings of the ancients. One who believes in the existence of paranormal or metaphysical reality.

oracle: person or system who divines the future. A mystic or psychic can be an oracle. Divination tools are considered oracles, like the tarot, I Ching, Runes.

out of body experience: OOBE. sensation of floating outside of one's body and in some cases, seeing one's physical body outside oneself.

parapsychology: interdisciplinary field for the study of all forms of extra sensory phenomena.

past life regression: process of hypnosis or meditative visualization for reliving or discovering previous experiences of one's previous lives.

pendulum: crystal or weighted object on a chain or string used as a communication method with divine entities, hovering or swinging side to side, over words, letters or a yes/no while a question is posed

precognition: forecasting the future, obtained through ESP

psi: generic term referring to all psychic phenomena, experiences, or events related to the psyche, or mind, and which cannot be explained by established physical principles.

psi-gamma: ability to acquire information through non-sensory or nonphysical methods (telepathy, **clairvoyance** and **precognition**)

psi-kappa: ability to affect or move physical objects through nonphysical methods (telekinesis and psychic healing).

psychic: ESP. precognition, *premonition* and *precognitive dreams* – Perception of events before they happen.

psychography: automatic writing technique producing information by means of extra sensory perceptions of spiritual dimensions.

psychometry: psychic sense of touch. A psychometrist obtains intuitive impressions and information by holding or connecting with an object or person.

pyrokinesis: is the ability to start and control fires with the mind.

psychokinesis/telekinesis: ability to manipulate objects by the power of thought.

radiesthesia: dowsing with rods or a pendulum. Radiesthesia is a Latin origin meaning sensitivity to radiation. The rod or pendulum can amplify a dowser's sensitivity to electromagnetic fields.

remote viewing: astral projection in that it involves the projection of consciousness to remote locations.

retrocognition or *post-cognition*: Perception of past events.

Runes: were first used over 1500 years ago in Scandinavia. They formed an early alphabet known as Futhark after its first six letters: F –U-th-A-R-K. The name 'rune' originally meant secret or mystery, were considered magical signs for charms and divination.

scrying: psychic gazing or seeing. As in gazing into a crystal ball or seeing through a reflective surface.

smudging: a symbolic exercise found in feng shui practice, many Native American traditions, and alternative healing practices. It involves burning selected herbs or other materials to clear negative energy.

telekinesis: see psychokinesis

telepathy: origin means distant-feeling. Using extra sensory perception for communication between minds over distance or through any barrier. Transfer of thoughts, words, or emotions in either direction.

transfiguration: spirit superimposes its face on the medium's face, and those in the room can see the visible characteristics of a deceased person's face

Voodoo, vodun: African word for "spirit" often misrepresented by popular movies; i.e., sticking pins in voodoo dolls was a means of teaching a healing technique by identifying pressure points like acupuncture. Hollywood has created the myth of Voodoo being a method of inflicting a curse.

Wicca: western esotericism drawing upon a diverse set of ancient pagan and 20th century hermetic motifs for theological and nature based ritual practices.

Ying Yang: Chinese philosophy of two primal opposing but complementary forces found in all things in the universe.

Zen: means meditative concentration. Zen Mind is an ideal state of mind for developing psychic awareness.

BIBLIOGRAPHY

Article, T. W. (n.d.). *Initiation*. Manila: Copyright by the Theosophical Publishing

Avalon Malibu Psychiatrist, (. (2017, July 25). Retrieved from Ghosting In Dating Could Be A Sign Of Mental Illness: https://www.avalonmalibu.com

Besant, A. (1923). *Initiation - The Perfecting of Man*. The Theosophical Press.

Bowden, H. (1977). *The Dictionary of American Religious Biography*. London: Greenwood Press.

Britannica, E. (1956). The Barnum Effect. (263-272). Meese, *Wanted A Good Cookbook*

Cayce, E. (1971, 1993 -2007). *Edgar Cayce Readings*. Retrieved from Area for Research and Enlightenment, Edgar Cayce Foundation.

CIA. (1998, December 8). *Is an ancient form of energy providing China's children with the miracle of second sight?* Retrieved from CIA.gov: https://www.cia.gov

Dr. Erickson, B. H. (2017). *What is Ericksonian*. (2012, January 28). Retrieved from World Records Academy: https://www.worldrecordacademy.com

Forbes. (n.d.). Medium Helps Law Enforcement Solve the Unsolvable. 165-166.

Freud, S. (1914). *The Psychopathology of Everyday Life*. NYC: The Macmillan Co.

T. T. (1973). *Helena Petrovna Blavatsky*. Krotona, CA: Theosophical Publishing

Gray, E. (1970). *A Complete Guide to the Tarot*. Bantam.

Hypnosis Motivation Institute, H. N. (2019). *Hypnosis Terms and Definitions*.

Ingo Swann. (2014). Retrieved from Psi Encyclopedia: https://psi-encyclopedia.spr.ac.uk/articles/ingo-swann

Jim Popkin. (2015, November 12). *Former Pentagon Scientist Who Says Psychics Can Help American Spies*. Retrieved from newsweek.com:

Kaleej Times. (2013, April 2). Retrieved from Mind reading Sharjah Girl 'exceedingly rare' savant: https://www.khaleejtimes.com

Leadbeater, C. W. (1992). *The Masters and the Path, Part III. The Great Initiations*. Adyar, Madras: Theosophical Publishing.

Masters, R. A. (n.d.). Spiritual Bypassing: When Spirituality Disconnects Us From What Really Matters. In R. A. Masters.

Michael Tompkins, E. (2014, August 24). Difference of Sociopath-Psychopath. (M. By Kara Mayer Robinson Reviewed by Joseph Goldberg, Interviewer)

Newton, D. M. (1995). *Journey of Souls*. Woodbury, MN: Llewellyn Publications.

Nostradamus. (1555). *Little, Brown and Company*. Lyon.

O'Donnell, D. P. (1972). *Johnny, We Hardly Knew Ye;*. United States of America: Little, Brown and Company.

Parapshychology Foundation, I. (2017). *Parapsychology Basic Terms*.

Paul Dong, T. E. (n.d.). *China's Super Psychic Children*. Da Capo Press.

PSI Encyclopedia. (n.d.). Retrieved from D.D. Home, Stefan Ossowiecki, Etta-Wriedt: https://psi-encyclopedia.spr.ac.uk/articles/

Pyrokinesis: *3-Year old Child from Iloilo* . (2011, March 24). Retrieved from Philipine News: https://philnews.ph

Riis, J. (1890). *How the Other Half Lives: Studies among the Tenements*. New York. New York: Charles Scribner's Sons.

Roberts, J. (1970). *The Seth Materials*. Englewood Cliffs, NJ: Prentiss Hall.

Smith, O. (2015, November 5). *Copyright ©2019 Daily Express*. Retrieved leading scientists that 'telepathy exists': https://www.express.co.uk

Socieity, T. (n.d.). *The Comte St. Germain*. Retrieved from Introduction quote: www.wikipedia.com

Starlab Institute, A. R. (n.d.). Thought Transfer.

Stearn, J. (1967). *The Sleeping Prophet*. New York: Doubleday.

Surowiecki, J. (1998). What Psychic Friends Failed to Foresee. *Slate Magazine Online*, slate.com/articles/arts/the_motley_fool

Talbot, M. (n.d.). The Convulsionairres. In M. Talbot, *The Holographics Universe*.

The Psychic Children. (n.d.). Retrieved from psychicchildren.co.uk/1-3-ChinaSuperPsychics.html

The Rider-Waite Tarot Deck. (n.d.). Retrieved from www.wikipedia.com

Times, L. A. (1987). Woman Wins False Arrest Suit Against LAPD. *Psychic Vision*, p. 166.

University of California Museum of Paleontology. (2019, January 3). *ESP: What can science say?* Understanding Science : <http://www.understandingscience.org

Vries, b. M. (2021, April 8). *Managing a Chronic Complainer*. Retrieved from managing-a-chronic-complainer: https://hbr.org

INDEX

5th dimension, 107, 117
Akashic Records, 109, 130, 138
Andromeda's Muse, 23, 181
Angels, 158, 186, 256, 274
   angelic host, 205
   angelic choir, 150
   angelic realm, 157
   Michael, St., 101, 155, 158
   Seraphim, 159
Ascended Masters, 67, 149, 161, 186
astral plane, 61, 101, 113, 117, 155
astrology, 11, 93, 102, 137, 248
   Jupiter, 101
   sun, planets, moons, 102
Atlantis, 177, 179
Barnum Effect, the, 251
bilocation, 109
book of life, 88, 112, 130, 138, 153
central nervous system, 107
chakras, 57, 111
China's Super Psychic Children
   Omni Magazine, 231
Christ Consciousness, 68, 149
CIA, 226, 229
clairvoyance, *(see senses)* 60, 277
collective shifts, 186
conscious, 99, 276
   subconscious, 56, 69, 78, 108, 120, 212
   super unconsciousness, 109, 113
   universal consciousness, 59, 105, 187
cosmic assistance, 111
   Anunnaki, 186
   Arcturian, 129, 163, 186, 247
   Centurions, The, 126
   Germain, St. Comte, 11, 46, 98, 124
   Kumara, Sanat, 113, 141
   Pleiadians, 163, 186
death, 124, 137, 276
déjà vu, 121
divination, 115, 249, 277
   augury, 92
   crystal ball, 92
   palmistry, 93, 265
   tarot, 96

divine law, 142, 155, 247
DNA, 89, 107, 117, 137
dreams, 18, 164, 170, 179, 205, 224, 277
electromagnetic fields (EMF), 279
energy, 61, 98, 247, 274
   auras, 177
   energy signature, 106, 117, 183
   holographic, 61, 106
   vampires, 51
   vibrations, 72, 98, 106, 126
ESP, 60, 108, 115, 230, 237, 277
Forbes, 228
fortune teller, 13, 92, 248
free will, 179
gate keepers, (see spirit guides) 111
ghosts, 205 (see paranormal)
God, 32, 63, 70, 88, 113, 121, 129, 203,
   217, 248, 256, 265
   godhead, 36, 110, 151, 156, 269
Harvard Medical School, 226
healing, 177, 274
heaven, 36, 83, 120, 137, 170
hypnosis, 9, 119, 262, 275
Jupiter, 130 *(see Astrology, way stations)*
karmic journey, 139
key of souls, the, 112
key word sectors, 127, 143
kinesiology, 111
mediums, 20, 35, 61, 215, 264, 275
   celebrity, 79
   cryptic messages, 34
   grief/grieving, 32, 78
   family reunions, 33
   meditation, 58, 64, 69, 115, 277
   newly departed, 31
   trance-communication, 108, 111, 108
mind mapping, 66
mental matrix, 108, 121
multi-verse, the, 98, 155
natural intuition, 52, 97, 114, 152
NDE, 31, 124, 128
New Age, The, 9, 55
occult arts, 9, 67, 113
out-of-body experience, 185, 206, 276

paranormal, 278
  activity, 57, 77, 164, 192, 263
  affecting emotions, 199
  animals as, 208
  apparition categories, 206
  children, 196
  crossing over, 194, 197
  dead time, 195
  negative energy, 199
  overlapping dimension, 195
  spiritual task, 194
Planting Seeds on Concrete, 133, 170
POST wisdom, 8
prana, 277
psychic, 46, 61, 97, 109
  experience, 56, 217
  fraud, 15, 80, 93, 239 - 254
  hotlines, 246
  interpretation, 68
  participation, 33, 72 - 76, 168
  social setting, 29
psychic ability, 60, 106
  empathic, 216
  levitation, 109
  Pi/Q, 109 - 111
  precognition, 14, 61, 152, 275, 278
  predictions, 179, 275
  remote viewing, 225, 230, 279
  telepathy, 5, 16, 185, 226, 278
  tools (clairs), 18, 78, 214 - 220
Reader's Digest, 229
readings, 178, 274, 277
  asking about others, 26
  cherry picking, 50
  cold readers, 248
  helping, 25
  infidelity, 44
  in-person, 24
  others joining, 28
  recordings, 28
  validation, 14, 20, 37, 116, 135, 168,
    250 - 262
Reiki, 9, 274
reincarnation, 29, 35, 40, 64, 87, 96
112, 134, 143, 177
relationships, 134, 137
  personality disorders, 39, 43, 49
sensory perception, *(see ESP)* 110 - 117

clairs, 57, 72, 75, 98
signs from
  Archangels, 158
  Ascended Masters, 163
  cosmic guides, 164
  God, 162
  departed loved ones, 165
silver cord, 55, 146
skeptics, vigilantes, 177, 230, 238
soul
  advanced, 36, 128, 146, 154
  agreement, 122
  beginner, 125, 132, 147
  contracts, 141
  crossing over, 167
  groups, 32, 36, 112, 120, 132, 137
  intermediate, 97, 106, 117, 256, 269
  kingdoms, 36
  levels, 122
  mirrors, 46
  review, 122
  soulmate, 126, 132, 140
  transiting, 132
  twin, 36, 134, 136, 137
spirit guides, 26, 41, 68, 115, 140, 156,
  218, 255
  Ancients, The, 131, 150, 269
  angelic choir, the, 149
  Ascended Masters, 110, 155
  gatekeepers, 36
  light energy guides, 149
  mediator, 35
  Nina, 145, 153
  Sage, 110, 139
  universal guides, 151
tarot, 45, 63, 248, 275 *(see divination)*
  myths, 95
  Rider-Waite, 94
timelines, timing, 85
  destiny, predestined, 89, 180
  splitting, 65
  ignoring intuition, 86
  vertex points, 90
universal timestream, The, 112, 113
veil, the 31, 98, 105, 195, 207, 211
Voodoo, 247, 279
walk-ins, 142
weigh-way stations, 128

PEOPLE CITED

Alliette, Jean-Baptiste, 93
Armagan, Esref, 223
Bjorling, Joel, 142
Blavatsky, Helen H.P., 67, 171
Brennan, Barbara, 174
Cayce, Edgar, 130, 138, 177, 263
   Davis, Gladys, 179
   predictions, 180
Child, Irvin L., 240
Churchill, Winston, 48, 225
Convulsionnaires, The, 174
Dajo, Mirin, 173
Dryer, Carol, 174
Gibson, Dr. Edward, 224
Freud, Sigmund, 56
Home, D.D. 239
Hume, David, 175
Hunt, Valerie, 111
Ingo Swann, 229
Kennedy, John F. 234
Layne, Al, 178
Lévi, Éliphas, 95
May, Edwin, 230
Mesmer, Franz, 178
Mirabelli, Carlos, 234
Newton, Isaac, 143
Newton, Michael, 125
Kahunas of Hawaii, The, 173
Nostradamus, 92, 98, 234
Nurse Melanie Uribe, 228
Piper, Leonora E., 191
Plato, 173
Powell, Dr Diane, 226
Price, Pat, 225
Roberts, Jane, 9
Sanguino, Ramses, 226
Schwarz, Jack, 173
Sun, Chulin, 228
Tesla, Nikola, 105
Twain, Mark, 224
Unnikrishnan, Nandana, 226
Yongsul, Nong, 228
Western Visayas, 226

FEATURED INTERVIEWS
   Germain, St. Comte, 186
   Jenkins, David, 193
   Nina, 148

www.ingramcontent.com/pod-product-compliance
Lightning Source LLC
Chambersburg PA
CBHW011318080526
44589CB00020B/2742